COVERING the period from 1⸱
to A.D. 700, when printing was about ⸱⸱
begin in China, T. H. Tsien has made
the first comprehensive study of early
Chinese writing and writing materials,
including inscriptions on bones, shells,
metals, stone; books made of bamboo,
wood, silk, quasi-paper, and paper;
such tools of writing as the brush, ink,
inkslabs, and book knife. The author
has made careful use of archeological
and textual evidences and has not forgotten the social and intellectual factors which shaped the development of
communication in China.

About the author . . .

T. H. TSIEN is associate professor of
Chinese and librarian of the Far Eastern Library, University of Chicago.

W9-BCC-544

THE UNIVERSITY OF CHICAGO
STUDIES IN LIBRARY SCIENCE

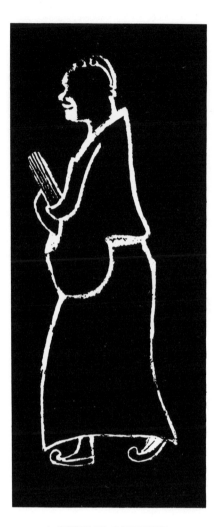

A SCHOLAR CARRYING
A VOLUME OF
BAMBOO BOOKS IN HIS ARMS

Reproduced from a tomb tile of the third century B.C.
in the Collection of the Royal Ontario Museum,
Toronto

WRITTEN
ON
BAMBOO AND SILK

*The Beginnings of Chinese Books
and Inscriptions*

BY TSUEN-HSUIN TSIEN

Chien, Ts'un-hsun.

THE UNIVERSITY OF CHICAGO PRESS

Library of Congress Catalog Card Number: 61-11897
The University of Chicago Press, Chicago and London
The University of Toronto Press, Toronto 5, Canada
© 1962 by The University of Chicago. Published 1962
Printed in the U.S.A.

"THE SOURCES OF OUR KNOWLEDGE

LIE IN WHAT IS WRITTEN ON BAMBOO AND SILK,

WHAT IS ENGRAVED ON METAL AND STONE,

AND WHAT IS CUT ON VESSELS

TO BE HANDED DOWN

TO POSTERITY."

Mo Tzu, fifth century B.C.

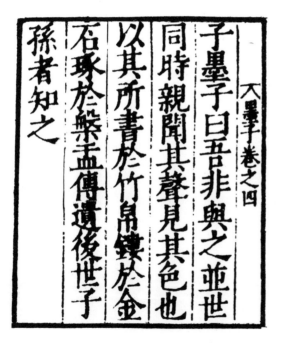

417
C434w

76709

PREFACE

"Written on bamboo and silk" was an old Chinese expression for books, documents, or other written records produced in ancient times. These words are therefore used to indicate a period in Chinese book history, running from antiquity to about the sixth century A.D., when bamboo and silk were used as writing material in China. The title also describes the general scope of this book, even though early writings on other materials, including paper, are discussed. In the language of the philosopher Mo Tzu, who lived around the end of the fifth century B.C., what is "written on bamboo and silk" is the source of our knowledge about the ancients whose voices and countenances we cannot hear and see.

Many studies of the development of Chinese books have dealt with the invention of printing and its subsequent history, but few have treated the period before the use of printing. The latter period is much more important for the origin of communication and scholarship in China and is much longer than that during which printing has been employed. Information about early Chinese records included in general histories of books is incomplete and inadequate, and the few investigations made by sinologists generally limit their scope to a certain phase. Because of this gap, a comprehensive study of the development of early Chinese records is needed not only by students of book history and of Chinese culture, but also by those in other disciplines who are seeking evidence of the early state of communication in Chinese civilization.

To investigate the early development of Chinese books without reference to that of inscriptions is not only illogical but also impossible. The word "book" is usually defined as "a collection of literary writings" and "inscription" as "writings on hard surfaces." Although inscriptions are hardly to be considered as books, nevertheless, there is no clear demarcation between these two kinds of written records. Not only are texts of literary writings and documents found to have been inscribed on hard materials, but also inscriptions have frequently been transcribed into books. Therefore, this study traces the origin and evolution of all kinds of written records produced in ancient China, no matter whether they are called books or inscriptions.

vii

Since the end of the last century, a great quantity of inscribed objects and writing materials have been discovered at various sites in and outside of China. In more recent decades especially, the excavation of many unusual materials and tools for writing provides us with new evidence concerning the development of Chinese records during different stages. The present study is intended to reconstruct from available evidence a general picture of the Chinese written records from about 1400 B.C., when the earliest known Chinese writing is found to have been recorded, to about A.D. 700, when printing is believed to have been in process of initiation. This period of more than two thousand years prior to the invention of printing marks the early stage in Chinese book history, when the materials, contents, forms of writing and its arrangement, and certain characteristics of format gradually took the shapes which became traditional for Chinese books and culture during the following stage when printing was applied. While printing is used as a landmark of book history, it merely changed the method and thus increased the quantity of production, without changing the general substance and format of the records.

The introduction of this work includes a discussion of the value of early Chinese records and of social and intellectual factors underlying their development within a chronological framework. The main body is arranged according to the different materials most commonly used in successive periods. In addition, there is a chapter on the origin and evolution of the various tools and vehicles for writing. A concluding chapter summarizes the previous discussions, and gives some generalizations and interpretations under various topics of general interest. Special emphasis has been laid on the beginnings of inscriptions and books and on the development of such physical aspects as materials, format, and technology. The dates of the origin and existence of different materials are traced with special care from both archeological and literary evidence. No attempt, however, is made to discuss the authorship, dating, and contents of all literary materials, which belong in a separate work on literary history.

The sources of information for this study consist principally of various field reports of archeological excavations, reproductions of objects and inscriptions, and decipherments and interpretations of these by scholars of various disciplines. Examples of these materials and writings have been reproduced to illustrate the distinctive forms in which the early Chinese records are preserved. Sources of these pictures are acknowledged following each item in the list of illustrations. Literary materials are also used to interpret and supplement the archeological data. In some cases philological evidence is used, since the forms of early pictograms and ideograms throw some light on the objects and ideas of ancient times.

The dates for Chinese dynasties or particular periods are usually given upon their first appearance in the text, and their equivalents in the western calendar can be found in the Chronological Table following the end of the main text. The metric system is used throughout the book for modern measurement, whereas such words as "foot" and "inch" are reserved for translation of ancient units. Chinese characters for personal and place names, book titles, and special terms which are not given in the text can be found in the Glossary or in the Bibliography. A brief reference to the sources is given in the footnotes; details are in the Bibliography. Abbreviations of book titles can be found at the beginning of the Bibliography. Corresponding characters for authors and titles, translation of titles or description of the contents and particular editions used for citation are all given in the Bibliography.

In the preparation of this study, I wish to express my sincere gratitude to Professor H. G. Creel for his inspiration and encouragement that has enabled me to undertake this investigation. He has read the entire manuscript and offered many valuable suggestions to eliminate my errors. I am also greatly indebted to Professor Howard W. Winger for his advice and criticism of the manuscript. To Professors Edward A. Kracke, Jr., L. Carrington Goodrich, and Ruth F. Strout, I am grateful for their reading and suggestions to improve the work. My thanks are also due to Mrs. H. G. Creel, Dr. Kenneth Starr, Dr. Babette M. Becker, Dr. T. L. Yuan, Dr. K. T. Wu, Dr. Shu-ch'ing Lee, and Dr. Cho-yün Hsü for their reading of whole or part of the manuscript and for their help in one way or the other.

Dr. Kenneth Starr of the Chicago Natural History Museum and Mr. E. D. Grinstead of the British Museum have generously provided me with many pictures from their respective collections for illustration. Professors Tung Tso-pin and Lao Kan of Academia Sinica were especially kind in sending me otherwise unobtainable materials and photographs. I also wish to express my appreciation to Dr. Lester E. Asheim, Dr. Herman H. Fussler, and members of the Graduate Library School of the University of Chicago for their interest in sponsoring the publication. To Miss June Work I owe gratitude in many ways in the preparation of the book. Finally, my wife, Wen-ching, has written the calligraphy in the glossary and bibliography. Without her encouragement and constant help, this work could not have been completed.

Chicago, Illinois
January, 1962

T. H. T.

CONTENTS

ILLUSTRATIONS

I

INTRODUCTION

THE LEGACY OF EARLY CHINESE RECORDS

There are many reasons why the history of Chinese books should especially command our attention. Not only were the Chinese the first printers, having invented block printing early in the eighth century and used movable type four hundred years earlier than Gutenberg,[1] but even before the invention of printing, they were also distinctive contributors to the development of human records. From very ancient times, some unusual materials, such as bamboo and silk, were used for writing exclusively by the Chinese; others, including bone, bronze, and stone, also used by the ancient peoples of other civilizations,[2] were inscribed by the Chinese much more extensively and with greater refinements. Paper, the most popular material for writing, was invented in China early in the second century A.D. and gradually spread over other parts of the world before the modern age. This invention is generally recognized as one of the most important contributions toward the progress of human civilization. The use of the brush pen and lamp-black ink as the basic vehicle for committing thoughts to writing can be traced back to remote antiquity in China. The brush has not only influenced the styles and arrangements of Chinese writing but also made calligraphy, along with painting, an outstanding branch of Chinese art; and the quality of Chinese ink is so superior that "for centuries it was employed by artists of Europe under the misnomer 'India Ink' and is still unrivalled."[3]

From very ancient times, the Chinese had already made attempts toward the mechanical multiplication of writings. The use of stamping seals cut in relief and obtaining duplicate inscriptions from molds or matrices indicate efforts to make copies other than by handwriting as

---

[1] Carter, *The Invention of Printing in China and Its Spread Westward* (2d ed. rev.), pp. 41, 212.

[2] Diringer, *The Hand-produced Book*, pp. 23–52, 79–112.

[3] Wiborg, *Printing Ink*, p. 2.

1

early as a millennium before the Christian era. As soon as paper and ink were perfected, several centuries before printing, the technique of taking inked impressions from stone inscriptions was developed. This made possible the multiplication of writings on a much larger scale and was very close to the technique of the block print.

Chinese records are also distinguished for their unique continuity as the carrier of an old and ingenious civilization which bound the Chinese people together as the largest homogeneous cultural group of mankind. The continuous use of Chinese writing as a living medium of communication has maintained Chinese ideas and aspirations and perpetuates the memory of successes and failures in a long tradition that has been carried forward triumphantly from generation to generation so that the origins of many aspects of modern life and institutions can be traced back to ancient times. Even books printed by modern techniques sometimes preserve the narrow vertical columns on a printed page (see p. v) which are believed to have derived from the old system of bamboo and wooden tablets. This unbroken tradition of Chinese civilization is largely due to the uninterrupted use of ancient literature in fundamental education and also to the fact that assiduous study of the books preserved from antiquity was for many centuries the main way to achieve prominence in society.

Chinese writing was not used only by the Chinese; many other peoples in East Asia, though they spoke different languages, also used Chinese characters as part of their writing. Books written in Chinese and produced in China were introduced to many of her immediate neighbors as early as they came into contact with the Chinese civilization. In some of these countries, especially Indo-China, Korea, Japan, and Liu-ch'iu, Chinese was the language of books and writing for long periods. Even today, Chinese characters still constitute part of some of these languages.

The production of books and documents in China was especially remarkable both in quantity and quality. Chinese classical literature is believed to rank among the greatest written by the human race. In terms of volume, China at the close of the fifteenth century A.D. probably had produced more books than all other countries put together.[4] Even during very early times books were numerous and varied in subject matter. An elaborate system of book classification in seven divisions was introduced as early as the first century B.C., and a modified fourfold scheme made in the third century A.D. has been used by Chinese bibliographers for over

[4] Cf. Latourette, *The Chinese: Their History and Culture* (3d ed. rev.), pp. ix, 770. My estimate is that more pages existed in China as late as 1500, whereas Professor Latourette has suggested 1700 or even 1800.

1,500 years. The four divisions of classics, philosophy, history, and belles-lettres may have influenced the triad scheme of Francis Bacon (1561–1626), which is the basis of modern western classification.[5]

The development in quantity and quality of early Chinese records reflects the splendid state of communication, scholarship, and literary history of ancient China which constitute the basis of Chinese civilization. It is obvious that the origin and progress of that civilization can be intelligible only through an understanding of the manner in which the early records were developed. On the other hand, an understanding of the state of written records and book production depends upon a knowledge of the social and intellectual background of the period in which the records were produced, preserved, transmitted, or dispersed.

COMMUNICATION WITH THE SPIRITS

Ancient writings in China were used to communicate not only among human beings but also between human and spiritual beings. The latter use was probably even more important in the early development of written records in ancient times. It is well-known that the ancient Chinese writings on bones and shells are primarily records of divination by the Shang people. The Shang dynasty (1765?–1123? B.C.) ruled an agricultural society characterized by a highly developed culture. Religion had a very significant role in the life of the state. Different kinds of supernatural beings are known to have been worshipped, especially the royal ancestors, whose help, advice, and blessings were constantly needed by their descendants. It is believed that the lavish funeral ceremony, rich deposits in the tombs, and constant sacrifice to the dead were meant to win their favor and to provide more blessings.

Writing was used to communicate with the spirits on various occasions. When sacrifice was held, the spirits were usually advised in writing to receive the offerings. If blessings were asked, prayers were also made in the form of a written message. Foretelling the future by consulting the spirits, divination, was practiced and its data were later recorded. The media used for these purposes were generally tortoise shells and ox bones, on which the oracular and other records of the Shang people are preserved.

After the Shang was conquered by the Chou dynasty (1122?—256 B.C.)

[5] Tsien, "A History of Bibliographic Classification in China," *Library Quarterly*, XXII (1952), 308.

divination by shells and bones is believed to have continued; but inscriptions were recorded, in general, separately on bamboo and silk. Stalks of the milfoil plant were also used for divination. Formulas and their interpretations are well preserved in the *I ching*, or the *Book of Changes*, which is a handbook of divination used by official fortunetellers of the early Chou period.

The most numerous inscriptions of the Chou dynasty left today are those made on bronze vessels. These inscriptions usually include names of ancestors receiving sacrificial offerings and also prayers to be presented to the ancestors, asking for protection of their descendants, the continuation of their families, long life, or other blessings. The philosopher Mo Tzu said that the reason for engraving inscriptions on vessels and cutting on metals and stone was the fear that if the perishable materials should rot and disappear, the descendants might not be reverent and obtain blessings.[6]

Prayers for blessing from the nature spirits are also found recorded on stone tablets. The inscription, "Inscribed Curse on the Ch'u State," of the fourth century B.C. was a prayer addressed to the nature spirits of three different rivers which the Ch'in state worshiped. Even bamboo and wooden tablets, which are known as materials for records of human communication, were also used for sacrificial purposes. In the bone inscriptions, we have found that the character *ts'e* (see Table I, *6d*) for "book," resembling the form of a bundle of tablets, is sometimes combined with an element signifying "spirit" and that the term *kung tien* means "to place the tablets before the ancestors for sacrifice."[7] Ancient documents which recorded agreements between feudal states were usually presented to the spirits as guarantors. Treaties, including such statements as "whoever shall violate this covenant, may the bright spirits destroy him," were usually made in triplicate; and one copy was buried on the spot, filed with the spirits.[8]

Silk, commonly associated with bamboo as book material, is also frequently mentioned by ancient philosophers as the material on which the records of spirits and ghosts were preserved.[9] As soon as paper was invented, in the second century A.D., it was used as a cheap substitute for expensive funeral objects to be buried with the dead. Paper money bearing writings for ghosts has been used until recently in the sacrifice to

[6] Mei Yi-pao, *The Ethical and Political Works of Motse*, p. 167.
[7] Tung Tso-pin, "Chung-kuo wen-tzu ti ch'i-yüan," *TLTC*, V (1952), 349.
[8] Creel, *Studies in Early Chinese Culture*, pp. 37–38.
[9] Mei, *Motse*, p. 167.

ancestors. The extensive use of written messages instead of oral prayer to communicate with spiritual beings, who were supposed to be able to read, was an important factor in adding a great number of written records in ancient times.

GOVERNMENT DOCUMENTS AND ARCHIVES

The development of the government system under the Chou dynasty encouraged the extensive use of documents and the establishment of archives in the royal court as well as in the feudal states. The enormous quantity of written records produced during these early days was apparently due to the increasing demand for communication among the various feudal states, between the royal court and the feudal princes, between the ruler and his subordinates, and among the various branches of the government. The pattern of interstate relations during the Ch'un Ch'iu period (722–481 B.C.) added to the legal importance of the documents. The emphasis on moral conduct in political and social life increased the value of ritual and historical writings. Even communications of a minor nature were frequently put into writing.

The proper relationship between the ruler and the feudal lords and relations among the states had to be legalized by written documents. The princes, when selected as feudal lords, were granted land, slaves, goods, and, among other things, books and writers. The feudal lords, in return, had the responsibility of giving homage, tribute, counsel, and military service to the Chou kings. Those who failed to observe these duties were subject to legal or moral punishment. The *Tso chuan*, a supposed commentary on the *Spring and Autumn Annals*, records that when the Chou conquest was completed, "lands were apportioned [to the Duke of Lu] on an enlarged scale, with priests, superintendents of the ancestral temple, diviners, historiographers, all the appendages of state, the tablets of historical records, the various officers and the ordinary instruments of their offices."[10] When conferences or covenants between the states were convened, copies of written documents were held by each of the parties to the agreement. If disputes should arise, reference was made to the documents in the archives. In 634 B.C., when Duke Hsiao of Ch'i invaded the borders of Chou, the marquis of Ch'i asked whether the people of Lu were afraid. The reply was that "they rely on the document . . . preserved in the archives of covenant, under the care of the grand-

[10] Legge, *Ch'un Ts'ew with the Tso Chuen*, p. 754.

master."[11] Sometimes such documents and treaties were cast on bronze vessels for permanent preservation. A bronze plate of the ninth century B.C. was inscribed with a treaty of some 350 words defining the boundaries between two states.[12] Many other inscriptions also record documents of a legal nature.

The abundance of diplomatic documents is the result of frequent interstate communications. The *Tso chuan* records that, in a period of twenty years between 722 and 703 B.C., there were fifty conferences, forty warlike operations, thirty-five court visits and missions, sixteen treaties, and many other diplomatic affairs.[13] Many documents, including treaties and diplomatic correspondence, must have been produced upon each of these occasions.

At the royal court and in various feudal states, official records of such occasions as military conquests, appointments, conferment of honors, and royal proclamations were also frequent. Draft orders are mentioned as having been written on tablets and dispatched to the peasants for service in war.[14] Records of victories on the battlefield and captures during the campaign were not only written on bamboo and silk but also cast on bronze and engraved on stone for long commemoration. Tablets of jade, ivory, or bamboo were worn at the girdle by officials for taking notes when the king met them at court.[15] Official appointment by a written document was usually made on bamboo or wooden tablets.

Records of many such activities are well preserved in ancient literature. The *Shang shu*, or the *Book of Documents*, consists largely of decrees, speeches and addresses on various occasions by kings and ministers of ancient dynasties. The *Shih ching*, or the *Book of Poetry*, includes folk songs, odes, and hymns which were collected or composed by court historians and sung at occasions of entertainments and sacrifice. The *Ch'un-ch'iu*, or the *Spring and Autumn Annals*, which is a brief chronicle of the state of Lu between 722 and 481 B.C., contains political and interstate affairs, wars, and activities of historical personages. The rituals of the aristocratic class are recorded in the *I-li*, or *Book of Etiquette and Ceremonial*, and the *Li-chi*, or *Records of Ceremonial*. Even a minor event such as a plea addressed by the Duke of Chou to his brother is recorded. As

---

[11] *Ibid.*, p. 198.

[12] Kuo Mo-jo, *Liang-chou chin-wen-tz'u ta-hsi: k'ao-shih*, pp. 129a–131a.

[13] Britton, "Chinese Interstate Intercourse before 700 B.C.," *American Journal of International Law*, XXIX (1935), 615–35.

[14] Legge, *She King*, p. 264.

[15] Legge, *Li Ki*, I, 16; II, 12–13.

Creel says, "That such a request should be put into writing at all is remarkable. . . . We simply have to accept the fact that the Chous were a people who liked to write books."[16]

RECORDERS, USERS, AND CUSTODIANS

Prior to the time of Confucius, the literati, who were primarily responsible for the production, use, and care of books and documents, were largely aristocrats. How large the literati class was is unknown, but it is believed that the total number of literate persons was not small, since every member of the aristocracy was expected to have been trained in reading and writing.[17] The education of aristocratic sons was primarily directed toward their preparation for service in various branches of the government. As Confucius said: "The student, having completed his learning, should apply himself to be an officer."[18] The subjects to be taught included the reading of ancient literature, besides such skills as archery and charioteering. The *Kuo-yü*, or *Discourses of the States*, mentions several categories of reading materials to be studied by a prince of the state of Ch'u around 600 B.C. These include the state annals, chronicles of other states, poetry, rituals, music, law, quotations and discourses, ancient records, and official documents.[19] After an extensive training, the students were expected to serve in government functions.

The officers concerned with recording were generally called *shih* (see Table I, 7f). This character, which represents an object held by a right hand, occurs frequently in bone and bronze inscriptions of the Shang and Chou dynasties. Although the sign for this object has been interpreted differently, most scholars agree that this character originated from and has been used in connection with records. It was said that the *shih* specialized in preserving, reading, and making books.[20] As used in inscriptions and in ancient literature, the character *shih* seems to mean both the high and lesser ranks of recording officers. The T'ai Shih, which may be translated "Grand Historiographer," held a very important post in charge of documents, equivalent to the rank of ministers appointed by the king. There were many other *shih*, who may be called scribes, serving in

---

[16] Creel, *The Birth of China*, pp. 254–55.
[17] *Ibid.*, pp. 256–57.
[18] Legge, *Confucian Analects*, p. 208.
[19] *Kuo yü*, 17/1a–2a.
[20] Wang Kuo-wei, "Shih shih," 6/4a, in *WCAIS*, ts'e 3.

various branches of government offices, as recorders, writers, or keepers of documents. Another official title for recorders is Tso Ts'e, or Maker of Books; these were employed by the lesser rulers in the aristocratic household for literary or clerical work.

The chief duty of the historiographers or scribes was probably to record important affairs of the court, speeches of the king or the princes, and activities of government offices. Many bronze inscriptions and much ancient literature bear the formula, "The King agrees in saying . . . ," which means the record was not written by the king himself but by the historiographer at the king's order.[21] In other words, the *shih* were members of a technical profession specially trained and engaged in writing, copying, reading, and caring for official records.

The office of court historian or scribe was usually held by inheritance in one family. The family which engaged in this profession sometimes had a clan name relating to books or documents or to their service as recorder or keeper of the documents. Many surnames which appear frequently in Chinese history and are borne by modern families, such as Chien (tablets), Chi (documents), Shih (scribes), and Tung (custodian) are probably related to this profession. An interesting story of 526 B.C. in the *Tso chuan* charged that a court historian of the Chin state, named Chi T'an, was ignorant concerning his family history. The king said: "Father Chi seems not to leave any posterity. [Chi T'an] must have run through the documents, and yet he has forgotten [the works of] his ancestors!"[22]

The importance of historiographers in ancient government was probably due to their power over the production and communication of official records. The historiographers were responsible for making records, and what was written therein was of great concern to the rulers or feudal princes. In order to be sure that no injurious words were kept, not only were the most reliable officials selected for this office, but they were also sent to the states to supervise their records and possibly supply intelligence to the king. The *Tso chuan* says, as we have mentioned before, that documents and historiographers, along with many other presents, were sent as gifts to the Duke of Lu when he was appointed feudal lord after the Chou conquest of the Shang dynasty.

The frequent removal of documents in emergencies and flights of historiographers to other states further illustrates the political importance of official records. The *Tso chuan* records that in 517 B.C., when the army of Chin drove out the late Chou king's son Ch'ao, he fled to the state of

[21] Creel, *The Birth of China*, p. 257.

[22] Legge, *Ch'un Ts'ew with the Tso Chuen*, p. 660.

Ch'u, along with other members of the royal house, "carrying with them the archives of Chou."[23] The great historian Ssu-ma Ch'ien (*ca.* 145–86 B.C.) said that his ancestors had charge by inheritance of the historical archives of the Chou dynasty, and in the middle of the seventh century B.C. the Ssu-ma family left Chou for Chin.[24]

Another story tells not only of the importance of the documents but also of the power of their custodians, who could sometimes run away with the documents in their custody. The *Lü-shih ch'un-ch'iu*, written about the third century B.C., says that "the Grand Historiographer Chung Ku of the Hsia dynasty wept after taking out the documents and regulations . . . and fled to Shang . . . When [the tyrannical last Shang king] became more and more reckless and deceitful, the historiographer Hsiang Chih of the Shang dynasty fled to [the state of] Chou bringing with him the documents."[25] Although literary sources stood on the side of the historiographers and laid the blame on the rulers, these flights, especially at the end or during the decline of the dynasty, imply that these documents may have included information which might be useful to rival rulers, and thus might hasten the overthrow or weakening of the dynasty.

PRIVATE WRITINGS AND COLLECTIONS

Toward the end of the fifth century B.C., a new era began in Chinese history, with many changes taking place in political, social, and economic institutions. This epoch is known as the Chan Kuo or Warring States period (468–221 B.C.) and was characterized by numerous wars among the many feudal states. Feudalism was gradually disintegrating as a result of the land and other reforms. Social mobility became freer and more rapid as the lower classes began to acquire education and enter the service of government. Thus the aristocratic monopoly of learning was no longer possible. The popularization of education was probably pioneered by Confucius (551–479 B.C.), who was the first one in Chinese history to engage in private teaching to a group of disciples of humble origin. "In education," he said, "there should be no class distinctions."[26] In the past, the training of sons of aristocrats was primarily aimed to prepare them for the service of the government in traditional functions. Confucius,

---

[23] *Ibid.*, p. 717.
[24] *Shih chi*, 130/1a.
[25] *Lü-shih ch'un-ch'iu*, 16/1b.
[26] Legge, *Confucian Analects*, p. 305.

however, planned to produce "gentlemen" who should possess the superior qualities of wisdom, courage, and capability and be well versed in courtesy, ceremonial, and music. Through both moral influence and education, they could lead the common people with kindness and justice and bring about enlightened rule in government.

Against the background of institutional reforms and popular education, a great diffusion of knowledge became possible. Various schools of philosophy and scientific thought developed in this period and took the shape that became the traditional pattern of Chinese culture during the next two thousand years. Later historians classified these different schools according to the characteristic content of their thinking—the Confucians, the Taoists, the yin-yang or cosmologists, the legalists, the logicians, the Mohists, the diplomatists, the eclectics, and the agrarians. The various schools of philosophers were traditionally described as having been derived from different official institutions of the early Chou dynasty, but modern scholars doubt the theory. Nevertheless, the flourishing of plebeian writers in philosophy, science, and literature demonstrates diffusion of knowledge from the aristocratic class to private scholars of lower status.

It is generally supposed that Chinese writing prior to the time of Confucius consisted primarily of official documents and collected works with no private authorship. None of the writings mentioned in works of pre-Ch'in philosophers or quoted in early historical works surviving today is found to have contained information concerning private writings before the Warring States period.[27] Even in this period the concept of authorship was not so clear as in later times. A book bearing the name of a certain person was not necessarily "written" by this person. It might be a record of his "sayings" written by his followers or a collection of writings by many persons of a similar school of thought but attributed to the most famous name of the school. Since most of the pre-Ch'in books transmitted today have been revised by Han scholars, it is often difficult to know what part of a book is original and what part is later addition.

The rivalry for power among the various states encouraged the feudal lords to employ distinguished scholars, statesmen, and military strategists to serve their interests. The most important work required of them was probably extensive reading, discussion, and writing, as well as contributing plans and schemes to their respective sponsors. At the court of Ch'in, it is said, Lü Pu-wei (290–235 B.C.) assembled as many as three

---

[27] Lo Ken-tse, "Chan-kuo ch'ien wu ssu-chia chu-tso shuo," *Ku-shih pien*, IV, 9–14, 29–61.

thousand scholar-politicians and asked them to write what they had learned. Lü then collected their discussions into a book of more than 200,000 words, covering all of the subjects. When completed, the book was displayed at the gate of the market place in the capital, and a reward of one thousand pieces of gold was offered to anyone if he could change a word of this writing.[28] This story tells us not only that a complete, full-length, and systematically organized book existed during this period but also that the number of persons who could read had increased considerably.

It was common during the Warring States period for private scholars to possess collections of books in connection with their teaching and writing. Mo Tzu said: "The books belonging to the scholars of the world of the present day are too many to be conveyed."[29] When scholars traveled from state to state, they carried their books with them. Mo Tzu, for example, "brought numerous books in his wagons on his southern journey as an envoy to Wei," intended for reading during his travel.[30] Hui Shih, a logician who lived around the fourth century B.C., was described as a man with many plans who possessed books sufficient to fill five carts.[31] Of Su Ch'in, the famous diplomat who died in 320 B.C., it is told that, after the failure of his repeated efforts to persuade King Hui of Ch'in to make plans against six other states, he searched among several tens of his book trunks and discovered a book of military strategy.[32] After thorough study of this book, he finally succeeded in forming a federation against Ch'in with himself as the leader. It seems to be a common pattern in the development of libraries in China, as in Greece, that private collections flourished after the establishment of official archives but before that of the centralized libraries by the government.

BURNING OF BOOKS

The feudal period in Chinese history ended in 221 B.C., when the six contending states were finally conquered by the powerful state of Ch'in and the empire was unified. Although the dynasty lasted for only fifteen years, it nevertheless introduced many sweeping changes and for the first time achieved unification. Feudalism was formally abolished, economic

---

[28] *Shih-chi*, 85/5a–b; Cf. Bodde, *Statesman, Patriot, and General in Ancient China*, p. 6.

[29] Mei, *Motse*, p. 140.

[30] *Ibid.*, p. 226.

[31] *Chuang-tzu*; or *Nan-hua chen-ching*, 10/38a.

[32] *Chan-kuo ts'e*, 3/3b.

measures were standardized, and writings were unified under the Ch'in style. To enforce unification, a series of preventive measures including, among other things, censorship and thought control were introduced. A great many ancient books were destroyed, but certain kinds of writings were preserved for government monopoly. The well-known story about the "burning of books" was but a part of this authoritarian policy of the new government.

The censorship of literature as an effective measure of thought control, however, was not a Ch'in invention; it had precedents in history and a justification in legalist philosophy. The early legalist Shang Yang (d. 338 B.C.), known as Lord Shang, who lived more than two centuries before the famous book-burner Li Ssu and introduced reforms in Ch'in which led to the later victory of the state over the whole country, "taught Duke Hsiao of Ch'in . . . to burn books in order to manifest the law and statutes."[33] A later legalist, Han Fei Tzu (d. 233 B.C.), said: "In the state of an intelligent ruler, there is no literature of books and bamboo tablets, but the law is the only doctrine; there are no sayings of the former kings, but the officials are the only models."[34] This method of censorship had probably already been used by some of the feudal lords, since literary documents have been insufficient and missing from the time of Confucius.

In 213 B.C., seven years after the crowning of Shih Huang Ti, or the First Emperor of Ch'in, a recommendation was made by the Grand Councilor, Li Ssu, concerning the simplification and standardization of writing and also the censorship of literature. He suggested that "all books in the historical archives, except the records of Ch'in, be burned; that all persons in the empire, except those who held a function under the control of the official scholars, daring to store the classical literature and the discussions of various philosophers, should go to the administrative or military governors so that these books may be indiscriminately burned."[35] Many books were undoubtedly destroyed, but the damage done to ancient literature by this order was probably not so extensive as supposed, since certain categories of books were clearly stated in the decree to be exempt. The statement specified that the state records, books in the possession of officials of learning, and technical works on medicine and pharmacy, divination, agriculture and horticulture were not included.

Furthermore, many privately owned books are known to have been saved from the censorship. Also, the order was in force only a short period

---

[33] Duyvendak, *The Book of Lord Shang*, pp. 125–26.
[34] *Han-fei-tzu*, 4/7b.
[35] *Shih chi*, 6/22b; cf. Bodde, *China's First Unifier*, pp. 82–83.

and probably relaxed in 208 B.C., when Li Ssu died. It is believed that the damage done in 206 B.C., when the imperial palaces were captured and burned by the rebels, was much greater and more extensive than that of the Ch'in rulers. Since no pre-Han records are available for checking, it is difficult to say how many were destroyed through censorship and how many were damaged by the following catastrophes.

RESTORATION OF ANCIENT WORKS

The Ch'in empire, overthrown in 207 B.C. as the result of a peasant revolution, was succeeded by the Han dynasty. Through four hundred years of internal development and external expansion, the Han dynasty (206 B.C.–A.D. 220) became one of the most glorious periods in Chinese history. It also laid down the foundation for a national culture. Confucianism emerged triumphant over other schools of thought and became influential in the government. Confucian scholars entered government offices through the operation of the imperial university and the civil service examination systems. Since Confucian teachings were primarily based on a corpus of ancient literature, the triumph of Confucianism resulted in the restoration of ancient books after the Ch'in destruction. In 191 B.C. the criminal law against possession of books, which had been initiated by the First Emperor of Ch'in was abrogated.[36] The next few decades brought the beginning of the restoration of the Confucian classics destroyed by the Ch'in.

Systematic, large-scale recovery of ancient works was not begun, however, until the reign of Emperor Wu (r. 140–87 B.C.), who "set plans for restoring books and appointed officers for transcribing them, including even works of various philosophers and the commentaries, all to be stored in the imperial library."[37] It is said that after the strenuous efforts made by his minister Kung-sun Hung, books were piled up like hills.[38] Official agents were sent to search out all the surviving books, giving rewards, so they could borrow the books from private collections for transcribing. In ancient times, books were preserved in archives which were usually attached to the government offices where the documents were produced. Now, for the first time in Chinese history, a centralized imperial library was established, where a wide range of materials was systematically collected and administered.

[36] Dubs, *The History of the Former Han Dynasty*, I, 182.
[37] *Han shu*, 30/1b.
[38] *T'ai-p'ing yü-lan*, 619/1a.

The search for books throughout the country continued while they were being collated and arranged in systematic order. In 26 B.C. a special decree ordered Liu Hsiang (*ca.* 80–8 B.C.), a state counselor, to head a commission of prominent scholars, including a military commander, a historiographer, and a physician, to examine these materials. Liu was responsible for collating the classics, philosophical works, and poetical writings. On the completion of each book, Liu would record the headings of chapters and write a summary of the book to be presented to the emperor.[39] The result of these summaries was a collection of critical bibliographies, known as *Pieh-lu,* or *Separate Records.* Liu Hsiang served in the imperial library for nineteen years until 8 B.C., when he died with the task unfinished. His son, Liu Hsin (d. A.D. 23), then succeeded him in the work. Being a distinguished scholar of the Confucian classics, Liu Hsin arranged all of the books then in the imperial library into seven categories and compiled a classified catalogue, known as *Ch'i-lüeh,* or *Seven Summaries.* This scheme was composed of seven main divisions, including the general summary, the six classics, the various philosophers, poetry and rhymed prose, military works, science and occultism, and medicine, with thirty-eight subdivisions.[40] Liu Hsiang's work is the earliest known bibliography in China and Liu Hsin's the first system of subject classification and descriptive cataloguing of Chinese books.

Both of these early records have since been lost, but Liu Hsin's catalogue is known to have included some six hundred titles in more than 13,000 "volumes."[41] About a century later, Pan Ku adopted this catalogue as the bibliographical section in his *History of the Former Han Dynasty,* which contains a similar number of titles and volumes.[42] About one-fourth of these works are preserved in whole or in part, including some reconstructed from other sources.[43] Although most of the writings listed in this history no longer survive today, this record nevertheless represents the books then extant in the imperial library written prior to and around the Christian era. The writings in this catalogue reflect the general state of scholarship when Confucianism had begun to make its influence felt in China.

---

[39] *Han shu,* 30/1b.

[40] Tsien, *op. cit.,* pp. 309–10.

[41] *Kuang hung-ming chi,* 3/12a.

[42] *Han shu,* 30/33b. The total number as given at the end of this section includes 596 works in 13,269 chüan.

[43] It is estimated that 47 works have been preserved almost in complete form, 41 incomplete, and 65 in quotations from other sources; see Teng and Biggerstaff, *An Annotated Bibliography of Selected Chinese Reference Works* (rev. ed.), p. 12.

The collection of books was engaged in not only by the government but by individuals as well. Royal princes, high officials, and noted scholars were all interested in book-collecting. Among them, Liu Te (d. 131 B.C.), the prince of Ho-chien, and Liu An (d. 122 B.C.), the prince of Huai-nan, are said to have offered valuable gifts, together with a transcribed copy of the original, to the donor, to acquire whatever fragments of the pre-Ch'in period they could.[44] Another noted scholar, Ts'ai Yung (A.D. 132–192), is said to have possessed over 10,000 rolls in his private library.[45] Bookstores are known to have existed in China before the Christian era. The term *shu-ssu* for "book shop" first appears in the work by Yang Hsiung (53 B.C.–A.D. 18),[46] although it may have existed earlier. It is said that when the philosopher Wang Ch'ung (*ca.* A.D. 27–100) was young, he was poor and could not afford to buy books but only read them in the bookstores in the capital, Lo-yang.[47] Apparently books were still a luxury of the upper classes.

During the entire Han period, literary, historical, and other writings were increased tremendously. An authorized version of the Confucian classics was engraved on stone and the voluminous commentaries of many scholars became the standard interpretation followed by later students. The first comprehensive Chinese dictionary, *Shuo-wen chieh-tzu*, compiled by Hsü Shen about A.D. 100, preserves 9,353 characters as written in the third century B.C. and some archaic forms from an even earlier date. The foundation of Chinese historiography was established during the period by two monumental histories, the *Shih chi*, or *Records of the Grand Historiographer* by Ssu-ma Ch'ien (*ca.* 145–86 B.C.), and the *Han shu*, or *History of the Former Han Dynasty* by Pan Ku (A.D. 32–92), which became the models of later official histories. Ballads and folk songs, which survive as a new genre of poetry, were collected by the music bureau established by Emperor Wu. Also significant are many philosophic and scientific works produced during this dynasty, including those on astronomy, mathematics, botany, medicine, agriculture, and technology.

Books were produced and accumulated on a large scale, but great losses were suffered during the several political disturbances. At the beginning of the Christian era, the well-catalogued imperial library was destroyed during the insurrection against Wang Mang when the Former

[44] Wu, "Libraries and Book-collecting in China before the Invention of Printing," *T'ien Hsia Monthly*, V, (1937), 246.

[45] *Ibid.*, p. 247.

[46] Yang Hsiung, *Fa-yen*, 2/3a.

[47] *Hou-han shu*, 79/1a.

Han capital was razed by fire. After the restoration of the Later Han dynasty by Emperor Kuang-wu (r. A.D. 25–57), the quest for ancient literature was revived. When his capital was moved from Ch'ang-an to Lo-yang, it is said that over 2,000 vehicles were laden with written records.[48] Later, in the early second century, the original collection in the imperial library was even tripled.[49] But during the closing years of the Later Han another catastrophe took place when the capital, Lo-yang, was destroyed by the warlord Tung Cho and innumerable books were looted and burned. During the evacuation, when the capital was moved again in 190 to the former capital, Ch'ang-an, many books written on silk rolls were used as tent curtains and receptacles during the journey; others were either destroyed in the capital or sank in the river when they were shipped westward. Many of those which survived were destroyed during the new disturbances in A.D. 208.[50] These destructions during the last two hundred years of the Han dynasty constitute two of the five major bibliothecal catastrophes in Chinese history up to the close of the seventh century, as discussed by the Sui scholar Niu Hung.[51]

POPULARIZATION OF RELIGIOUS LITERATURE

From the collapse of the Han in A.D. 220 until the reunification in 590 under the Sui, a period known as the "Dark Ages," caused by political disunion, warfare, and barbarian invasions from the north and west, fell over China. In the south the Chinese ruled over several kingdoms, and learning and culture continuously flourished there. In the north the Turks, Mongols, Tibetans, Hsien-pi and Hsiung-nu seized control of parts of the nation. The continuity of Chinese civilization was not broken, however, and Chinese language and literature remained the common means of communication even in the north where the barbarians ruled. Confucianism continued among the intellectual classes; Taoism emerged and developed as a religion; and Buddhism, which was first introduced to China at the beginning of the Christian era, flourished during this period. When barbarian incursions and political turmoil were prevalent, people began to seek solace in the new faith which advocated withdrawal from the disorderly world.

[48] *Ibid.*, 109a/3a–b.
[49] *Ibid.*, 109a/3b.
[50] *Ibid.*, 102/17b.
[51] *Sui-shu*, 49/2a–3b.

The introduction of Buddhism was an important milestone not only in the history of Chinese thought and religion but also in the development of Chinese scholarship and the popularization of literature. At first, Buddhism had little influence in Chinese scholarly circles but was propagated among the masses. With the need of literature to aid the spread of the religion, tremendous efforts were made in the translation of Buddhist texts into Chinese. The first translations of Buddhist scriptures appeared in the second century A.D., and the amount greatly increased in the third century. Translations by one Buddhist scholar named Dharmaraksha amounted to 149 works.[52] Not only in the Northern Dynasties, where many rulers became devout converts, but also in the Chinese domain of the Southern Dynasties, Buddhist literature became part of the imperial collections. In A.D. 279, when Hsün Hsü (231–289) compiled the imperial catalogue of the Chin dynasty, sixteen rolls of Buddhist works were already included.[53] In the middle of the fifth century, the imperial library of the Sung dynasty (420–479) contained 438 rolls of Buddhist sutras.[54] In the early sixth century, a private scholar named Juan Hsiao-hsü (479–536), of the Liang dynasty, compiled a comprehensive catalogue called *Seven Records,* in which two main divisions were given to Buddhist and Taoist literature. The catalogue listed 2,410 works of Buddhist writings and 425 Taoist works.[55] At about the same time one of the earliest Buddhist catalogues, compiled by Seng Yu in 505–515, contained as many as 2,162 works in 4,328 rolls.[56]

The greatest period of production of Buddhist literature was under the Sui dynasty (581–618), when the empire was again unified. Transcription of Buddhist literature was encouraged, and a special agency for translation was established. In 581, during the reign of Emperor Wen, a decree was issued to have all of the Buddhist works copied for deposit in the temples in large cities, with a specially prepared copy to be kept in the imperial library.[57] During his reign, more than 130,000 rolls were transcribed; and "the copies of Buddhist canons in private hands were ten or a hundred times as many as those of Confucian classics."[58] The most comprehensive and earliest extant Buddhist bibliography, compiled by

[52] Yao Ming-ta, *Chung-kuo mu-lu-hsüeh shih,* p. 230.
[53] *Kuang hung-ming chi,* 3/12b.
[54] Yao, *op. cit.,* p. 230.
[55] *Kuang hung-ming chi,* 3/17b–18b.
[56] Yao, *op. cit.,* p. 260.
[57] *Sui shu,* 35/36a.
[58] *Ibid.*

Fei Ch'ang-fang under imperial auspices in 597, lists 2,146 works in 6,235 rolls.[59]

In 606, Emperor Yang ordered the establishment of the bureau of translation of Buddhist canons in the imperial park of the capital and appointed a number of scholars to this agency.[60] The bibliographical section of the *History of the Sui Dynasty*, which was a register of important literature known and extant in the period, contains an appendix of Buddhist and Taoist works besides the four main divisions. It is recorded that there were 377 titles in 1,216 rolls of Taoist writings and 1,950 titles in 6,198 rolls of Buddhist writings.[61] The latter category comprises almost one-half of the total titles or one-sixth of the total volumes of the register. It is not surprising that the quantity of Buddhist literature had challenged that of Confucian and Taoist writings. Following the great diffusion of Buddhism during this period, the demand for mass production of Buddhist literature became the motivating force which encouraged printing in the following century.

[59] Yao, *op. cit.*, p. 273.
[60] *Ibid.*, p. 268.
[61] *Sui shu*, 35/27b; 31b.

II

RECORDS ON BONES AND SHELLS

ORIGIN AND NATURE OF BONE AND SHELL INSCRIPTIONS

The earliest known Chinese documents preserved in the original form today are written or incised on animal bones and tortoise shells. They are primarily records of the later portion of the Shang dynasty (1401?–1123? B.C.), which represent perhaps a part of the royal archives produced more than three thousand years ago. The extensive use of bones and shells in Shang for making vessels, implements, and ornaments, and especially for divination and writing has been regardèd as a unique characteristic of ancient Chinese culture.[1] The use of bone materials in divination, however, did not originate in the Shang period, but can be traced back to greater antiquity. In various Neolithic sites in China, many bone objects have been recovered, including pieces of animal bones and tortoise shells with scorched marks but no inscriptions.[2] The Shang people probably inherited this tradition of using both bones and shells for divination but added inscriptions to these oracle materials.

According to early literature, tortoise shells were also used for divination in the Chou dynasty (1122?–256 B.C.), but oracle inscriptions were said to have been recorded separately either on tablets or on silk and not directly on the shells.[3] No bone inscriptions of the Chou period are known to us except a piece of ox scapula inscribed with eight characters discovered in 1954 at Hung-chao, Shansi,[4] and dated from about 500 B.C.[5] This casual evidence seems to indicate that oracle records were also made on bone materials by the Chou people, but they probably did not follow the entire Shang tradition on an extensive scale.

The bone and shell inscriptions may be generally grouped into two dif-

[1] White, *Bone Culture of Ancient China*, p. 24.
[2] Shih Chang-ju, "Ku-pu yü kuei-pu t'an-yüan," *TLTC*, VIII (1954), 267–69.
[3] *Chou-li chu-su*, 24/22b–23a.
[4] *Wen-wu ts'an-k'ao tzu-liao*, 1956, No. 7, p. 27; Plate 20.
[5] Tung Tso-pin, "Ch'un-ch'iu Chin pu-ku wen-tzu k'ao," *TLTC*, XIII (1956), 271–74.

ferent kinds of records, namely, oracle and non-oracle. Non-oracle inscriptions are, however, comparatively few and, in some cases, considered part of the oracle statement. The most common among the oracle inscriptions are those concerning sacrifice, warfare, hunting, journeys, sickness, rain, and other spiritual, natural, and human affairs in connection with the royal house. When rulers needed to make decisions or forecast what might happen during the coming evening or next ten days, they usually asked their ancestors or the deities for advice through the medium of bones and shells. After divination, the queries, answers, and sometimes a statement of verification might be recorded by the diviners or scribes on these oracle materials. The inscribed bones and shells so far discovered are primarily such records of divination of the Shang dynasty.

Despite the controversy over the chronology of ancient China, a large part of the bone and shell inscriptions can be roughly dated by the established criteria within the range of certain reigns. It is generally agreed today that the material covers a period from the early fourteenth century B.C., when the nineteenth sovereign P'an Keng of the Shang dynasty is believed to have moved his capital to An-yang during the fourteenth year of his reign, to the late twelfth century B.C. when the last Shang king, Ti Hsin, was conquered by the Chou dynasty. The traditional chronology[6] dates the Shang dynasty as 1765–1123 B.C., and the fourteenth year of P'an Keng as 1388 B.C.[7] Thus the bone and shell inscriptions so far discovered were generally produced within the range of this period, covering twelve reigns in eight generations of the Shang royal house. Scholars are not quite certain, however, whether we have any bone inscriptions as early as P'an Keng, since the few pieces thus dated are debatable.[8]

DISCOVERY AND STUDY OF BONE RECORDS

The discovery of these relics occurred at the end of the nineteenth century, when fragments of inscribed bones and shells were found by farmers on their land at An-yang in modern Honan Province. They were

[6] Since no absolute chronology of China before 841 B.C. has been established, the traditional chronology as adopted in Mathias Tchang, *Synchronismes chinois* (Shanghai, 1905) is used throughout this writing unless otherwise stated.

[7] According to the chronology reconstructed by Tung Tso-pin, P'an Keng moved his capital to An-yang in 1385 B.C., and the Chou conquest occurred in 1112 B.C. See his *Yin-li p'u*, Part II, 1/1a.

[8] Ch'en Meng-chia, *Yin-hsü pu-tz'u tsung-shu*, pp. 33–34.

first sold at drugstores as "dragon bones" for medical use and later found their way into collections of antiquarians when a patient discovered ancient inscriptions on the bones of his remedy in 1899. During the first half-century since their appearance, it has been estimated, more than 100,000 pieces[9] of inscribed bones and shells were unearthed, including 72,000 pieces obtained from at least nine major diggings by private undertaking before 1928 and 28,000 pieces excavated by official agencies since then.[10] Since the bones and shells are very brittle, most of the materials are broken pieces bearing inscriptions from a single character to more than one hundred.

Although private finds are more numerous than official excavations, the latter have been more valuable in research as archeological data became one of the important criteria for dating the material. The work of scientific excavation was undertaken by the Institute of History and Philology of the Academia Sinica from 1928 to 1937. A total of 24,918 pieces of inscribed bone and shell were discovered during its fifteen excavations in this period.[11] The area of excavation was centered at Hsiao-t'un village near An-yang, Honan. Although it was later extended to neighboring areas, almost all of the discoveries came from Hsiao-t'un.

The most important and representative discovery was the thirteenth excavation, in 1936, when a full pit of 17,096 specimens was unearthed.[12] Except for a few pieces of inscribed bones, the pit contained almost nothing but tortoise shells, which indicates that the preservation or storage was probably intentional. While discoveries in other sites were primarily broken pieces, this pit contained nearly three hundred complete tortoise shells, dating back to the Wu Ting period (1324–1266 B.C.), with a few pieces probably earlier. Besides these unusual specimens, many others were written on with a brush, using cinnabar and black fluid; some carved ones were inlaid with red and black pigments for decoration. Carapaces and reshaped carapaces, which were rare in previous discoveries, were also found in this site. Among the deposit of tortoise shells was found a human skeleton. It is suspected that this man was a custodian of the shell archives, but why he was buried with them is not known.[13]

In 1929–30, when the third excavation by the Academia Sinica was in progress, the Honan Provincial Museum discovered 2,673 pieces of

[9] Tung Tso-pin, *Chia-ku-hsüeh wu-shih-nien*, pp. 185–88; Hu Hou-hsüan's estimate is 161,989 pieces, see his *Wu-shih-nien chia-ku-wen fa-hsien ti ts'ung-chieh*, p. 65.

[10] Tung Tso-pin, *Chia-ku-hsüeh wu-shih-nien*, pp. 177–78.

[11] *Ibid.*, pp. 31–61.

[12] Hu Hou-hsüan, *Yin-hsü fa-chüeh*, pp. 98–101.

[13] Shih Chang-ju, "Yin-hsü tsui-ching chih chung-yao fa-hsien," *KKHP*, II (1947), 43.

inscribed shells and 983 inscribed bones, totaling 3,656, from two further excavations.[14] The excavation at the sites of An-yang has been resumed since 1950 under the auspices of the Institute of Archeology of the National Academy of Sciences and other agencies set up by the new government. Although bones and shells have frequently been found, only a few pieces are inscribed.[15]

The study of bone and shell inscriptions has developed into a highly specialized field of science which requires a knowledge of many disciplines —philology and epigraphy, ancient history and geography, archeology, anthropology, astronomy, and chronology. It is reported that up to 1949, in the first half-century since the discovery, a total of more than 800 works in this field were written in various languages on different subjects by some three hundred scholars of many nationalities.[16] The deciphering and philological study of the bone inscriptions have laid the foundation for further research. The interpretation of the formation of the characters has been generally aided by the old lexicon, *Shuo-wen chieh-tzu*, compiled by Hsü Shen about A.D. 100. Many of the forms preserved in this work, however, are closer to the bronze than to the bone inscriptions. But through comparison and analysis of different forms and deduction of the meaning from context, many inscriptions have been deciphered even though the pronunciation of some characters may be unknown.

The bone inscriptions have also been used to elucidate and verify ancient literary texts, some of which are thus proved to be reliable to a very large extent, while others do not agree with the inscriptions. With the establishment of criteria for dating the inscriptions, the bone material has been used for the study of the controversial chronology of the Shang dynasty. Another approach is the sociological study of the inscriptions. This has resulted in an interpretation of the ancient society, especially the social structure and the family system, of the Shang dynasty. It is said that two contending parties alternatively held power at the court, influencing successive changes and restorations of many cultural procedures of the Shang dynasty, including the systems of sacrifice and calendar and the styles of writing.[17] But the material is too scanty for generalization and thus the results are controversial. More recently, attention is being given to reconstruction of the broken pieces of bones and shells into complete specimens, so that longer inscriptions can be

[14] Hu Hou-hsüan, *Yin-hsü fa-chüeh*, pp. 113–14.
[15] *Ibid.*, pp. 134–35; 140.
[16] Hu Hou-hsüan, *Wu-shih-nien chia-ku-hsüeh lun-chu mu*, Preface, pp. 7–10.
[17] Tung Tso-pin, *Yin-li p'u*, Part I, 1/2b–4b.

read and more data assembled for the more accurate and meaningful interpretation of the material.

VOCABULARY AND FORMS OF THE SHANG WRITING

We do not know how large the vocabulary of the Shang dynasty was. The total number of characters in the known bone inscriptions may be well over one million, but a large portion of the inscriptions consist of formulas repeating the same words again and again. Thus the whole vocabulary represented by the published bone inscriptions is estimated at more than 2,500 individual characters. Among them, about one-half are legible today and the rest, including many personal and geographical names, have not yet been deciphered.[18]

Some scholars suggest that long works of literature could not have been produced in the Shang dynasty because the limited number of characters was not sufficient for this purpose. This argument is certainly not valid, since the vocabulary contained in the bone inscriptions is not too small to write longer pieces of literature than those produced in the Chou dynasty. The bronze inscriptions, covering a period three times longer than that of the bone materials, include a vocabulary not much larger than that of the bone inscriptions.[19] Some of the single pieces of Chou literature transmitted today are estimated to include a vocabulary of no more than 3,000 characters.[20] Because the oracle inscription was a special kind of record used only for particular events, it needed only a limited portion of the whole language. On the other hand, the longer writings in books and documents of the Shang dynasty must have been written with more characters than those represented in the bone inscriptions. Thus the scarcity of Shang literature today may well be due to failure to be preserved through the centuries rather than to limitations of vocabulary.

Among the inscriptions on various materials so far discovered, we can see that at least two major forms of writing were used in the Shang dynasty. The inscriptions on Shang bronzes (Plate IV), which will be

[18] Sun Hai-po, *Chia-ku-wen pien* (1934) lists 1,006 legible and 1,112 illegible characters, making a total of 2,118. Chin Hsiang-heng's supplement, *Hsü chia-ku-wen pien* (1959), increases the total to 2,630 characters, including about 1,300 deciphered.

[19] Jung Keng, *Chin-wen pien* lists a vocabulary of 2,969 characters, 1,804 legible and 1,165 illegible, in bronze inscriptions of the Shang and Chou dynasties.

[20] Erkes, "The Use of Writing in Ancient China," *JAOS*, LXI (1941), 127–30. He mentions that the *Spring and Autumn Annals* contains 950 characters, the *Confucian Analects* 2,200, and the *Book of Poetry* 3,000.

discussed in the following chapter, are generally more ornamental and picturesque and seem to have a greater affinity with the original pictography than the more simple and conventional form of the bone and shell inscriptions. Since most of the characters appearing on the Shang bronzes cannot be clearly understood, it is difficult to draw any conclusion about their ages. However, the more picturesque writing on bronzes probably represents a more ancient form of writing used in the Shang dynasty for ornamental purposes just as ancient forms of writing are employed on seals and other objects in modern times. It is assumed that the inscriptions on bone materials were the current form of writing popularly used in the Shang dynasty.[21]

Although the bone inscriptions are the earliest known examples of writing in China, they indicate that it had already reached a very advanced stage of development and included almost every principle of the formation of Chinese characters[22] (Table I). The dominant category is that of pictograms representing concrete objects, such as the human body, animals, and natural and manufactured objects. They are not crude pictures of objects but conventionalized symbols abbreviated to emphasize distinguishing details. For example, the animal symbols are all written with highly simplified lines and, in most cases, give side views of the object placed vertically with heads facing the direction in which the order of columns moved. The next common category in the bone inscriptions is that of ideograms, which transfer the symbols for objects to those of ideas. They suggest a physical action, indicate a position, or assemble ideas from their components. The less common category in the bone inscriptions is that of phonograms, which are either a combination of a pictogram with a phonetic element or a phonetic loan, using a word of similar sound to express an additional idea. The scarcity of phonograms in the bone inscriptions[23] indicates their late development in Chinese writing. Most of the new characters later added to the language are based on the principle of the phonograms.[24]

The forms of the bone writing were generally less stable than those of the later writing. In some characters, the construction varies a great deal; in others, the position of the elements was sometimes changeable.

---

[21] Tung Tso-pin, "Chung-kuo wen-tzu ti ch'i-yüan," *TLTC*, V (1952), 349.

[22] Creel, *The Birth of China*, pp. 159–60.

[23] For examples, see Tung Tso-pin, "Chia-ku-wen tuan-tai yen-chiu li," *TYPLWC*, I, 414.

[24] Among the 9,353 characters in the *Shuo-wen chieh-tzu*, more than 80 per cent are phonetic compounds; in the monograph on "six scripts" of the *T'ung-chih*, compiled by Cheng Ch'iao (1104–1162), the whole vocabulary was increased to 24,235 characters, among which 90 per cent are phonetic compounds, 7 per cent ideograms, and 3 per cent pictograms.

TABLE I

Principles and Forms of Shell and Bone Inscription

Principles	Examples								Explanation
Pictograms	man	woman	child	mouth	nose	eye	hand	foot	a. Whole or parts of human body
	horse	tiger	dog	elephant	deer	sheep	silkworm	tortoise	b. Side or front view of animals
	sun	moon	rain	lightning	mountain	river	grain	wood	c. Symbol of natural objects
	vase	tripod	bow	arrow	silk	book	oracle	omen	d. Symbol of artificial objects
Ideograms	two men against each other — fighting		man and a plough — ploughing		weapon and animal — hunting		woman nursing child — suckling		e. Combination of pictograms suggesting action
	sun setting among grasses — sunset		moon-light on window — bright		hand holding brush — writing brush		hand holding object — scribe		f. Assembling ideas
	above	below							g. Indicating position
Phonograms	horse + li — black horse		spirit + ssu — sacrifice		woman + jen — pregnancy		river + huan — Huan River		h. Combination of pictogram and a phonetic element
	lai wheat for lai — to come		feng phoenix for feng — wind						i. Phonetic loan of a word with the same sound to express another idea
	1	2	3	4	5	6	7	8	

Since the bone inscriptions were incised with a stylus, the characters contain more straight lines than curves, which are more common in the bronze inscriptions. The strokes are usually forceful with sharp ends as a result of the swift carving by the stylus.

The styles of bone writing changed from period to period. In the early periods, including the reign of Wu Ting (1324–1266 B.C.) which probably produced the largest part of the oracle records, the inscriptions are generally cut in quite large characters with heavy and vigorous strokes. The bones and shells are usually smooth and glossy, and some of the carvings are filled with vermilion or black pigments for illumination. This early style gradually gave way to weak and irregular strokes. Except for a short period in the reign of Wen Wu Ting (1194–1192 B.C.), the inscriptions of the later period are generally cut in particularly small script with very fine lines; but the strokes are well balanced and columns properly arranged. The characteristics and styles of the inscriptions are among the criteria by which bone inscriptions may be dated.

TYPES OF BONE MATERIALS AND METHODS OF INSCRIBING

The materials used for divination and writing include animal bones and tortoise shells, which are known to have been specially collected and prepared in the Shang dynasty. The animal bones were primarily those of cattle, especially water buffaloes, and a few deer, sheep, pig, and horse bones. The bones of cattle were undoubtedly supplied locally. The Shang people used cattle a great deal, not only in agriculture but in sacrifice as well. The oracle inscriptions tell us that the number of cattle used for sacrifice reached several hundred or even one thousand head at one time.[25] Except for a few which were destroyed in such ceremonies as drowning, burying, or burning, their meat must have been used as food and certain parts of the bones saved for divination after sacrifice.

Tortoises, on the other hand, probably appeared only in the south and were presented to the Shang court as tribute by many vassal states and individuals. According to ancient literature, the tribute of tortoises was presented from regions in the present Yangtze Valley.[26] Specimens discovered at An-yang have been identified as species native to the same regions and to coastal provinces farther south.[27] The oracle inscriptions

[25] Hu Hou-hsüan, "Yin-tai pu-kuei chih lai-yüan," *CKHSSLT*, 1st ser., IV, 5b–6a.

[26] Legge, *Shoo King*, pp. 116–17; *She King*, p. 620.

[27] Bien, "On the Turtle Remains from the Archeological Site of Anyang, Honan," abstract in White, *op. cit.*, p. 51.

also contain such divinations as "there will be tortoises presented from the south" or "no tortoises will be presented from the south."[28] There are some five hundred occurrences of similar records concerning the tribute of tortoises in the oracle inscriptions. They reveal that as many as one thousand tortoise shells were presented at one time, while a total of more than 12,000 shells were recorded as having been received by the Shang court.[29]

The proportion of bones to shells discovered at An-yang is said to be about equal. The quantity of specimens and the nature of inscriptions all indicate that there has been no discrimination in the use of bones and shells for different occasions of divination. Some scholars have suggested, however, that the tortoise shells were the major material and that the bones were a substitute when there were not enough tortoise shells.[30] The most common bone used for divination was the ox scapula, which provides a wide and smooth surface for writing. Other bones were occasionally used, including the socket end of the scapula, ribs, skulls, and horns, but they seem to have been used for records of historical events and not for oracle inscriptions.

The tortoise shells used in divination include the plastron, carapace, and reshaped carapace. The plastron was most common and usually used whole, but the carapace was sawed into halves because the spinal ridge was so protuberant that a flat surface could not be obtained otherwise. The use of the carapace was rare; sometimes it was remodeled into a long oval shape, often with a hole in the center, apparently for stringing. Specimens were discovered during the thirteenth excavation consisting of the right half of small carapaces which had been reshaped by cutting the edges of the shell.[31]

The tortoise plastrons vary from 14 cm. to 45 cm. in length and from 7 cm. to 35 cm. in width. In general, the medium size of 28 cm. long, 20 cm. wide, and 6–7 mm. thick is more common. The halves of the carapace vary from 27 cm. to 35 cm. in length, and 11 cm. to 15 cm. in width, the smaller size being more common. The reshaped carapace, of which there are fewer specimens, is from 12 cm. to 16 cm. in length and 5 to 6 cm. in width.[32] A large plastron, which measures about 45 cm. in length and 35

---

[28] Hu Hou-hsüan,"Wu-ting shih wu-chung chi-shih k'o-tz'u k'ao," *CKHSSLT*, 1st ser., III, 55a.

[29] Hu Hou-hsüan, "Yin-tai pu-kuei chih lai-yüan," *op. cit.*, pp. 11b–12b.

[30] White, *op. cit.*, p. 25.

[31] Shih Chang-ju, "Yin-hsü tsui-ching chung-yao fa-hsien," *KKHP*, II (1947), 42; Plates. 8:2, 9:2.

[32] Tung Tso-pin, "Shang-tai kuei-pu chih t'uei-ts'e," *AYFCPK*, No. 1(1929), pp. 73-78; Hu Hou-hsüan, "Chia-ku hsüeh hsü-lun," *CKHSSLT*, 2d ser., II, 3a.

cm. in width, was identified with similar species which can be found in the Malay Peninsula.[33] The medium and small sizes are supposed to have been fresh-water tortoises probably brought from the Yangtze Valley to An-yang where the people could breed them for oracle use.[34]

When the gelatinous matter had been removed from the shells, they were scraped flat and smooth, ready for use. On the inner side of the shell, oval cavities about 10 mm. long with round holes connected with them were then chiseled or bored. The preparation of cavities on bones for divination was similar. Each piece of bone or shell had from two or three cavities to more than 200. The great tortoise shell of the Wu Ting period, discovered in 1929 by Academia Sinica, has 204 drilled and chiseled cavities of which 50 were used.[35] They were arranged in orderly rows, and in tortoise shells they were balanced on each side of the central line of the plastron.

When heat was applied to them, the oval cavity would produce, on the other side of the shell, a long vertical crack and the round hole a short horizontal crack branching from it. The character *pu*, for oracle (see Table I, *7d*), which is a long vertical line and a shorter horizontal line slanting at either the right or left side, is actually the form of the crack signs; and its pronunciation as *pu*, *p'u*, or *pou* is the sound of cracking. The character *chao*, which means "omen" or "foretelling" (see Table I, *8d*), is a group of crack signs appearing on one piece of bone or shell.[36]

After cracks were made on the outer side of the shell, inscriptions recording the divination were sometimes written or incised by diviners or scribes. Although most of the bone inscriptions were engraved, some specimens were found to have been written with a brush and cinnabar or black ink on the inner side of the shell. While at least twenty examples of written inscriptions have been found,[37] none seems to have been written on the outer side of the shell. During the excavations in 1929, three inscribed bones were found bearing written characters that were incompletely carved. This suggests that the inscriptions were first written with brush and ink and then carved with stylus.[38] The carved inscriptions were sometimes illuminated with cinnabar or black pigments, especially popular during the Wu Ting period, and some were inlaid with turquoise for decorative purposes.

[33] Tung Tso-pin, "Ten Examples of Early Tortoise-shell inscriptions," *HJAS*, XI (1948), 122.

[34] White, *op. cit.*, p. 51.

[35] Tung Tso-pin, "Ten Examples," *op. cit.*, p. 122.

[36] Tung Tso-pin, "Shang-tai kuei-pu chih t'uei-ts'e," *op. cit.*, pp. 107–10.

[37] Ch'en Meng-chia, *Yin-hsü pu-tz'u tsung-shu*, p. 14.

[38] Tung Tso-pin, "Chia-ku-wen tuan-tai yen-chiu li," *op. cit.*, pp. 417–18.

The sequence of strokes in each character was generally the same as that followed by modern writers. For vertical strokes, it is from top to bottom and for horizontal strokes, from left to right. The method of engraving, however, as revealed by photographic enlargement and microscopic examination of the inscriptions, was different from the order of writing. It seems that engraving was easier in the vertical position, so that the engraver usually rotated the bones or shells in different positions when different kinds of lines were carved. Probably the vertical lines of all the characters were first carved at one time and then the bone was rotated so that horizontal strokes could be cut in the same way. For small characters and thin strokes, the lines were made with only one cut by a sharp stylus. But for large characters and heavy strokes, each line was cut twice, at its left and right side, so that a groove would be made by removal of the fragments.[39] The tool for engraving was most likely a knife or a burin made of bronze, although jade and rodents' teeth are also suggested.[40] During the third excavation in 1929, two small knives made of bronze were reported to have been discovered; but whether they were tools for cutting or engraving the shells and bones is uncertain.[41]

CONTENT AND ARRANGEMENT OF ORACLE INSCRIPTIONS

The subject matter of oracle inscriptions generally included heavenly phenomena such as solar and lunar eclipses, rain, wind, snow, or a clear sky; periodical forecasts about the happenings during the ten-day period, the evening, or the year; predictions for forthcoming travels, hunting, fishing, or military campaigns; human fortunes such as birth, illness, death, and dreams; and sacrifice to the ancestors, deities, and other spiritual beings. The most common category among these inscriptions is divination concerning the ten-day period, performed on the last day of each period to ascertain the good or bad things that might happen during the next ten days. The unit of a ten-day period was used by the Shang people as we today use the seven-day week. Since divination was performed every ten days, there must have been 36 such divinations each year. This practice seems to have been a tradition continued throughout the reigns of all the kings of the Shang dynasty.

The oracle inscriptions are usually written in certain formulas. These

---

[39] Tung Tso-pin, "Ten Examples," *op. cit.*, p. 128.

[40] White, *op. cit.*, p. 29.

[41] Li Chi, "Yin-hsü t'ung-ch'i wu-chung chi ch'i hsiang-kuan wen-t'i," *TYPLWC*, I, 90–91.

include the scattered characters for numerals used to indicate the different locations on the bone or shell for the order of divinations made on it.[42] There are also phrases of two or three small characters in a column, inscribed beside the crack signs or alongside the main inscription. They are probably technical terms in divination to indicate the degree of auspiciousness.[43] The most important part of the oracle inscriptions is the main body of complete or incomplete descriptions concerning the divination. They were usually written in very simple sentences with several sets of formulas.

A complete oracle inscription may be divided into four parts: (1) an introductory statement including the date of divination and the name of the diviner; (2) the queries, including the subject matter and the period to be divined; (3) the interpretation, including the spirits' answers to the queries as observed from the crack signs; and (4) the verification indicating whether later events were identical with the interpretation of the divination. In most cases, however, inscriptions on bones and shells are found in incomplete form. A long inscription of the Wu Ting period, which is translated below, may be used as an illustration. It says:

> Divined on the day *kuei-ssu*, X [name of diviner] asked: (introduction)
> "Will there be any calamities within the [next] ten days?" (query)
> The king read the oracle and said: "There will be calamities and messengers continuing to come." (interpretation)
> On the fifth day, *ting-yu*, there really were messengers coming from the west. Chih-kuo reported saying [the state of] T'u-fang invaded our eastern territory and attacked two of our towns. [The state of] [?]-fang also pastured on our western land.[44] (verification)

This inscription, which runs to 51 characters, is one of the few long inscriptions so far discovered. It appears on the left side and constitutes one of three paragraphs on one piece of bone. The one in the middle includes 45 characters and another on the right, 32, making a total of 128 characters[45] (Plate II). Inscriptions of similar length can also be found on other bones, including one of 54 characters which was reconstructed from two separate pieces by Kuo Mo-jo.[46] In many cases, the inscriptions on one piece of bone or shell may include several hundred characters, but

[42] Kuo Mo-jo, *Pu-tz'u t'ung-tsuan*: *k'ao-shih*, II, 4b.

[43] Wu Ch'i-ch'ang, "On the Marginal Notes Found in Oracle Bone Inscriptions," *TP* XLII (1955), 34–74.

[44] Tung Tso-pin, *Yin-li p'u*, Part, II, 9/4b, No. 43.

[45] Lo Chen-yü, *Yin-hsü shu-ch'i ching-hua*, Plate 2.

[46] Kuo Mo-jo, *op. cit.*, No. 592; *k'ao-shih*, III, 129b.

PLATE I
A WHOLE INSCRIBED PLASTRON

The oracle statements concerning a good or bad harvest in the upper part of the shell and the numerals in the order of divination at the lower part were arranged symmetrically (*ca.* 1300 B.C., 20 × 11.5 cm.).

PLATE II

AN INSCRIBED SCAPULA

This piece includes three long inscriptions in 128 characters concerning divination of happenings during next ten-day periods (*ca.* 1300 B.C., 22 × 19 cm.).

they are usually divided into many independent paragraphs made at different times. For example, one of the four largest pieces of tortoise shell discovered in 1929 by the Academia Sinica includes 277 characters; but they are divided into 28 units, the longest unit containing not more than 15 characters.[47]

The longest paragraph so far discovered is probably one which, continuing from the front to the back of the bone, totals 93 characters.[48] In most cases, the longer inscriptions appear on bones for divination concerning a ten-day period, with records of important happenings, primarily belonging to the Wu Ting period.[49] On the average, each fragment includes about ten characters. Because the bones and shells are very brittle, they are in most cases broken pieces.

The oracle inscriptions on bones and shells are generally read from top to bottom, in the same order that we follow today. But there seem to have been no definite rules for the arrangement of the vertical lines, since they are read sometimes from right to left and sometimes from left to right. As an example (Plate I), the inscriptions on a whole inscribed plastron concern divination about a good or bad harvest during the year, with an affirmative query on the right half, reading from left to right, and a negative query on the left, reading from right to left. Some of the characters are written in reverse on different halves. This symmetrical arrangement is believed to have been used only in oracle records in order to balance the inscriptions on the writing surface and also to suit the positions of their respective "oracular signs."[50] Since inscriptions on many other bones and animal skulls, on stone and jade implements, and on bronze vessels of the Shang dynasty are all written from right to left in vertical columns, it is believed that this arrangement was the regular form of writing by the Shang people and that irregularities in the oracle inscriptions are only exceptions.[51]

NON-ORACLE BONE RECORDS

Most of the inscriptions on animal bones and tortoise shells are, as indicated in previous discussion, oracle records. We have found, how-

[47] Tung Tso-pin, "Ta-kuei ssu-p'an k'ao-shih," *AYFCPK*, III (1931), Plate I; "Chia-ku-wen tuan-tai yen-chiu li," *op. cit.*, p. 402.

[48] Lo Chen-yü, *Yin-hsü shu-ch'i ching-hua*, Plates 3, 5.

[49] Tung Tso-pin, "Chia-ku-wen tuan-tai yen-chiu li," *op. cit.*, p. 403.

[50] Tung Tso-pin, *An Interpretation of the Ancient Chinese Civilization*, pp. 24–25.

[51] *Ibid.*, p. 25.

ever, some inscriptions which are non-oracular in nature. They pertain to miscellaneous matters inscribed on oracle materials or are records of historical events on non-scorched bones, all of which have nothing to do with divination. Miscellaneous records include registers of bone materials. The gift of tortoise shells to the Shang court from various vassal states or individuals was considered very important, and such records are usually found on the margin of the carapace and on the bridges or tails of the plastron. A brief statement about the donor and the amount of the tribute was recorded. For example, such registers as "Ch'üeh presented 150" or "Hua presented 100" are very common in the marginal inscriptions. Records are also sometimes found on the socket end or near the edge of scapulas. More than 800 such records of receipts belonging to the Wu Ting period are found in such locations among the inscriptions.[52]

Historical records may either be included in oracle inscriptions or found on independent objects. In the oracle inscription itself, the queries are the subject matter to be divined and the verification statements are actually records of historical events. When the king asked: "Will Heaven send down more rain to save the crop?" a statement that: "It rained on a certain day" sometimes followed. In a complete tortoise shell discovered in the thirteenth excavation by the Academia Sinica, a record on the left bridge of the shell says: "It rained in the ninth month from the *ting-yu* to the *chia-yin* day, for eighteen days."[53] Since this was unusual, it was especially recorded with reference to a previous inquiry. This kind of inscription, however, is considered a part of the oracle statement and not an independent historical record.

Independent records of historical events are generally found on bone materials which were apparently not used for divination. They were neither scorched nor inscribed with oracle data, but contain statements concerning events that happened to the royal court. Several inscriptions regarding hunting and military campaigns are found on pieces of bone tablets. The survival of long, narrow bone tablets used for historical records suggests that similar tablets made of bamboo and wood might have been used for ordinary documents and books in the Shang dynasty. At least two complete and several broken pieces of such bone tablets, carved with decorative designs on the front and inscriptions, are inlaid with turquoise. One large animal rib, 22 cm. long, now in the collection of the Royal Ontario Museum at Toronto, bears an inscription of 22

---

[52] Hu Hou-hsüan, "Wu-ting shih wu-chung chih-shih k'o-tz'u k'ao," *CKHSSLT*, 1st ser., III, 67a.

[53] *Ibid.*, p. 2b.

PLATE III

NON-ORACULAR RECORDS ON BONES

A

B

Records of royal hunting expeditions. (A) Inscription on bone spatula, ca. 1152 B.C., is inlaid with turquoise (21.5 cm. long). (B) Inscription on two deer skulls, ca. 1160 B.C.

characters, stating that on the *hsin-yu* day the king went hunting in the foothills of the Cock Mountain and was successful in the chase, and in the tenth month of the third year supplementary sacrifice was offered[54] (Plate III.A). This piece is dated the third year of Ti Hsin,[55] the last Shang king, which corresponds to 1152 B.C., according to the traditional chronology. Another complete piece, 28 cm. long, and two fragments carry a similar inscription on the capture of a rhinoceros.[56] The complete rib bears the date "in the fifth month of the sixth year," which is attributed to the sixth year of Ti Hsin, or 1149 B.C. These inscriptions were probably made on bones of animals captured during the hunting expedition in order to celebrate the successful mission and to reward the officials.[57]

Another historical record of a military campaign is found on a fragment of bone tablet dating from the first half of the twelfth century B.C. The original size of the tablet was probably 20 cm. in length and 5 cm. in width; but only one-third of it survives, bearing an inscription of 56 characters arranged in five lines.[58] The inscription says that a military campaign took place against a certain state in the west, and the prizes of war included 1,570 prisoners, two chariots, 180 shields, 15 pieces of armor, and a certain number of arrows.[59] Since the fifth line does not complete the statement, there must have been another line in the inscription. It is estimated that there were more than 160 characters in the whole inscription.[60]

On the back of this tablet is an inscription comprising a table of cyclic days, which was computed by the ten stems and the twelve branches to make a cycle of sixty for use in calendars.[61] A similar table of cyclic characters, but with mistakes in combinations and order, is found on another piece of bone, believed to have been carved by beginners practicing the technique of incising.[62] Tables of names and dates for the sacrifices to the ancestors are also found on separate pieces of bone, probably used by the diviners as memoranda.[63] Certain genealogical tables are also recorded on bone tablets.[64]

---

[54] White, *op. cit.*, pp. 28, 97.

[55] *Ibid.*, p. 97.

[56] Shang Ch'eng-tso, *Yin-ch'i i-ts'un*, Nos. 426, 427; *k'ao shih*, 62b–63a; 71b.

[57] *Ibid.*, 63a.

[58] Tung Tso-pin, "Chung-kuo wen-tzu ti ch'i-yüan," *op. cit.*, p. 349.

[59] *Ibid.*

[60] *Ibid.*

[61] Ch'en Meng-chia, *op. cit.*, Plate 16.

[62] *Ibid.*, p. 44.

[63] Tung Tso-pin, "Chung-kuo wen-tzu ti ch'i-yüan," *op. cit.*, p. 349.

[64] Ch'en Meng-chia, *op. cit.*, p. 44.

Some historical records are also found inscribed on human and animal skulls. An inscription about a sacrifice to Ti I was inscribed on a piece of a human skull.[65] Three fragments of inscribed bones from An-yang, formerly in a private collection, have recently been certified by a paleozoologist as the frontal pieces of a human cranium.[66] At least three inscriptions concerning hunting expeditions have been found on three separate pieces of animal skulls.[67] One specimen, 54 cm. long, 22 cm. wide, and 19 cm. deep, is probably the skull of a white rhinoceros, since the characters for that animal appear in the inscription.[68] The other two specimens are deer skulls which bear similar inscriptions except that the name of the animal is not mentioned (Plate III.B). It is believed that the animals were captured during a hunting expedition by Ti I, who used them in sacrifice to his father Wen Wu Ting, whose name appears on one of these two skulls.[69]

Single characters are found on stag horns from An-yang which were used for utensils.[70] Inscriptions are also found on ornamental implements and other objects of bone. A hairpin bearing three characters, saying "two [pins] were presented by [a certain] lord," was found at An-yang.[71] Ivory was decoratively carved in the Shang dynasty, but no inscription has been found to indicate that it was used for writing.

[65] Tung Tso-pin, "Chung-kuo wen-tzu ti ch'i-yüan," *op. cit.*, p. 349.

[66] *Wen-wu ts'an-k'ao tzu-liao*, 1954, No. 4, p. 5; Plates 1–3.

[67] Tung Tso-pin, *Yin-hsü wen-tzu: chia-pien*, Nos. 3939–41.

[68] T'ang Lan, "Huo pai-ssu k'ao," *Shih-hsüeh nien-pao*, I, No. 4 (1932), 119–24.

[69] Kuo Mo-jo, *op. cit.*, *k'ao-shih*, pp. 125a–126a.

[70] Tung Tso-pin, *Yin-hsü wen-tzu: chia-pien*, No. 3942.

[71] Hu Hou-hsüan, "Yin-tai pu-kuei chih lai-yüan," *op. cit.*, p. 10b.

III

INSCRIPTIONS ON METALS AND CLAY

Inscriptions were also made on various kinds of metallic objects, pottery, and clay materials. While a few writings are found on gold, iron, and pewter, the extensive inscriptions are primarily on bronze. Although bronze inscriptions were used as early as the Shang and as late as the Han, their importance as historical documents is generally more significant during the Chou dynasty. Since the iron age did not begin in China until the seventh or sixth century B.C., bronze was the most important metal in ancient Chinese civilization.

Pottery, although an altogether different kind of material, seems to have a close relationship with bronze. Not only are the important types of bronze vessels believed to have sprung from those of pottery,[1] but their inscriptions also show some resemblance in origin. As time went on, pottery inscriptions remained short, and were primarily marks for identification, while bronze inscriptions developed into lengthy records of historical events. This is probably because the bronze vessels were made of enduring material, while pottery was too fragile for permanent preservation. When stone tablets came into extensive use for monumental and commemorative inscriptions in the Later Han dynasty, bronze inscriptions almost completely ceased to function as historical records.

Another example of a close relationship between metal and earth is the use of the seal and its impression on clay. It was primarily used to insure privacy of bamboo and wooden documents. Stamps were sometimes also applied to other earthen objects such as bricks and tiles used as building materials. Many such clay inscriptions belonging to the Warring States and Han periods survive today.

---

[1] Creel, *The Birth of China*, p. 105.

NATURE AND TYPES OF BRONZE INSCRIPTIONS

The ancient Chinese bronzes are not only technically and artistically exquisite objects, but their inscriptions are equally important as original documents of ancient times. They are valuable for the understanding of the development of Chinese writing, and their content adds to our knowledge of ancient history and institutions. The style and content of the inscriptions, in turn, have become important criteria in determining the age of the objects.

Inscribed bronzes generally include sacrificial vessels, musical instruments, military weapons, measurement standards, mirrors, coins, seals, and other tools and articles. Among them, ritual vessels constitute the most important category on which the longer inscriptions of historical significance were usually cast. The vessels have different uses and shapes which include some thirty or forty major common types. Traditionally, they were given names found in ancient literature or inscribed on the objects themselves. Because of the great variety of forms and designs in relation to their uses, which are sometimes difficult to differentiate from one another, the earlier bronze catalogues merely list similar objects together without a logical grouping.

A more recent classification groups them into major categories according to their uses, such as food vessels, wine vessels, water and miscellaneous vessels, and musical instruments.[2] Another classification, based on the shape of the bottom of the vessel,[3] divides them into those having round, flat, and circular bases, and three or four legs. No matter how these objects are classified, the vessels generally include two important parts: the body which may be round, square, or rectangular, and the determinative features such as handles, legs, and lids. In general, vessels with round bodies usually have three legs, and square or rectangular ones, four.

There seem to be no definite rules concerning the location of inscriptions. Although some were inscribed either by casting or engraving on the outside, probably for decorative purposes, the basic position for earlier inscriptions is usually inside the body, no matter whether the vessel is round or square with three or four legs. They also appear occasionally on the cover or handle if there is one, and are comparatively scarce, but not unknown, on ears, mouths, necks, spouts, or legs.[4]

[2] Jung Keng, *Shang Chou i-ch'i t'ung-k'ao*, I, 21–23.

[3] Li Chi, "Chi Hsiao-t'un ch'u-t'u chih ch'ing-t'ung-ch'i," *KKHP*, III (1948), 3–4.

[4] Shih Chang-ju, "Shang Chou i-ch'i ming-wen pu-wei li lüeh," *TLTC*, VIII (1954), 129–34; 180–85; 211–19.

The bronze vessels and implements were excellently cast. Some early specimens of the Shang dynasty contain approximately 80 to 85 per cent copper and 15 to 20 per cent tin, with small quantities of lead and other minerals.[5] The bronze was cast in molds either by the direct process of pouring the molten metal into the molds or by the so-called lost wax process in which the mold was made on a wax model which was melted out, leaving the mold ready for casting.[6] Many fragments of pottery molds discovered at An-yang are believed to have been used for casting in the Shang dynasty.[7]

Ancient bronzes are generally objects for sacrificial, funeral, or daily use which were sometimes buried in graves of aristocratic families as a gift to the dead. They were unearthed from time to time either by accident or by grave robbers, who have always been attracted by unprotected wealth buried underground. It is said that even before the countries of the feudal princes were conquered by others, their ancestors' tombs had already been broken into and robbed.[8] Under the Han dynasty, even royal princes employed professional diggers to collect underground treasures from the ancient tombs.[9]

The discovery of bronze vessels, which were treasured as emblems of sovereignty, was usually considered a lucky omen, an occasion for the reigning monarch to make special rewards to the officials or to change the reign title of the dynasty in commemoration or celebration. In 116 B.C., Emperor Wu of the Han dynasty changed his reign title to Yüan Ting because a *ting*, or tripod cauldron, was found near the Fen River in Shansi.[10] Such finds during the successive dynasties were usually considered somewhat sacred, but the details of discoveries are generally unknown.

During the last thirty or forty years, however, a number of important bronzes either have been scientifically excavated or are known to have been found in some identified sites. These include many districts such as Hsin-cheng, Lo-yang, Chün-hsien, An-yang, Cheng-chou, and Hui-hsien in Honan; Hun-yüan in Shansi; Shou-hsien in Anhui; and Ch'ang-sha in Hunan. The objects were usually found at the site where they were originally manufactured, but there was also transfer before burial by gift, in trousseaux, and by capture in war.

[5] Carpenter, "Preliminary Report on Chinese Bronzes," *AYFCPK*, IV (1933), 679.
[6] Yetts, *The Eumorfopoulos Collection Catalogue*, I, 34–39.
[7] Karlbeck, "Anyang Moulds," *BMFEA*, VII (1935), 39–60; Plates 1–7.
[8] *Lü-shih ch'un-ch'iu*, 10/7b.
[9] *Hsi-ching tsa-chi*, 6/1b.
[10] *Han shu*, 6/17b; Dubs, *The History of the Former Han Dynasty*, I, 71–72; note 17.9.

Although bronze objects are numerous, those bearing inscriptions probably amount to no more than six or seven thousand pieces extant today.[11] Among them, some one thousand are said to date from the Shang,[12] another one thousand from the Ch'in and Han,[13] and some four thousand or more from the Chou dynasty.[14] While the majority of these inscriptions are very brief, they are much longer and more complete than those on the bones and shells. They contain an average of from 20 to 50 characters, with a few having less than ten or over two hundred.[15] The longest one, of about 500 characters, was cast on a tripod. The total vocabulary used in bronze inscriptions does not much exceed that of the bone inscriptions. According to the dictionary compiled by Jung Keng, the vocabulary of bronze inscriptions used in the Chou and pre-Chou periods includes 1,804 legible and 1,165 illegible characters. Those of the Ch'in and Han periods contain 951 legible and 33 illegible characters.[16] However, the characters as revealed either on bones or on bronzes do not represent the whole vocabulary used in ancient books and documents during their respective periods, since the inscriptions were used only in recording certain particular events on certain special occasions and are limited to those which have been discovered.

The earlier inscriptions of the Shang and Western Chou dynasties were all cast on bronzes, but some, of later date, were incised. It is especially common to find vessels and implements from the Ch'u state with engraved inscriptions. The size of characters is generally about 2 cm. in the square form, although there are cases of larger characters in the oblong form. They are generally arranged vertically and from right to left in the traditional order as in other documents. We have found, however, at least ten cases in which the text is read from left to right. One example even shows that the text is read in alternate lines, that is, the first, third, and fifth lines read from top to bottom, but the second and fourth lines from bot-

[11] There is no complete census available for the total number of bronze inscriptions. Liu T'i-chih listed 6,456 in his *Hsiao-chiao-ching-ko chin-wen t'o-pen*, which is considered to be the most complete collection, although some of them are believed to be forgeries.

[12] Lo Chen-yü listed in his *Yin-wen ts'un* 755 inscriptions and Wang Ch'en added to it 1,167, which were believed to have been from the Shang dynasty but many are proved to be from the Chou period. Bernhard Karlgren said that some 450–500 are definitely from the Shang; see his "Yin and Chou in Chinese Bronzes," *BMFEA*, VIII (1936), 23.

[13] Jung Keng recorded in his *Chin-wen hsü-pien* 88 inscriptions of Ch'in and 749 of Han date.

[14] Kuo Mo-jo, *Ku-tai ming-k'o hui-k'ao*, I, appendix, 1a.

[15] Creel, "Bronze Inscriptions of the Western Chou Dynasty as Historical Documents," *JAOS*, LVI (1936), 338.

[16] Jung Keng, *Chin-wen pien* includes inscriptions of Shang and Chou; *Chin-wen hsü-pien* includes those of the Ch'in and Han periods.

tom to top.[17] There are also cases of duplicated or missing characters in the text, indicating that the inscriptions on the molds might not have been well checked or collated.

STYLES AND USAGE OF BRONZE INSCRIPTIONS

The development of bronze inscriptions, like that of bronze implements, may be generally divided into four periods : the Shang or Yin (1401?–1123? B.C.), the Western Chou (1122?–771 B.C.), the Eastern Chou (770–256 B.C.), including the Ch'un Ch'iu (722–481 B.C.) and most of the Warring States (468–221 B.C.) periods, and the Ch'in and Han dynasties (221 B.C.– A.D. 220). The inscriptions used during different periods vary to a certain extent in their forms of writing, styles of composition, and grammatical usage. These, in addition to the motifs and forms of the vessels, have been used for dating.

The inscriptions on Shang bronzes are generally short, simple, and written in formulas, with more pictorial elements in the scripts. These characteristics suggest that they are generally different from the inscriptions of the Chou dynasty and later. These short inscriptions usually include different kinds of names, such as the name of the clan or person, of the ancestor receiving offerings, of the vessel, or of the maker. There are many such simple inscriptions as Fu I, "Father I," or Tso Fu Ting, "Made for Father Ting," containing personal names composed of cyclical characters. It is believed that the Shang people, in sacrificing to the dead, used the name of the date of birth or death as the posthumous name. Since this system also extended up to the middle of the Chou dynasty,[18] it is difficult to consider it as exclusive evidence of Shang date.

There are, however, many simple pictorial characters which are believed to be peculiar to the Shang dynasty.[19] They are written in such forms as animals—horses, elephants, pigs, dogs—or human figures with vessels and implements, indicating sacrifice, manufacture, warfare, or other actions of social and economic life[20] (Plate IV). These characters are, as a rule, more crude in form and less conventionalized than those in the bone and shell inscriptions. It is believed that this script was probably a more ancient form of Chinese writing that the Shang people utilized for inscribing vessels.[21]

[17] Jung Keng, *Shang Chou i-ch'i t'ung-ka'o*, I, 94; Figure 54.
[18] *Ibid.*, I, 75.
[19] Karlgren, "Yin and Chou in Chinese Bronzes," *BMFEA*, VIII (1936), 20.
[20] Cf. Karlgren, "Some Early Chinese Bronze Masters," *BMFEA*, XVI (1944), 4–7.
[21] Tung Tso-pin, *An Interpretation of the Ancient Chinese Civilization*, p. 24.

PLATE IV

INSCRIPTIONS ON SHANG BRONZES

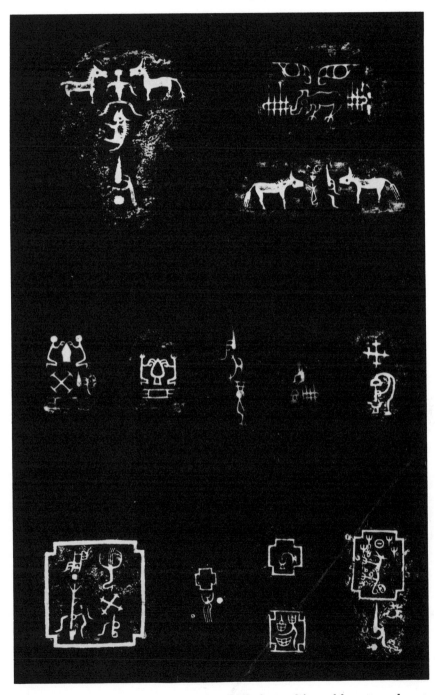

Figures in the upper row represent animals; middle, human life, and lower row, elements of a hollow cross.

The bronze inscriptions of the Western Chou dynasty include some long narrative compositions. These are primarily records of military campaigns, covenants, treaties, appointments, rewards, ceremonial events, and other political and social affairs of the times. Many of them are very similar in style of composition and grammatical usage to the literary documents transmitted from the Chou dynasty. The longest inscription, of some 500 characters, on a tripod cauldron for the prince of Mao, which is generally dated to the period of King Ch'eng (1115–1079 B.C.), discloses a literary similarity, for example, to some chapters in the *Book of Documents*.[22] This inscription, five paragraphs all beginning with the statement "The King said," might have been composed and written by the court scribe to be inscribed on the prince's vessel as a record.

A number of legal documents are found preserved on bronze vessels of the Western Chou period. Because of the permanent nature of the material, bronzes seem to have been considered especially suitable for this purpose, as the *Rituals of Chou* says: "Treaties were written on tripods and ritual vessels."[23] The *Tso chuan* also contains several references to the casting of penal codes on tripod vessels.[24] A treaty cast on a shallow plate, dating from the ninth or eighth century B.C., concerns the boundary between the fiefs of two neighboring clans.[25] Similar inscriptions of a legal nature include records of the exchange of four horses for thirty lots of land,[26] a contract relating to the purchase of five slaves,[27] and litigation about a land dispute.[28]

The characters of the Western Chou inscriptions are generally well balanced, and their lines are very regular and heavy. An example, reproduced in Plate V, shows a medium-sized inscription of sixty-five characters arranged in eight lines inside the bottom of a *kuei* vessel. The inscription says: "In the third month, the King solemnly ordered Tai and the *nei-shih* saying: Replace the Marquis of Hsing in his duties. I give you three groups as subordinates: the men of Chou, Tung and Ching. . . ." The vessel was dedicated to the Duke of Chou and is dated to the Western Chou period. Most inscriptions of this period are written in well-executed calligraphy.

The removal of the Chou capital from modern Shensi to Honan in

---

[22] Kuo Mo-jo, *Liang chou chin-wen tz'u ta-hsi: k'ao shih*, p. 135b.

[23] *Chou-li chu-su*, 36/4b.

[24] Legge, *The Ch'un Ts'ew with the Tso Chuen*, pp. 609, 732.

[25] Kuo Mo-jo, *Liang-chou chin-wen tz'u ta-hsi: k'ao shih*, pp. 129a—131a.

[26] *Ibid.*, pp. 81b–82a.

[27] *Ibid.*, pp. 96b–99b.

[28] Kuo Mo-jo, *Chin-wen ts'ung-k'ao*, II, 165a.

PLATE V

INSCRIPTION ON A BRONZE VESSEL

A four-handled *kuei* with inscription cast inside the bottom (enlargement below), dedicated to the Duke of Chou, *ca.* eleventh century B.C. (diameter across the brim 27 cm.).

770 B.C. marked the decline of the power of the royal house of Chou over the feudal states, and its leading part in ceremonial activities was shifted to the various feudal courts. This fact is reflected in the superseding of vessels from the royal Chou by those from the various feudal states. The inscriptions of the Eastern Chou period extant today come from at least forty-eight states, as compared with none or few from the royal house of the Chou dynasty.[29] These states may be generally divided into two cultural groups. The northern group included those states north of and along the Yellow River, while the southern group lay along the Yangtze and the Huai rivers. It appears from the vessels and their inscriptions that neighboring states shared similar characteristics in their cultures. In general, inscriptions of this period are characterized by their use of rhymes in composition and of ornamental style in calligraphy. They are usually shorter and contain more formulas than the Western Chou inscriptions.

More than seventy Chou inscriptions written with rhymed verses have been found.[30] Most of them came from such states as Ch'i, Ch'in, Chin, and Hsü in the Ch'un Ch'iu period. The inscriptions of this period were sometimes used for decorative purposes. A *t'an* vessel of the Ch'i state, dating from 589 B.C.,[31] bears an inscription of fifty-three characters spreading like a fan over the upper part of the surface of the vessel. Not only were the writings used for adornment, but individual characters were sometimes written in ornamental styles.

One of the most interesting styles is the bird script, in which a decorative bird sign is affixed to the ordinary characters, or the individual strokes of a character are written in the form of bird feathers (Fig. 1). Variations of

Shang script   Script of Warring States period

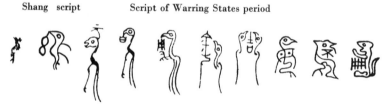

FIG. 1—Styles of Bird Script

this style include a form in which one or two bird signs are added to ordinary characters,[32] or that in which the bird signs are combined with the regular strokes of a character.[33] Although the use of the bird script

[29] Karlgren, "Yin and Chou in Chinese Bronzes," *op. cit.*, pp. 56–77.

[30] Kuo Mo-jo, *Chin-wen ts'ung-k'ao*, II, 127–30.

[31] Kuo Mo-jo, *Liang-chou chin-wen tz'u ta-hsi: k'ao-shih*, p. 202.

[32] Cf. Yetts, "Bird Script on Ancient Chinese Swords," *JRAS*, 1934, pp. 547–52.

[33] Jung Keng, "Niao-shu k'ao," *YCHP*, XVI (1934), 195–203; XVII (1935), 173–78.

can be traced back to the bone and bronze inscriptions of the Shang dynasty,[34] the extensive use of this style is found only in the Warring States period and primarily on weapons from the southern states. At least eighteen out of some twenty-nine inscriptions written in different styles of bird script are found from the Warring States period.[35] This probably marks the beginning of the wide use of artistic styles in Chinese writing.

The inscriptions on bronzes during the Ch'in, Han, and subsequent dynasties developed into definite formulas. They are different from the earlier styles of either prose or rhymed compositions. Beginning with the Ch'in dynasty, when the feudal system was abolished, the use of bronze vessels in court rituals gradually became unimportant. With the unification of the empire by the First Emperor of Ch'in, all metal objects in the country were collected by the government, and the manufacture of bronze vessels for use in ceremonials practically ceased. Almost all of the inscribed metal objects of the Ch'in period extant today are measuring vessels and objects with statements concerning the Emperor's efforts toward standardization. The inscribed bronzes of the Han dynasty usually include the name of the caster, measurement of the piece, the date of its casting, the name of the owner, and formalistic expressions of good will.

MIRROR INSCRIPTIONS

Bronze mirrors, usually circular in form with extremely fine decorations and inscriptions on the back, were in common use among the ancient Chinese. A piece of bronze mirror is said to have been found at An-yang.[36] Both literary and archeological testimony indicates their exquisite designs as well as their extensive use in the Chou dynasty. A moralizing inscription ascribed to King Wu, saying "Look to the past, but take thought of the morrow,"[37] has been thought to imply the use of mirror inscriptions as early as the twelfth century B.C., but this may be a legend. A poem dated about the ninth century B.C. says:

> My mind is not a mirror,
> It cannot [equally] receive [all impressions].[38]

Few mirrors of the Western Chou period survive, but many fine specimens

[34] Tung Tso-pin, "Yin-tai ti niao-shu," *TLTC*, VI (1953), 345–47.
[35] Jung Keng, "Niao-shu k'ao," *op. cit.*
[36] Kao Ch'ü-hsün, "Yin-tai ti i-mien t'ung-ching," *BIHP*, XXIV (1958), 685–719.
[37] *Ta-tai li chi*, 6/2b.
[38] Legge, *She King*, I, 38.

of Eastern Chou are extant today. Among them, a group of eleven bronze mirrors said to have been found in the royal tombs at Lo-yang, Honan,[39] and dating from about 550 B.C., shows masterly technique and exquisite artistic feeling. One of them is inlaid with gold and silver decoration and others bear a background of fine designs. Similar mirrors of the Warring States period are also reported to have been found at the site of Ch'ang-sha, Hunan.[40] None of these early specimens, however, is inscribed.

The earliest known inscription on an extant specimen is probably the one dating from the third century B.C. The inscription of seven characters reads: "May we long think of each other, I wish that we may never forget each other."[41] Other pre-Han inscriptions are, like this one, generally limited to shorter phrases of good wishes, greetings, or maxims. They are usually considered to be love gifts from men to women, with the wish that the lover should be as close as the image in the mirror. These early inscriptions, which express human desires for both spiritual and material satisfaction, set a pattern that later inscriptions on mirrors usually followed. One common example says:

> May you have great joy, prominence and wealth;
> may you obtain what you love;
> may you have a thousand autumns and ten thousand years;
> may you have extended years and increased longevity.[42]

The inscriptions on the Han mirrors not only followed the earlier formulas of greetings and good wishes but also added many variations. For instance, the phrase "May you have sons and grandsons" was very common. Dates and names of manufacturers were frequently inscribed. It is estimated that more than one hundred mirrors of the Han period extant today are inscribed with dates from A.D. 6 onward.[43] Political propaganda is also found on mirror inscriptions, especially those made during the period of Wang Mang (A.D. 9–23), the usurper of the Han dynasty.[44]

During the Later Han dynasty, allusions to various folk beliefs and Taoist cabalistic ideas came into mirror inscriptions. A typical example is found in a very fine decorated mirror inscribed with 55 characters forming an inner circle surrounding a square, in which the twelve cyclical

---

[39] White, *Tombs of Old Loyang*, 86–89; Plates 120–30.

[40] Hsia Nai, "New Archeological Discoveries," *China Reconstructs*, 1952, No. 4, p. 18.

[41] Liang Shang-ch'un, "Chung-kuo ku-ching ming-wen ts'ung-t'an," *TLTC*, II (1951), No. 3, p. 2.

[42] Cf. Karlgren, "Early Chinese Mirror Inscriptions," *BMFEA*, VI (1934), 20; No. 32.

[43] Liang Shang-ch'un, *op. cit.*, II, No. 4, 19.

[44] Karlgren, *op. cit.*, p. 38; No. 123.

PLATE VI

INSCRIPTION ON A BRONZE MIRROR

A fine decorated mirror with inscriptions forming an inner circle surrounding a square
(Later Han dynasty, diameter 18 cm.).

characters are distributed on the four sides (Plate VI). The inscription says:

> This gift mirror, made at Shang Fang (Board of Manufacture),
>   is true and without blemish;
> Its decoration is engraved with skillful craftsmanship.
> On the left the Dragon, and on the right the Tiger ward off ill-
>   luck;
> The Scarlet Bird and the Sombre Warrior combine the *yin* and
>   *yang* principles harmoniously.
> The twelve branches, all complete, occupy the centre; and the
>   necessary fairies are present.
> May joy, wealth, and prosperity long be ensured to both parents;
> May their lives outlast metal and stone, and may [their lot be
>   like that of] nobles and kings.[45]

The mention of animals, fairies, immortals, positive and negative principles, and the five elements correspond to the beliefs and superstitions popular in the Later Han dynasty.

Mirror inscriptions of the post-Han period, especially since the Sui and T'ang dynasties, represent a type entirely different from those of early mirrors. They repeat formulas of four or five characters over again in different inscriptions, most of them using similar phrases. Although many of the T'ang mirrors imitated Han designs, the inscriptions are usually of a different type.[46]

Mirror inscriptions are generally located in the inner or outer circle among the designs on the back of the mirror. The characters are all written in a decorative style adapted to the space provided for designs. The earlier forms of the Warring States period are more cursive, similar to the seal style, and those on the Han mirrors are modified *k'ai* or model script. There are numerous borrowed characters of similar pronunciation but different meanings. Many erroneous characters occur because of ignorance on the part of the scribe or ineptitude on the part of the engraver. Moreover, the characters are often severely maltreated variants of older forms, probably because of the artistic stylization.

NUMISMATIC INSCRIPTIONS

Inscriptions on metal coins, which flourished in the Chou dynasty, have been prized by epigraphists, numismatists, and students of economic

---

[45] Cf. Yetts, *The Eumorfopoulos Collection Catalog*, II, 53.

[46] Liang Shang-ch'un, "Sui T'ang shih ching chih yen-chiu," *TLTC*, VI (1953), No. 6, 189–91.

history. Except for a few special types, almost all of the early and late metal coins bear inscriptions. They are generally different in writing style from other bronze inscriptions and sometimes vary from one type to another because of regional diversity. The inscriptions are primarily geographical names, numerals for the denomination and units of the coins by which the coin types, dates, and areas of their circulation can generally be established. There are, however, many coin inscriptions which are either uncertain or entirely undecipherable.

Ancient Chinese coins include at least five major types: cowry shells, spade coins, knife coins, metal plates, and round coins. No inscriptions are found on cowry shells, which were used in the Shang and early Chou dynasties. The date of the earliest use of metal coins with inscriptions is controversial, but it is generally believed that metal coins could not have been used earlier than the eighth century B.C. Some opinion, however, suggests the possible use of the spade coins as early as the late Shang or early Chou dynasty.[47] Metal coins were tokens made of bronze, copper, or brass in the shape of spades, knives, or other things. The spades or knives were agricultural implements for weeding but must have been used in early times as a medium of exchange.

The spade coins were circulated among the states of Yen, Chao, Lu, Wei, and Han, north of and along the Yellow River. In general they are of four shapes classified according to their top or foot, such as the hollow-handle, pointed-foot, square-foot, or round-foot. They usually bear inscriptions such as An-i, T'un-liu, or Shan-yang (Plate VII.B), indicating the towns where the coins were manufactured. Others bear longer inscriptions including names of the mint, numerals for the denomination and the units of the money. They generally contain six to eight characters which may be read as "Liang standard superior money equal to one *lieh*," or "Liang money to be used as one *chin* and equal to one *lieh*"[48] (Plate VII.C). Liang was the capital of the Wei (Liang) state located on the eastern plain of Chou China around the fourth century B.C. The *chin* and *lieh* are the monetary units used during that time. Many of these inscriptions, however, are meager, and the actual meaning is sometimes difficult to interpret.

Most interesting and well cast are the knife coins from the state of Ch'i. The inscriptions are more legible than those of the other types. They include such inscriptions as "Legal money of Ch'i" or "Everlasting legal

[47] Wang Yü-ch'üan, *Early Chinese Coinage*, p. 114; *Wo-kuo ku-tai huo-pi ti ch'i-yüan ho fa-chan*, p. 34.

[48] Wang Yü-ch'üan, *Early Chinese Coinage*, p. 138.

PLATE VII

INSCRIPTIONS ON ANCIENT COINAGE

(A) Knife money bearing inscriptions "Everlasting legal money of Ch'i at the establishment of the state." (B) Spade money bearing the place name Shan-yang. (C) Spade money with inscription "Liang standard superior money equal to one *lieh*." (D) Round-hole coin. (E) Square-hole coin. (F) "Wu-shu" coin.

money of Ch'i at the establishment of the state" (Plate VII.A). The latter one is believed to be the earliest of all Ch'i knives.[49] Other knife coins bear inscriptions including local names, such as "Legal money of Chi-mo" or "Legal money of An-yang." Both Chi-mo and An-yang were important principalities of the state of Ch'i, where the mints were situated.

Metal plates were probably the only money which circulated in the state of Ch'u in the Yangtze and Huai valleys. They were made of gold, copper, or other metals in various sizes and were stamped with the name of the mint and the monetary designation. Stamps, from two to sixteen, on the metal plates are of three varieties: *Ying yüan, Ch'en yüan,* and *Shou-ch'un. Yüan* was a monetary unit of the metal plates. Ying, Ch'en and Shou-ch'un are names of the three places which served as the capital of Ch'u at the end of the Warring States period in the third century B.C. The presence of names of capitals of Ch'u in the stamps indicates that metal plates were the official currency of the state.

Theories of the origin of round coins vary. Traditional opinion is that round coins with a square hole in the center, bearing the inscription *pao huo,* "precious money" (Plate VII.E), were issued in 524 B.C. by King Ching of the Chou dynasty. Modern scholars, however, believe this account to be legendary; and they date these round coins with such inscriptions as *pao huo, pao ssu huo,* or *pao liu huo* from the later part of the Warring States period.[50] They also believe that the hole in the earliest round coins was round (Plate VII.D) and later was changed to square.

The first round coins with a square hole bearing the inscription *pan liang,* "half a *liang*" (each *liang* equals 24 *shu*), were cast by the Ch'in state and later circulated throughout the country after the unification of the empire in 221 B.C. After the Ch'in was overthrown by the Han dynasty, round coins of lighter weight, bearing the same inscription *pan liang* but varying in weight from three to five *shu,* were used in the second century B.C. Although there were changes and revisions of the monetary system from time to time during the successive dynasties, the coins bearing the inscription *wu shu,* "five *shu*" (Plate VII.F) later became the most popular currency, persisting until the beginning of the T'ang dynasty (A.D. 618–907) when a different system was adopted. The inscriptions on these round coins are generally written in the small seal style and are easy to recognize. Although they are interesting to numismatists, the later inscriptions are generally less valuable for the comparative study of Chinese writing than those of the earlier period.

[49] *Ibid.,* p. 153.
[50] Cf. Yang Lien-sheng, *Money and Credit in China,* pp. 20, 21.

INSCRIPTIONS ON SEALS AND SEALING CLAY

Ancient seals were made of various materials, including metal, jade, stone, earthenware, ivory, and horn. The technique of carving or casting seals and stamping their inscriptions on other objects[51] is probably the earliest attempt by the Chinese to duplicate writings by a mechanical device. This process, according to Carter, was one of the prerequisites for the invention of printing in China.[52] He believed that the use of private seals began slightly before the beginning of the Ch'in dynasty (255 B.C.) and that cutting seals in relief, which was vital in the prehistory of printing, began around A.D. 500.[53] Archeological evidence, however, indicates that the use of private seals, the cutting of seals in relief, and their impressions with ink, were all developed very early. At least three seals cast in relief on bronze are said to have been found at An-yang.[54] One, about 2.5 cm. square, bearing a hollow cross sign and an inscription with a bird symbol (Plate VIII.A, left), is very similar to those inscribed on Shang bronzes.[55] It is believed that the inscription was the name of a military general of the Wu Ting period.[56] Thus the use and cutting of seals in relief can be traced back as early as the Shang dynasty.

Other early specimens include a group of bronze and jade seals said to have been found in the ancient tombs of the late Chou period at Lo-yang, Honan. They bear inscriptions either carved or cast in relief.[57] Other seals of similar period were found at I-hsien, Hopei, and at Ch'ang-sha, Hunan.[58] Those from Ch'ang-sha, of gold, bronze, turquoise, and soapstone, are especially important to show the development and changes of the shapes and inscriptions during the Chou, Ch'in, and Han dynasties. The one made of gold is also inscribed in relief. The bronze seals include a square one with an inscription of four characters cut into the surface and two round ones with designs of animal figures.[59] The one made of turquoise bears an inscription in bird script.

Seal impressions with red ink are believed to have been made no earlier than the fifth or sixth century A.D.;[60] the earlier ones were black. A seal

---

[51] The system of sealing documents is discussed in Chapter VI.

[52] Carter, *The Invention of Printing in China and Its Spread Westward*, (rev. ed.), pp. 11–18.

[53] *Ibid.*, pp. 13, 16, note 4.

[54] Yü Hsing-wu, *Shuang-chien-i ku-ch'i-wu t'u-lu*, II, 11–13.

[55] Wang Ch'en, *Hsü yin-wen ts'un* I, 37b, 53a, 85a; II, 67a.

[56] Tung Tso-pin, "Chung-kuo wen-tzu ti ch'i-yüan," *op. cit.*, p. 347.

[57] White, *Tombs of Old Loyang*, p. 102; No. 187.

[58] *Ch'ang-sha fa-chüeh pao-kao*, p. 51, Plate 19. 5–7.

[59] *Ibid.*

[60] Cf. Carter, *op. cit.*, pp. 16–17; note 10.

PLATE VIII

INSCRIPTIONS ON SEALS AND SEALING CLAY

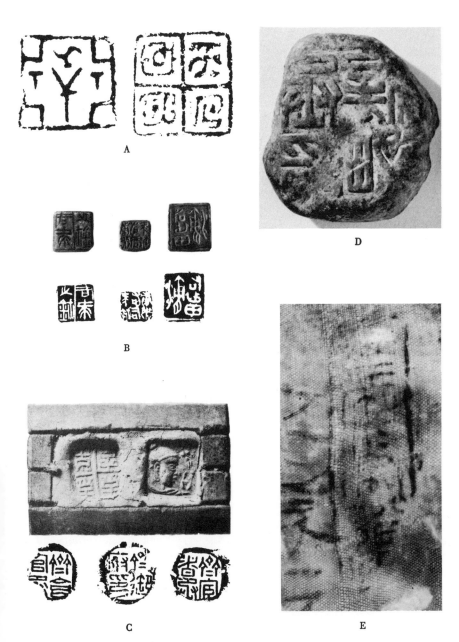

(A) Impression of bronze seals from An-yang. (B) Bronze seals and their impressions (*lower row*) of the late Chou period (½ size). (C) Sealing clays. (D) A clay seal of the Han dynasty. (E) Seal impression of silk from Jen-ch'eng, *ca.* A.D. 100 (enlarged two times from Plate XIX.B).

impression with black ink (Plate VIII.E) is found on a silk strip from Tun-huang dated about A.D. 100.[61] Although the inscription is unreadable this specimen seems to be the earliest known seal impression on soft material. Since silk, seals, and ink all existed as early as the Shang dynasty, there is reason to believe that they could have been used together long before the Han dynasty.

Because the ancient seal was used for identification, it was usually worn attached by a string to the knob. Seals were usually square but sometimes round or oblong. Each seal is usually carved with two, three, or four characters, the last indicating the type of seal. Seals were carved on one side, or sometimes on two, with the family name on one and the personal name on the other. A single seal may have as many as five or six sides inscribed on separate surfaces for different purposes.

The total number of characters in the ancient seal inscriptions includes more than 1,200 for the pre-Han period and over 2,500 for the Han period.[62] The style of inscriptions on the pre-Ch'in seals is generally close to that on coins, pottery, weapons, and bronze vessels of the Warring States period. The style of seal inscriptions varied from one state to another and were written in different forms. Those on the Ch'in and Han seals generally follow the style called *mo-yin* or *miu-chuan*, which is one of the six styles of writing mentioned in the *Shuo-wen*. This style, somewhat between the small seal and the clerical style, has been followed by seal engravers throughout later centuries even until today. It seems to be an established practice that seal inscriptions should use an archaic style, perhaps not only for ornamentation but also to make imitation more difficult.

Seal inscriptions, besides their application on silk and paper, were usually stamped on small pieces of clay affixed to the bamboo or wooden documents used for official and private communications in ancient times. In order to insure the secrecy and authenticity of the message, the tablet was covered with a board and bound with cords on which the sealing clay was affixed (Plate VIII.C, upper). Even when tablets have decomposed through long years of underground burial or have been burned as waste by government offices, the sealing clay has been preserved in certain sites that have come to the attention of modern archeologists. Such materials were first discovered in 1822 in Szechuan and later found in Sian, Shensi; several hundred pieces were collected from the two

---

[61] Chavannes, *Les documents chinois*, p. 118, No. 539.
[62] Cf. Lo Fu-i, *Ku-nien wen-tzu cheng*; *Han-yin wen-tzu cheng*.

sites.[63] The most recent and abundant discovery was made at Lin-tzu, Shantung, where pottery inscriptions were also found. In 1934, this site yielded more than 500 pieces, which are now in the possession of the Shantung Provincial Library.[64] They generally bear inscriptions of titles of administrative officials, feudal princes, and other nobles, as well as private seals of personal names. Most of them are from the Han dynasty; a few are from the late Chou and Ch'in, and some are dated as late as the Chin dynasty. Although we have evidence that seals were used in the Shang dynasty, we do not know how early clay was used for sealing. The earliest reference is found in the *Tso chuan*, in which a sealed letter is said to have been sent to Duke Hsiang of Lu in 544 B.C.,[65] but clay is not mentioned. The *Lü-shih ch'un-ch'iu* says: "The relationship between the people and the ruler is similar to that of seal and clay, which may be shaped square or round according to your wishes."[66] The *Huai-nan-tzu* also mentions "the seal impressed on clay."[67] These sources, as well as the actual discovery of sealing clays from the late Chou period, seem to indicate that clay was a popular medium for seal impressions when documents made of bamboo and wood were used.

The sealing clay was not ordinary earth but a kind of sticky, fine, soft material. It was probably refined by a process, similar to that for making pottery, of cleaning and washing the material in a sieve and then crushing it into a soft paste. Of the specimens collected, the material used during the Chou dynasty was generally thick and heavy, that in the Ch'in and Han thin and brittle, and that in the Chin dynasty light and fine. It seems that the later the period, the more convenient and lighter the material. Colors distinguished different uses: purple and blue for emperors; brown, gray, and black for officials; and clay mixed with mercury and gold for sacrificial purposes.[68] Since the inscriptions on the sealing clay are primarily titles of central and local administrative units, they are one source for the study of ancient geography and the civil service system, especially of the Han dynasty. They bear such titles as *ch'eng* (district magistrate), *hsiang* (county official), and *i* (city magistrate), which are not included in literary sources.[69] The same is true of the local titles of the Ch'i state

[63] Wang Hsien-t'ang, *Lin-tzu feng-ni wen-tzu*, Introduction, p. 27a.

[64] *Ibid.*, p. 1a.

[65] Legge, *Ch'un Ts'ew with the Tso Chuen*, II, 548.

[66] *Lü-shih ch'un-ch'iu*, 19/12b.

[67] *Huai-nan-tzu*, 11/4b.

[68] Wang Hsien-t'ang, *op. cit.*, p. 12a.

[69] *Ibid.*, Part II, catalog, 7a–16b.

(Plate VIII.C, lower), with its sealing clay especially abundant in various collections.[70]

INSCRIPTIONS ON POTTERY VESSELS

Inscribed objects made of clay or earth materials comprise three important groups: pottery, sealing clay, and bricks and tiles. They were made primarily from soft and fusible earth or from hard and plastic clay. Unlike those on stone, inscriptions on clay or earth objects were not engraved but were cast in molds or impressed by carved seals while still soft or scratched on the surface after they were baked. Such inscriptions are usually short, but useful for comparative study of the development of Chinese writing.

The earliest known pottery in China, such as painted vessels discovered in Honan and Manchuria, date from the late Neolithic period. They bear color designs in geometrical lines but no inscriptions. Although some scholars have thought that the few pictures on the pottery vessels of the Hsin-tien period, discovered by Andersson in Kansu and ascribed by him to about 1300–1000 B.C., were possibly a more primitive form of Chinese writing,[71] they are too few to be used for a conclusive study. A few specimens of Shang pottery discovered at An-yang bear some scratched inscriptions of a single character, generally a numeral or the name of the owner of the vessel. A very unusual case is a large character *ssu*, "sacrifice," written with ink and brush on a potsherd.[72] A number of potsherds incised with numerals and other characters were found in the upper stratum at Ch'eng-tzu-yai, Shantung, which was dated as of the Ch'un Ch'iu period.[73] The most interesting find among them was a fragment of a jar only faintly incised with nine characters after baking. The inscription has been deciphered as "a man of Ch'i caught six fish and a small turtle in a net" and is in a highly advanced style of writing.[74]

Most of the inscribed pottery discovered so far belongs to the Chou dynasty, especially the Warring States period, and later. Considerable finds were first made about 1876 at Lin-tzu and Tsinan in Shantung and I-hsien in Hopei in the ancient states of Ch'i and Yen respectively during

[70] Cf. Wu Shih-feng, *Feng-ni k'ao-lüeh.*

[71] T'ang Lan, *Ku wen-tzu-hsüeh tao-lun* I, 27a–b.

[72] Shih Chang-ju, "Ti-ch'i-tz'u yin-hsü fa-chüeh," *AYFCPK,* IV (1933), 724; Creel, *Studies in Early Chinese Culture,* p. 45.

[73] Li Chi, *Ch'eng-tzu-yai,* pp. 70–72.

[74] *Ibid.,* p. 72; Plate LII, Figure 5; Table 14.

PLATE IX
INSCRIPTIONS ON POTTERY AND CLAY

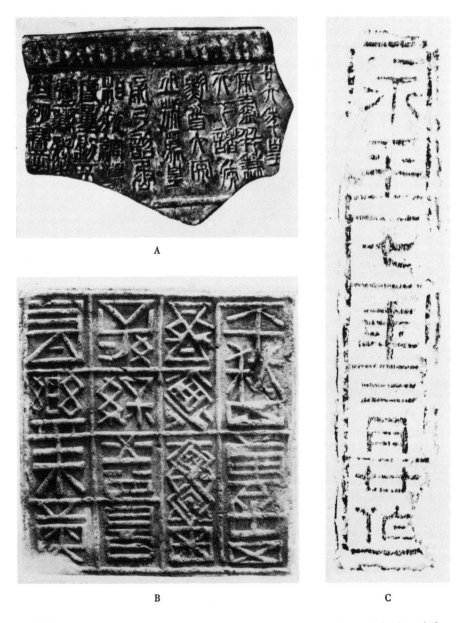

A

B   C

(A) Fragment of an earthenware measure bearing inscription of imperial edict of the First Emperor about standardization, 221 B.C. (B) Inscription on a brick, Han dynasty. (C) A brick inscription, A.D. 64.

the late Chou period.[75] Specimens have also been found more recently in Honan and Shensi. Ch'en Chieh-ch'i (1813–1884), the noted archeologist and collector who had the advantage of living near the site of discovery at Shantung, was the pioneer who recognized the value of the pottery inscriptions. Ch'en disclosed the discovery by farmers as they tilled their land and he paid for artifacts according to the length of inscriptions.[76] The objects are primarily eating and measuring vessels; and since they are very fragile, only a few complete specimens have been preserved, the rest being fragments. The inscriptions range from one to seventeen or eighteen characters, with a few longer ones produced in the Ch'in dynasty. The total vocabulary represented by the pottery inscriptions is only a little more than 800 characters; less than half have been deciphered because the brevity of the inscriptions and lack of context make them difficult to interpret.[77]

The pottery inscriptions generally include names of makers or owners, official titles, places, dates of vessels and their manufacture. Those of the Warring States period are similar to inscriptions on the bronze vessels and especially to those on weapons, coins, and seals. Since most of these pottery inscriptions are seal impressions, their styles of writing agree closely with each other.[78] The potteries of the Ch'in dynasty generally bear inscriptions about imperial edicts of the First Emperor, who ordered the standardization of measures. The inscription on one of these fragments, bearing 40 characters in the small seal style, reads: "In the twenty-sixth year [221 B.C.], the emperor had completely laid the country under his sway. The feudal lords and the people enjoyed great peace. He took the title of Huang-ti (emperor) and then ordered the ministers [Wei] Chuang and [Wang] Kuan to make clear and uniform the rules, measures, weights and standards which were inadequate and doubtful"[79] (Plate IX.A). This same edict is referred to on many other measuring objects, made of metal, of the Ch'in dynasty. The Han pottery objects extant today, primarily food vessels of various sizes, bear inscriptions of dates, names of owner or maker, and "lucky wishes," written with vermilion, impressed with seals, or carved by knives. These inscriptions are also very similar to those which appear on the Han bronzes.

The arrangement of pottery inscriptions is even more irregular than

---

[75] Ku T'ing-lung, *Ku t'ao-wen i-lu*, author's preface, pp. 1a–4a.

[76] *Ibid.*, pp. 2b–3b.

[77] *Ibid.*, Wen Yu's preface, p. 1a.

[78] Sun Shih-po, *Chi-mu ts'ang-t'ao*, Ku T'ing-lung's preface, p. 1b.

[79] Chou Chao-hsiang, "Pottery of the Chou Dynasty," *BMFEA*, I (1929), 34–35.

that which appears on the oracle bones. There are vertical columns in a single line from top to bottom, in single or double lines from left to right or from right to left, horizontal columns from left to right or from right to left, and also inscriptions upside down.[80] The characters are sometimes written in peculiar forms and the position of radicals is especially irregular.[81] These irregularities indicate that during the Warring States period styles of writing were very flexible and that the forms were not standardized until the unification of writing in the Ch'in dynasty.

INSCRIPTIONS ON BRICKS AND TILES

Inscriptions are also found on various building materials made of earth. The most common of these are the bricks and roof tiles used for palaces, terraces, houses, tombs, wells, and public roads. Inscriptions on bricks are usually made on the narrow side (Plate IX.C), but sometimes appear on the wide side (Plate IX.B) or on all four sides. Inscriptions were generally pressed with a patterned stamp on the surface of the brick before it was baked.

The most common inscriptions on bricks consist of dates, names, lucky omens, and miscellaneous records. For instance, one inscription records that it was "made in the second month of the first year of Yung-p'ing (A.D. 58)," and another, "good luck to the Prince of Kuang-han."[82] Some of the more than 500 inscribed bricks from Chekiang bear dates as early as 140 B.C.[83] Many bricks and tiles from ancient ruins are still prized by connoisseurs who use them for ink-slabs. The earliest known specimens seem to be a brick from the state of Ch'i and a broken roof-tile from the capital of the state of Yen, both probably belonging to the Warring States period.[84]

Inscriptions in decorative styles are also found on roof tiles, usually on the overhanging eaves of a roof. They sometimes bear pictures or inscriptions of lucky omens, names of palaces, temples, mausoleums, passages, granaries, or other public and private buildings commemorating their construction. The earliest known specimens are the fragments of roof tiles with inscriptions of "Yu-yang long life" from the Yu-yang

[80] Ku T'ing-lung, *op. cit.*, author's preface, pp. 9a–10b.

[81] *Ibid.*, Wen Yu's preface, p. 3b.

[82] Wang-Shu-nan, *Han Wei Liu-ch'ao chuan-wen*, ts'e 1–2.

[83] Feng Teng-fu, *Che-chiang chuan-lu*, chüan 1–2, dated inscriptions; chüan 3–4, undated inscriptions.

[84] Wang Chen-to, *Han-tai k'uang-chuan chi-lu*, postscript, p. 1b.

PLATE X

INSCRIPTION ON A ROOF TILE

A roof tile of the Han dynasty and inked squeeze (*above*) of its inscription in four characters, "Long happiness without end," divided equally into four sections (diameter 13.5 cm.).

Palace built in the middle of the fourth century B.C. by Duke Hsiao of Ch'in. Many other roof tiles bear names of such palaces as Chao-lin, Lan-ch'ih, T'o-ch'uan and of the imperial park Shang-lin, all of the Han dynasty.[85] One common inscription is the "ch'ang-lo wei-yang," or "long happiness without end," in which the term *wei-yang* was formerly considered to have been the name of the Han palace. Since the same inscription as that on roof tiles was found in many other sites, Lo Chen-yü says that it was just a lucky omen used for a decorative purpose. The inscription usually includes four characters arranged on the round end, divided into four sections, each section including one character in decorative style, with a circle at the center (Plate X). There are more than 3,000 pieces of such roof tiles extant today,[86] but the inscriptions usually repeat the same formula as the examples given above.

[85] Lo Chen-yü, *Ch'in Han wa-tang*, preface, p. 1a.
[86] *Ibid.*, preface, p. 2a.

IV

ENGRAVINGS ON STONE AND JADE

Inscriptions on bronze and stone, which are associated in the Chinese term for epigraphy, were the two major subjects of study in Chinese archeology before the discovery and study of those on bones and shells, pottery and clay, and bamboo and wood around the turn of the twentieth century. As historical documents, bronze inscriptions have been considered more valuable than stone because they come from an earlier period, but the study of stone inscriptions was developed much earlier than that of bronze. Therefore, earlier writings about ancient inscriptions include more material on stone than on bronze. The main reason for the neglect of bronze inscriptions was probably their inaccessibility, since they were usually kept in private or imperial collections.

For written records in general, inscriptions on stone have certain advantages over those on bronze. Stone inscriptions are usually longer, have been produced more abundantly, and are more easily accessible. Bronze objects, being movable, could be lost or destroyed by human agents; thus permanence of records was uncertain. Large and immovable stones, on the other hand, are generally less liable to such destruction. Since stone offers wider surfaces for inscription and the supply of material is inexhaustible, it seems to have been a better medium for long preservation of writing. For one reason or another bronze used for commemorative purposes completely yielded to stone; ever since the second or third century A.D., stone has been extensively used not only for monumental and commemorative inscriptions but also as a permanent material for preserving canonical literature by all of the Confucian, Buddhist, and Taoist disciplines.

STONE DRUMS AND MONUMENTS

Among the earliest inscribed stones of historical significance extant today are the ten so-called stone drums, which are still preserved in

PLATE XI

STONE INSCRIPTIONS ON CH'IN MONUMENTS

A

B

C

(A) One of the ten stone drums, *ca.* 770 B.C. (B) Inked squeeze of part of the inscriptions (each character about 5 cm. square). (C) Inked squeeze from a stone monument at Lang-ya, Shantung, 219 B.C. (500 cm. high).

Written on Bamboo and Silk

Peking. They are hard, dark-colored rocks roughly chiseled into their present form of drum-shaped boulders. This appears to have been the commonest form of monumental stone, known as *chieh* or rounded boulder, used before the Han dynasty, while the rectangular tablets or *pei* have been used only since that time.

These ten stones are irregular forms and sizes, varying from about 45 cm. to 90 cm. in height and averaging 210 cm. in horizontal circumference.[1] They are generally larger and flat at the base and smaller and round at the top, like truncated pillars, surrounded with inscriptions cut into the surface (Plate XI.A). Each of the ten stones bears a rhymed verse of about 70 characters arranged in 9 to 15 vertical columns with 5 to 8 characters in each column. Thus, the ten stones originally carried an inscription of about 700 characters; but because of successive injuries from natural and human causes, only 465 characters were left in the Sung dynasty, when ink squeezes which are still extant were made from the original stone (Plate XI.B). Three hundred and twenty-one characters, including incomplete ones and ditto signs remain today.[2]

Because of the incompleteness and obscurity of their text, the date, purpose, and even the proper order of the ten stones have been subjects of controversy ever since their discovery in the seventh century A.D. It is generally agreed, however, that the inscriptions were written in verse form by one of the dukes of the Ch'in state, probably in the seventh or eighth century B.C. The stones were traditionally dated from the period of King Hsüan (r. 827–782 B.C.) of the Chou dynasty.[3] One of the arguments was that the style of the poem agrees closely with that of one in the *Book of Poetry* dated from that time.[4] The opening lines of one verse on hunting in the inscription read:

> Our chariots were strong,
> Our steeds alike swift;
> Our chariots were good,
> Our steeds tall and sleek.[5]

The similarity in composition, however, is not conclusive evidence for dating, since the literary style could have been influenced by or modeled after that of earlier writings. Modern scholars definitely believe that the

---

[1] Bushell, "The Stone Drums of the Chou Dynasty," *JNCBRAS*, N.S., No. 8 (1874), p. 133.

[2] Kuo Mo-jo, *Shih-ku-wen yen-chiu*, I, 2b–3a.

[3] This theory was advanced by the T'ang poet Han Yü, who in 812 wrote a long poem in praise of this stone inscription. Many other poets and calligraphers inherited this theory and attributed the style of calligraphy to this period.

[4] Legge, *She King*, p. 288.

[5] Bushell, *op. cit.*, p. 147.

inscriptions were made in the Ch'in state because of their style of calligraphy and the locality where they were discovered. Ma Heng, a contemporary archeologist, has concluded that the stone drums must belong to the period of Duke Mu (659–621 B.C.), since a great amount of calligraphy similar in style was found on twelve other Ch'in vessels and stone engravings, especially one bronze dated from that period.[6] Others have dated them in 763 B.C.,[7] since the inscription corresponds with events described in the *Shih chi* as follows: "In the third year of Duke Wen (763 B.C.), a hunting expedition of 700 men was sent eastward and in 762 B.C. they reached the place where the Ch'ien River met with the Wei."[8] These stones were discovered in the early part of the T'ang dynasty in the present district of Feng-hsiang, Shensi, where the Ch'ien River flows northeastward to join the Wei. One verse on the stones describes the fishing in the Ch'ien River (Plate XI.B). The opening line says: "The Ch'ien was broad and overflowing."[9]

Kuo Mo-jo, however, does not believe that such an unusual record would have been made of a hunting or fishing expedition, a frequent occurrence in ancient times. He considers the inscription to have been made in the eighth year of Duke Hsiang (770 B.C.) of Ch'in, or the first year of King P'ing of the Chou dynasty, who moved his capital eastward to Lo-yang. He made a successful defense against the western Jung tribe with the help of Duke Hsiang of Ch'in. The Chou king then granted Duke Hsiang the territory east of Ch'i which had been occupied by the Jung, and these stone monuments may have been established on the mount to commemorate this significant occasion.[10]

Later than the stone-drum inscription were three stone inscriptions of prayers, also made by one of the Ch'in rulers in the late fourth century B.C. The inscriptions, known as *Chu Ch'u wen*, or inscribed curses on the Ch'u state, include three similar prayers addressed to the spirits of nature to which the Ch'in state sacrificed. The one addressed to the god Wu-hsien, discovered at Feng-hsiang, Shensi, in the middle of the eleventh century, originally carried an inscription of 326 characters; one to the spirit of the Chüeh-ch'iu, a river near Ch'ao-na, Shansi, where it was found at about the same time, bore 318 characters; and the third, to the spirit of the Ya-t'o River near Ling-ch'iu, Shansi, included 325 characters.[11] They

[6] Ma Heng, "Shih-ku wei Ch'in k'o-shih k'ao," *KHCK*, I (1923), 24–25.

[7] This theory was suggested by Lo Chen-yü, Ma Hsü-lun, and others.

[8] *Shih chi*, 5/5b–6a.

[9] Bushell, *op. cit.*, p. 148.

[10] Kuo Mo-jo, *op. cit.*, I, 9a–10a.

[11] Jung Keng, *Ku shih-k'o ling-shih*, p. 1a.

were all made by King Hui-wen (r. 337–311 B.C.) of the Ch'in state in 313 B.C., when disputes with King Huai (r. 328–299 B.C.) of the Ch'u state arose. The inscriptions were all written in a style similar to that of the stone drums, and 29 characters in exactly the same form appeared in both inscriptions.[12] The original stones no longer exist today, but the text of the first two inscriptions is preserved in rubbings made in the twelfth century from the original stones.[13]

Cursing another state by pronouncing invocation to the spirits of nature appears to have been an ancient practice. When one party to a covenant between states failed to observe its obligations, the offended party would present the case to the nature spirits for final judgment. The *Rituals of Chou* describes how the official Chu Tsu was charged with the duties of pronouncing invocations when conventions were agreed upon.[14] Although some actual cases as early as the eighth or sixth century B.C. are mentioned in the *Tso chuan*, [15] these three prayer inscriptions are the only surviving texts which represent this ancient practice of cursing.

Engravings on similar stones were made by the First Emperor of Ch'in, to praise the achievements of his administration, during his tours to the eastern territories after the unification of the empire. Between 219 and 211 B.C., seven stones were erected, including three made during his first visit in 219 B.C. on Mount I, the sacred mountain T'ai, and the terrace of Lang-ya, all located in modern Shantung Province. In the subsequent years, two more stones were erected on Mounts Chih-fou and Tung-kuan, also in Chih-fou, Shantung, in 218 B.C.; one on Chieh-shih in Hopei in 215 B.C.; and the last one on Kuei-chi in Chekiang in 211 B.C.[16] On the death of the First Emperor in 210 B.C., his son, accompanied by his minister Li Ssu, again made extensive tours throughout the empire and added supplementary inscriptions to those stones which had been engraved by his father. The original inscriptions by the First Emperor occupied three sides, and the additions were engraved on the fourth, all praising the illustrious virtue and the greatness of the First Emperor.[17]

The material of these stones was said to have been hard, dark-colored rocks, similar in shape to the stone drums. The one on the terrace of Lang-ya, which is probably the only one extant, is said to be 5 meters in height with a width of 2 meters at the bottom, about 1.7 meter in the

[12] Ma Heng, *op. cit.*, p. 21.
[13] Jung Keng, *op. cit.*, p. 5a.
[14] *Chou-li chu-su*, 26/6b–7a.
[15] Legge, *Ch'un Ts'ew with the Tso Chuen*, pp. 33, 452, 763.
[16] *Shih chi*, 6/14b–27a.
[17] *Ibid.*, 6/30b.

middle, and one meter at the top.[18] The original inscription by the First Emperor had already disappeared, leaving only the supplementary inscription by his son in 13 columns, with a total of 84 characters (Plate XI.C). Each character measures about 3 cm. square with horizontal lines at the upper and lower margins. These inscriptions were supposed to have been composed and written by Li Ssu, who used the so-called *hsiao-chuan*, or "small seal," style to standardize Chinese writing as one of the measures for the unification of the empire.[19] This style is generally simpler in construction than the "great seal," with fewer strokes; and every line is of equal thickness, smoothly curved and well-balanced. All characters were made to occupy almost equal spaces. From that time, all the irregularities of the earlier styles were dropped; and on this new basis were built the later styles of Chinese writing, such as the *li* or clerical script and the *k'ai* or model script, the latter still in use today.

STELE, PRECIPICE, AND GRAVE INSCRIPTIONS

Since the Han dynasty the shape of stone monuments has changed from rounded boulders to rectangular tablets. The boulders were apparently a more primitive form, since the rocks used for inscription were chosen locally and their surface was crude. On the other hand, the rectangular tablets or stele were sometimes selected at a distance, cut to the desired size, and polished to make a flat and smooth surface for engraving. This certainly required more labor and more advanced techniques than the crude boulders.

At one time many scholars believed that there was a hiatus of stone inscriptions in the Former Han dynasty, since no record of stone inscriptions made during this period was known to have existed in the eleventh century, when early collections of ancient inscriptions were compiled.[20] A few tablets are, however, ascribed to this period, although their authenticity has not been fully established.[21] Some scholars believe that the scarcity of stone inscriptions from the Former Han was due to Wang Mang's having destroyed all stone records of the period during his

[18] Jung Keng, "Ch'in-shih-huang k'o-shih k'ao," *YCHP*, XVII (1935), 128–29.

[19] Bodde, *China's First Unifier*, p. 177.

[20] Ou-yang Hsiu's *Chi-ku lu*, compiled in the middle of the eleventh century, includes no stone inscriptions of the Former Han period.

[21] Yeh Ch'ang-chih, a noted epigraphist of the Ch'ing dynasty, mentioned in his *Yü shih*, p. 2 four pieces of Former Han inscriptions, including a tablet erected in 131 B.C. on the occasion of Emperor Wu's birthday, one in 80–73 B.C. by the Prince of Kuang-ling, one at the Confucian temple in Ch'ü-fu, inscribed by Prince Hsiao in 56 B.C., and one by Piao Hsiao-yü dated in 25 B.C.

rebellion,[22] or that inscriptions on stone did not become popular until the Later Han period.

The stele has been used primarily to commemorate important historical occasions, to preserve the memory of noted individuals, and to inscribe miscellaneous records for permanency. The tablets were usually erected in such public places as before a monument, in the yard of a building, or above a grave; and they were usually supported by a base on the ground. Some of them have a circular hole, near the top of the stone, which probably originated from the ancient custom of using the tablet for fastening the sacrificial victim when it was led to the temple,[23] or for lowering the heavy coffins into the grave pits during the burial ceremony.[24]

The stele, which varies from less than one meter long to more than five or six meters, is usually divided into two parts, the upper part bearing the title decorated with various designs of tigers, dragons, or birds, and the lower bearing the inscription. The main portion of the text including the biographical sketch of the dead is inscribed on the front, and the names of his relatives are on the back. Two early specimens, one for Yüan An (d. A.D. 92) and another for his son Yüan Ch'ang (d. A.D 117), both high officials of the Later Han dynasty, were discovered in the 1920's.[25] The tablets, which have a circular hole at the center, measure 138 cm. high and 78 cm. wide and bear inscriptions in the seal style. This is unusual for Han stele inscriptions, for they are generally written in the clerical script.[26] The text of these two steles is a biographical sketch of the deceased, including his name, official title, positions held, and the dates of his death and burial.

While stone tablets erected above the ground are called *pei* or stele, those buried in graves are called *mu-chih* or grave inscriptions. A grave stone was originally similar to a stele (Plate XII.B), but it has been changed to and standardized in the present form since the sixth century A.D. It usually includes two pieces of stone—a base where the text of an epitaph is inscribed and a cover bearing a knob and the title. Earlier literature indicates that the grave inscription originated in the Former Han, but no specimen is extant today. The earliest known inscriptions are dated A.D. 106 and 163,[27] but the system was not popular until the fifth or

---

[22] Ferguson, *Survey of Chinese Art*, pp. 17–18.

[23] Legge, *Li Ki*, p. 218.

[24] *Ibid.*, p. 198.

[25] Jung Keng, *Ku shih-k'o ling-shih*, Parts 3–4, postscript by Ma Heng.

[26] For stone inscriptions in seal style, see Shang Ch'eng-tsu, *Shih-k'o chuan-wen pien*, which includes 2,921 characters from 95 different stones.

[27] Chao Wan-li, *Wei Chin Nan-pei-ch'ao mu-chih chi-shih*, I, 1a–b; Plates in Vol. III.

PLATE XII

INSCRIPTIONS ON GRAVE TABLETS

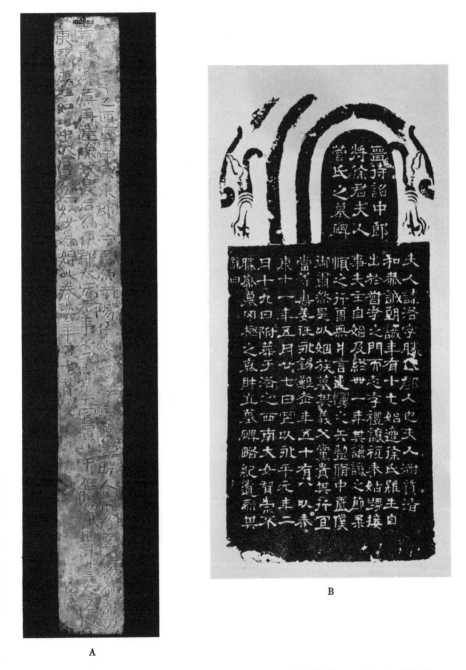

(A) Pewter deed to burial ground, A.D. 85 (33 × 3.5 cm.). (B) Stone epitaph of Madame Kuan Lo, A.D. 291 (58 × 24.4 cm.).

sixth century A.D., when the material was changed from stone to brick as the result of a proclamation prohibiting the use of stone to make luxurious burial tablets.[28]

In 1928–30, more than 120 brick epitaphs dating from A.D. 500, from the ancient kingdom of Kao-ch'ang, were found at Sinkiang.[29] These inscriptions on burial bricks, written with red or black ink and some engraved with vermilion filling, have enabled archeologists not only to construct a chronology for the Kao-ch'ang kingdom in the sixth and seventh centuries but also to trace Chinese influence upon neighboring states from the adoption of the Chinese burial system by foreign residents in Kao-ch'ang.[30]

Another type of inscription buried in graves is the deed to the burial site describing the boundaries, naming the owner of the land, and sometimes listing the details of transactions. This kind of deed was often inscribed on pewter (Plate XII.A) or iron tablets, but stone and bricks were also used. Specimens made of stone such as the one of P'an Yen-shou, dated A.D. 168, are still extant, and their use has been a funerary custom since the Han dynasty.

Besides being placed on tablets made of separate pieces of stone, inscriptions were also cut directly on mountains. This is known as *mo-yai*, or "cliff smoothing." The face of the cliff was first smoothed to a flat surface, then inscriptions were cut on the sides of precipices. Poems by distinguished writers and writings by visitors to historical spots were often engraved there for lasting memory.[31] This form became very popular in the fifth or sixth century A.D., when the enthusiasm for Buddhism approached its height in China. Numerous inscriptions of Buddhist incantations and passages from Buddhist sutras were engraved on precipices with characters of extraordinary size, apparently for the prestige of the religion.

The descriptive account of the construction of Buddhist iconography on mountainous sites is another form of stone inscription. The sculpture was usually contributed by private donors who hoped that they and their relatives would receive blessings as a result of the offering. The purpose of the construction and the names of contributors were therefore inscribed on stone beside the figures. Many famous Buddhist sites of stone grottoes, including those at Yün-kang in Shansi, Lung-men in Honan, Tun-huang in Kansu, were built from the fifth century A.D. and included many

---

[28] Feng Teng-fu, *Che-chiang chuan-lu*, postscript, p. 1a.

[29] Cf. Huang Wen-pi, *Kao-ch'ang chuan-chi*.

[30] *Ibid.*, chui-yen, pp. 3a–4a.

[31] Wang Ch'ang, *Chin-shih ts'ui-pien*, 21/33b.

thousands of Buddhist figures, some of which measure more than 15 meters in height.[32] Richest in inscriptions is the site at Lung-men, where more than 2,200 registers of donors, about two-fifths of them made before A.D. 618,[33] were inscribed on stone. The earliest one, a record of some 200 names, was engraved from 483 to 502.[34] It is recorded in the dynastic history that 802,366 man-days were employed between 500 and 522 to create the sculptures in three of these grottoes.[35] Inscriptions were also made on individual sculptures. A good example is a square pedestal now in the Pennsylvania University Museum, with three faces of the base in bas-relief carvings and on the fourth a well-cut inscription dated A.D. 524.

Inscriptions were also attached to public and private buildings of stone materials. The commonest of these are the decorated pillars in front of temples and graves. They vary in shape but usually occur in pairs, carved with designs and inscriptions. Some stone pillars of the sixth century were inscribed in reverse in the same manner as wooden blocks for printing.[36] Sometimes other constructions, such as well railings, bridge foundations, pagodas, tomb gates, and stone figures used for decoration, also bear early inscriptions.

CONFUCIAN CLASSICS ON STONE

One of the most gigantic projects of textual criticism, unprecedented in history, was the engraving on stone of the entire collection of Confucian classics, begun in the latter part of the second century A.D. and continued as late as in the eighteenth century. These inscriptions include two sets engraved in the Later Han and Wei dynasties and at least five more major undertakings that are known to have been made under successive dynasties.[37] They served as a permanent, standard text for the preservation and diffusion of ancient literature. These engravings,

---

[32] The largest figure is found at Yün-kang, where about 20 large and many small figures extend for about one mile.

[33] Kuan Pao-ch'ien, *I-chüeh shih-k'o piao*, first preface, p. 2a.

[34] The inscriptions in the grottoes of Lung-men are recorded and translated by Chavannes, *Mission archéologique dans la Chine septentrionale*, I, 320–576, with transcriptions in plates.

[35] *Wei shu*, 114/20a–b.

[36] Li Shu-hua, "The Early Development of Seals and Rubbings," *Tsing Hua Journal of Chinese Studies*, N.S., I (1958), No. 3, 82–4.

[37] The seven major inscriptions of stone classics include those made in A.D. 175–183 (Han), 240–248 (Wei), 833–837 (T'ang), 950–1124 (Shu), 1041–1054 (Northern Sung), 1134–1177 (Southern Sung), and 1791–1794 (Ch'ing).

enthusiastically carried on through so many centuries, testify to the continuing dominance of Confucian ideology in China.

In the second century B.C., when Confucianism was formally recognized as a state doctrine by the Han rulers, special chairs for scholars known as *po-shih,* or "scholars of wide learning," were established for the study of each of the classics. The classics were used as the principal textbooks for students for many centuries. As time went on, and the transmission of texts depended entirely on copying by hand, textual errors, in addition to different interpretations by scholars of various schools, inevitably caused controversy. As the *History of the Later Han Dynasty* says:

> Since being written by the sages, the canonical works have long been transmitted, and many errors have entered into the text. They have been wrongly interpreted by ordinary scholars, which confuses and misleads younger students. In the fourth year of Hsi-p'ing [A.D. 175], Ts'ai Yung [133–192] and others joined in a memorial to ask the emperor to collate and standardize the text of the Six Classics. Emperor Ling [r. 172–177] granted the request.[38]

This decision was extremely significant, since the project was not only a pioneer work in preserving the Confucian text permanently and accurately but also provided a stimulus for the later printing of Confucian works by the use of wood instead of stone.[39]

This project, started in A.D. 175, took eight years. The inscriptions were cut in the stone tablets on both sides. They were erected at the east side of the National Academy in Lo-yang, capital of the Later Han Dynasty, and arranged in rows in a U-shape with the opening toward the south. The classics were inscribed in such a way that the text read from the front of one stone to the front of the next throughout the series, and then in like order on the backs of the tablets. In T'ang and later inscriptions, however, each tablet was treated as a unit, the text being inscribed on the front and then the back of one stone before continuing to the next.

The tablets were covered with roofs, protected with balustrades around the four sides, and watched by special guards. These precautions were probably added later to protect them from the damage by the flood of visitors. The dynastic history says that, "when the tablets were first set up, the people flocked to the site to see or copy them; thousands of carts were driven there daily and they blocked the streets of the city."[40]

[38] *Hou-han shu,* 90b/8b–9a.

[39] The imitation of the idea is mentioned in a memorial of 932 by Feng Tao, who first printed the Confucian classics with wooden blocks. See quotation in Carter, *Invention of Printing in China and Its Spread Westward,* pp. 21–22.

[40] *Hou-han shu,* 90b/9a.

They seem to have been well publicized, so that later scholars and students all took these inscriptions as the standard text for reading and teaching.

Although many sources indicate that the number of classics engraved in Han was five[41] or six,[42] the inscriptions actually consist of seven classics[43] (Table 2). Those who counted six probably excluded the Confucian Analects, which was not established as one of the classics in Han times but was studied concurrently by students of other classics; and those who counted five also excluded the *Kung-yang Commentary*, which might be included with the *Spring and Autumn Annals*. The text cut in stone was selected from many versions studied during Han times. The standard version was inscribed as the main text, followed by the variations of other versions.

TABLE 2

HAN STONE CLASSICS AND NUMBER OF CHARACTERS INSCRIBED AND KNOWN TODAY

TITLES OF CLASSICS	VERSIONS	NUMBER OF CHARACTERS		
		In each Line	Total	Extant or Known Today
Book of Changes	Ching Fang (77–37 B.C.)	73	24,437	1,171
Book of Documents	Ou-yang Kao (first century B.C.)	73	18,650	802
Book of Poetry	Lu version	70–72	40,848	1,970
Book of Etiquette and Ceremonial	Tai Te (first century B.C.)	73	57,111	670
Spring and Autumn Annals	Kung-yang Kao (fifth century B.C.)	70	16,572	1,357
Kung-yang Commentary	Yen Peng-tsu (first century B.C.)	70–73	27,583	954
Confucian Analects	Lu version	73	15,710	1,333
Total		70–73	200,911 *	7,257†

* Chang Kuo-kan, *Li-tai shih-ching k'ao*, I, la–b.

† Ma Heng, "Han shih-ching kai-shu," *KKHP*, X (1959), 9.

Different records also disagree on the number of stones; one mentions 40 and others 46 to 48 pieces. Wang Kuo-wei believes that the total number of stones was 46. He derives this number by dividing the total number of characters inscribed by the number of characters in each tablet for different classics.[44] According to estimates from the reconstruction of

[41] Li Tao-yüan, *Shui-ching chu*, 16/24b.

[42] *Hou-han shu*, 90/9a.

[43] Seven titles are recorded in the Bibliographical Section of the *History of the Sui Dynasty* and recent discoveries confirm this record.

[44] Wang Kuo-wei, "Wei shih-ching k'ao," 3a, in *WCAIS*, t'se 8.

the discovered fragments, each tablet contained from 36 to 40 lines on each side and from 70 to 73 characters in each line. Thus, each tablet contained about 4,500 characters on two sides, making a total which approaches the figure of 200,911 characters for seven classics. Each tablet was about 175 cm. high, 90 cm. wide, and 12 cm. thick, and each character measured 2.5 cm. square.[45] There are no lines to separate the columns and characters. Each paragraph is separated by either one blank or one dot in order to save space; in only a few cases is a paragraph started with a new line.

A group of scholars, officials, and eunuchs participated in the collation, supervision, and writing of the text to be engraved on stone. Among them, at least twenty-five names are either recorded in history or inscribed in the postscripts at the end of each classic.[46] It is stated that the calligraphy in the clerical style was written exclusively by Ts'ai Yung, a famous calligrapher who initiated the project.[47] But the different classics are in varying styles of writing, and Ts'ai Yung was exiled in A.D. 178 when the work had just begun. Furthermore, it seems impossible that one hand could have written more than 200,000 characters. Although we do not know whether one person wrote a particular classic or one classic was written by many hands, in any case, many persons must have collaborated in the entire work of collating, writing, and engraving. The only engraver who is known to us is Ch'en Hsing, whose name is fortunately inscribed in the postscript to the *Confucian Analects*.

Shortly after the work was completed in A.D. 183, these stone tablets were damaged during the rebellion of Tung Cho in A.D. 190. When Emperor Wen of the Wei dynasty acceded to the throne in A.D. 220, he ordered the repair of the tablets. Recent discoveries of fragments of the *Book of Poetry* and the *Annals* indicate that some characters in these two classics were re-engraved. But ever since the middle of the sixth century A.D., they had been moved from place to place, and some were even used for building materials. It is recorded that in A.D. 546, when they were shipped from Lo-yang to Yeh-tu, one of the five capitals established by the Wei dynasty, a part of these tablets sank in the river.[48] Those remaining were said to have been transferred back to Lo-yang in 579, and again in 586 to Ch'ang-an, the capital of the Sui dynasty.[49]

---

[45] Chao T'ieh-han, "Tu Hsi-p'ing shih-ching ts'an-pei chi," *TLTC*, X (1956), 149.

[46] Ma Heng "Han shih-ching kai-shu," *KKHP*, No. 10 (1955), 3.

[47] *Hou-han shu*, 90b/8b–9a.

[48] *Wei shu*, 12/11b.

[49] *Sui shu*, 32/36b.

Most of the stone fragments discovered in the Sung dynasty and in recent years were found at Lo-yang, at the site of the National Academy. Only one fragment of the *Kung-yang Commentary* is said to have been found at Ch'ang-an, but the authenticity of the record is doubtful.[50] In the early part of the seventh century, when Wei Cheng (580–643), the compiler of the *History of the Sui Dynasty*, collected them, it was said that less than one-tenth of the text was preserved.[51]

No complete stone is extant today, but several hundred fragments are kept in many public and private collections. The remaining text of some 7,257 characters known to us is primarily based on tracings or rubbings from specimens discovered in the middle of the eleventh century and in the last thirty to forty years. The earlier discovery included inscriptions of 2,111 characters of the five classics (the seven works except the *Book of Changes* and the *Annals*,[52] and those discovered in 1922 to 1934 include several hundred fragments representing seven classics and a postscript on the preparation and collation of the texts, totaling more than 5,000 characters.[53] The largest piece ever discovered was found in the site at Lo-yang in 1934. It measures 49 cm. by 48.5 cm. on the front surface and 48 cm. by 47 cm. on the back; apparently the reason for this unevenness is that the stone was broken by natural forces. It contains a text of the *Kung-yang Commentary* in 624 characters inscribed on both sides.[54] (Plate XIII.A).

Although the dynastic history gives the fullest account of the stone classics inscribed in the Han dynasty, it is incorrect that the inscriptions were written in three styles.[55] Many later works, including the famous *Tzu-chih t'ung-chien* by Ssu-ma Kuang (1019–1086) and *Chi-ku lu-mu* by Ou-yang Fei (1047–1113) repeat the same error. Since the discovery of the original specimens, it has been possible to determine that the text engraved in Han was in one style and that made in the Wei dynasty in three styles.

The Wei inscription, which was engraved between 240 and 248, includes three classics, representing the old text versions of the *Book of Documents*, the *Annals*, and parts of the *Tso chuan*, which differ from the new text versions established in the Han dynasty. There were 35 stones, about 192 cm. high and 96 cm. wide, all inscribed in the *ku-wen* (archaic),

[50] Yao K'uan, *Hsi-ch'i ts'ung-yü*, 1/13b.
[51] *Sui shu*, 32/26a.
[52] Chao T'ieh-han, *op. cit.*, p. 153.
[53] *Ibid.*
[54] *Ibid.*, p. 145.
[55] *Hou-han shu*, 109a/3a.

PLATE XIII

STONE INSCRIPTIONS OF CONFUCIAN CLASSICS

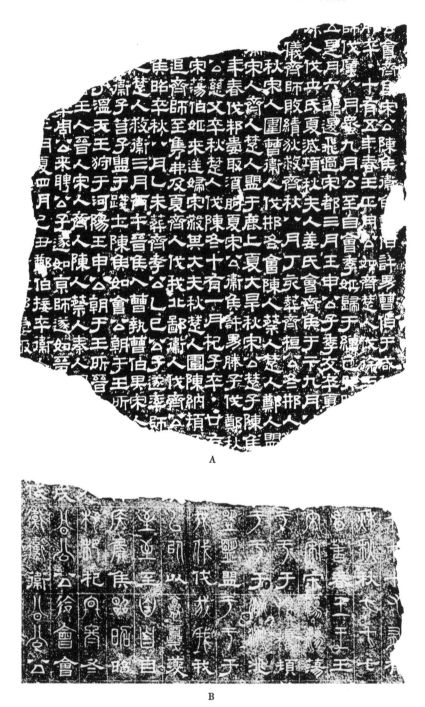

A

B

(A) Largest extant fragment containing the *Kung-yang Commentary* on both sides, A.D. 178–185 (49 × 48.5 cm.). (B) Text of the *Spring and Autumn Annals* in three styles of writing, A.D. 240–248 (52 × 42 cm.; each character is about 2.5 cm. square).

small seal, and clerical styles. There are two arrangements: in one, each character in the clerical style is accompanied by two in archaic and seal styles arranged horizontally under the first character forming a triangle; in the other, the three different styles in the order of archaic, seal, and clerical of the same character are engraved in a straight line (Plate XIII. B). The former arrangement included 74 characters in each line and 25 to 26 lines in one tablet, and the latter arrangement included 60 characters in each line and 32 to 34 lines in one tablet, all inscribed on both sides. Thus each tablet contained about 4,000 characters on both sides, with a total of the Wei inscription reaching some 147,000 characters.[56] These tablets were erected at the west side of the lecture hall of the National Academy and the stones were arranged in the form of an L, about 70 meters long.[57] Since they were established on the same site as the stones of the Han dynasty, they shared the fortunes of the Han stones when they were damaged, repaired, moved, or unearthed from time to time, and were thus confused by later scholars.

BUDDHIST AND TAOIST WRITINGS ON STONE

Engravings of Buddhist canons on stone came later than those of Confucian classics, but their scope and quantity are much greater. Although inscriptions in connection with Buddhist sculptures may be found as far back as the early part of the third century A.D.,[58] no Buddhist sutras, or canonical passages are known to have been engraved before the middle of the fifth century A.D. The Buddhists selected stone as a permanent material for inscriptions so that they might not be destroyed in a time when Buddhism might be suppressed. T'ang Yung, a high official of the Northern Ch'i dynasty who prefaced the engraving of a group of sutras in the sixth century A.D., says: "Silk will decay, bamboo is not permanent, metal seems hardly eternal, and vellum and paper are easily destroyed."[59] Stone was, therefore, the best medium for the preservation of Buddhist texts which had been laboriously translated from the Sanskrit since the second century A.D.

One of the earliest known inscriptions of the Buddhist canons is an incantation *O-mi-t'o-fo*, the Chinese version of Amitabba Buddha, or the

---

[56] Wang Kuo-wei, *op. cit.*, 3a–4b.

[57] Chang Kuo-kan, *op. cit.*, II, 16a.

[58] A register of donors for the sculpture of Buddhist images was engraved in A.D. 220. See Yang Tien-hsün, *Shih-k'o t'i-pa so-yin*, p. 297.

[59] Juan Yüan, *Shan-tso chin-shih chih*, 10/21b.

Immeasurable, which was engraved in A.D. 450 on the precipice of the Yün-lung Mountain at Hsü-chou, Kiangsu. The characters are in the *k'ai* style, or the modern book script, and the diameter of each character is 45 cm.[60] The complete text or selected passages of sutras were also engraved either on precipices or in grottoes. One of the famous engravings is the inscription of the *Avatamsaka sutra*, which was cut in A.D. 551 on the walls of a large grotto, 20 meters square, in the Feng-yü Mountain at T'ai-yüan, Shansi. Ku Yen-wu (1613–1682), a Ch'ing scholar and archeologist, said that he acquired a set of 124 ink squeezes from the 126 engravings in this grotto with 23 columns in each sheet and 57 characters in each column.[61]

In Shantung Province, at least five important engravings on precipices of different mountains were made in the sixth century A.D. One is the inscription of a partial text of the *Diamond sutra* in 296 characters written in the clerical style, engraved on T'ai-shan.[62] A group of inscriptions on three precipices, including an incantation and partial text of the *Paramita sutra* and the *Maha-prajna-paramita sutra*, was engraved in A.D. 570 on the Tsu-lai Mountain in T'ai-an.[63] Another group of inscriptions including seventeen different sutras was engraved on precipices of different mountains in Tsou-hsien.[64] The size of the surface used for engraving on these precipices varies from less than one meter to six or seven meters high and from one to four or five meters wide, with each character measuring as much as 60 cm. in diameter. Large inscriptions on precipices were undoubtedly used to impress upon visitors or pilgrims the immeasurable and splendid power of the Buddhist religion. They seem to have been used primarily to raise the prestige of Buddhism but not necessarily for the preservation of the texts, because these inscriptions are generally incomplete and selected versions.

Probably the most gigantic work among all stone inscriptions is the engraving of the complete texts of more than 105 Buddhist canons in some 4,200,000 words on 7,137 stone steles, preserved in the Mountain of Stone Sutras, southwest of Fang-shan, Hopei[65] (Plate XIV). This grotto library is situated in the eastern peak of the mountain where a large cave over 30 meters high, known as the Hall of Stone Sutras, and seven other caves are used for storing. In the large cave, there are 145 tablets re-

---

[60] Chiang-su T'ung-chih-chü, *Chiang-su chin-shih chih*, 3/21b.

[61] Ku Yen-wu, *Chin-shih wen-tzu chi*, 2/12b.

[62] Juan Yüan, *op. cit.*, 10/22b.

[63] *Ibid.*, 10/10b–11a.

[64] *Ibid.*, 10/20a, 27b.

[65] Chu I-tsun, *Ch'in-ting jih-hsia chiu-wen k'ao*, 131/4a–21a.

PLATE XIV
STONE INSCRIPTION OF BUDDHIST SUTRAS

One of the 7,000 tablets of Buddhist sutras in the grotto library of Fang-shan, Hopei, engraved since A.D. 550.

presenting 14 different sutras engraved on the walls and four pillars engraved with Buddhist images. A terrace in front of the cave is surrounded by stone balustrades; the doors, windows, and furniture are all of stone. The rest of the tablets are preserved in other caves and subterranean chambers. All of these tablets were cut successively from the sixth through the twelfth centuries.

The engraving of this huge collection was initiated by Hui-ssu, a Buddhist monk of the Northern Ch'i dynasty (A.D. 550–577), who made a vow to engrave twelve Buddhist sutras on stone in order to preserve them even if Buddhism should be suppressed. This task was carried out by his disciple Ching-wan (d. 639), who, from 605 to 631, completed the entire work of the *Maha-pari-nirvana sutra* in 120 tablets. Supplementary works and additions during the successive dynasties (Table 3) made this collection so remarkable that no other collection of stone inscriptions is comparable to it for size or for the labor involved. All of these stone tablets have been preserved because they were kept in grottoes, protected with stone gates and windows. One subterranean chamber was sealed and a pagoda built over it. The texts are all written in *k'ai*-style characters of very fine quality. A catalogue of the titles[66] was engraved on stone tablets, but no details about their format are known to have been given.[67]

TABLE 3

DEVELOPMENT OF STONE SUTRAS IN THE GROTTO LIBRARY IN FANG-SHAN, HOPEI*

DATE OF ENGRAVINGS	SPONSORS	No. OF SUTRAS	TITLES OF SUTRAS	No. OF CHÜAN	No. OF TABLETS
550–631	Hui-ssu and Ching-wan	1	Maha-pari-nirvana sutra	40	120
605–809	Ching-wan and 4 disciples	1	Saddharma-smartyupasthana sutra	70	210
		1	Avatamsaka sutra	80	240
		1	Maha-prajna-paramita sutra	520	1,560
		14	Saddharma-pandarika and other sutras	?	147
983–1100	Emperors of Liao	23	Dharani sutra and others	?	180
1026–1057	K'o-yüan	1	Maha-prajna-paramita sutra (continuation)	80	240
		1	Maharatnakuta sutra	120	360
1091	T'ung-li	62	Miscellaneous sutras	431	4,080
Total		105			7,137

* Data based on Chu I-tsun, Miao Ch'üan-sun, and Vaudescal.

[66] Miao Ch'üan-sun, *Shun-t'ien-fu chih*, 128/9a–10b; 128/42a–64a.

[67] Cf. Vaudescal, "Les pierres gravées du Che King Shan et le Yün Kiu Sseu," *JA*, 1914, pp. 375–459; *Wen-wu ts'an-k'ao tzu-liao*, 1954, No. 9, pp. 48–55.

The engraving of Taoist literature on stone was much later than that of Confucian and Buddhist works. The development of Taoism as a religion was in some ways stimulated by Buddhism, and the inscribing of Taoist canons on stone was probably also influenced by the engravings of Buddhist works. Most Taoist stone inscriptions were of the *Tao-te-ching*, the Taoist classic, of which at least eight different engravings are known to have been made in the T'ang dynasty or later. The earliest engraving was erected at I-chou, Hopei, in 708, and two others in the same place were set up in 738 and 893. Another version was erected in Hsing-t'ai in 739, and one in Chiao-shan, Kiangsu, was cut in 880.[68] There are other engravings of Taoist works, but they are much inferior in scope and quantity to both the Buddhist and the Confucian inscriptions.

INSCRIPTIONS ON JADE

Jade is the name given to two kinds of hard, precious or semiprecious stones, nephrite and jadeite, which were used by primitive men in making chisels, hatchets, ornaments, and other implements. While its hardness was useful to many peoples, jade has been especially prized by the Chinese for its coloration, translucency, lustre, and other aesthetic qualities. In ancient times, it was commonly used in China to make symbols of authority and religious worship, astronomical and musical instruments, and personal ornaments. It was also carved for mortuary purposes into various shapes, which were believed to possess the property of preserving the body from decay.[69] Jade was usually associated with bronze in sacrificial and ceremonial uses. Objects made of the two materials were similar not only in design and form but also in their use upon certain occasions. Bronze, however, had a more dominant part in ritualistic ceremonies, while jade was primarily decorative and auxiliary.

Jade was described in ancient literature as a material for writing, but few jade objects bearing genuine inscriptions are extant today. The earliest known inscriptions on jade came from the ruins at An-yang, excavated by the Academia Sinica and others. A jade tally, inscribed with three characters, is probably a passage identification for a certain Shang official.[70] A fish carved from jade of the Shang dynasty, with written

---

[68] Ma Heng, "Shih-k'o," *op. cit.*, pp. 51–52; Wang Chung-min, *Lao-tzu k'ao*, pp. 519–23; Carter, *op. cit.*, pp. 20–21.

[69] Laufer, *Jade*, p. 296.

[70] Hu Hou-hsüan, "Chia-ku hsüeh hsü-lun," *CKHSSLT*, 2d ser., p. 8, note 26.

vermilion characters, seems to have been used for driving away diseases.[71] A small jade ornament is inscribed with eleven characters in two lines, indicating that this object was given to an official named Yung by the Shang king on the cyclical day *i-hai*.[72] These evidences indicate that hard jade, like other materials, was already used for writing or carving inscriptions as early as the Shang dynasty.

Inscribed jade tablets played a prominent role in ancient sacrifice for such purposes as informing the deities of an accession to the throne, praying for the prosperity of a new dynasty, and obtaining blessings from the deities of nature. The messages of sacrifice were written or engraved on jade slips and preserved in stone chests.[73] A jade tablet of pure white, bearing an engraved inscription of 170 characters in the *li* style, is said to have been used by Emperor Kao-tsu (r. 206–195 B.C.) of the Han dynasty for the sacrifice to Heaven.[74] It is also said that Emperor Wu (r. 140–87 B.C.) drew, on the T'ai mountain, a jade tablet bearing the word "eighteen" but read as "eighty," which was taken to indicate his reign might last eighty years.[75] Such tablets were probably used for divination or magical purposes.

The funerary or sacrificial use of jade is attested by several recent discoveries of jade tablets. A set of some fifty tablets, 22.5 cm. long, 1.2 cm. wide, and 1.1 mm. thick, was recently found in an ancient tomb of the third century B.C. at Hui-hsien, Honan.[76] Although no writings are inscribed, the size and form indicate that they were intended for writing. A group of eleven inscribed tablets of jade and stone, dating from about the sixth century B.C., is said to have been discovered around 1940 at Ch'in-yang, Honan.[77] Among them, seven are made of pine-green and bluish-gray jade with white stripes, measuring about 1.4 to 1.6 cm. wide, 1.5 mm. thick, and the longest one is about 7 cm. Inscriptions, written in two or three lines with black ink on each tablet, are so blurred that all but a few of the characters are almost illegible. Another group of three dark-gray stone slips varies a great deal in size but they all have a wide end and pointed top. The largest piece, which measures 22.4 cm. long, 5.9 cm. wide at the end, and 5 mm. thick, bears a long inscription of

---

[71] Tung Tso-pin, "Ch'in-yang yü-chien," *TLTC*, X (1955), 108.

[72] *Ho-pei ti-i po-wu-kuan pan-yüeh-k'an*, No. 30 (1932), p. 2.

[73] *Shih chi*, 28/32a.

[74] Laufer, *op. cit.*, p. 117.

[75] Ying Shao, *Feng-su t'ung-i*, p. 10.

[76] *Hui-hsien fa-chüeh pao-kao*, p. 80., Plate 54:1.

[77] Tung Tso-pin, "Ch'in-yang yü-chien," *op. cit.*, pp. 107–8.

almost 50 characters in three or four columns; a small one, 2.3 cm. long, carries only one character.

The inscription includes the name Han Chieh and at least three occurrences of the name "p'i hsien Chin-kung," or "great splendid Duke of Chin." These two names occur together, indicating that these tablets probably belonged to the Chin state in the middle of the Ch'un Ch'iu period.[78] The inscription on the jade and stone slips bears similar names and writing style to those on a series of twelve bronze bells dated 550 B.C. The bells were said to have been discovered at Kung-hsien, Honan, south of Ch'in-yang, where the jade slips were found. These two sites are separated only by the Yellow River, and both belonged to the former state of Chin and its successor, Han. Judging from the evidence of the location where both the bells and jades were unearthed, of the relations between the Chin and Han states as revealed in the inscriptions, and of the similarity of writing styles, one might estimate that these slips were produced around the sixth century B.C.

Besides the sacrificial uses, jade tablets were also employed as a writing board for communication between the emperor and his subordinates when they met at the court. The *Records of Ceremonial* says: "For his memorandum-tablet, the Son of Heaven used a piece of sonorous jade; the prince of state, a piece of ivory; a great officer, a piece of bamboo, adorned with ivory at the bottom."[79] Tablets of different materials were apparently used for jotting down notes. When an official had an audience at court, he inscribed on the tablet what he had to say and added what the emperor replied or commanded.[80] The unusual quality and scarcity of jade made it exclusively for the emperor's use, while the less expensive materials were for the officials. The general names for such writing tablets were *kuei*, a rectangular tablet, and *hu*, a tablet in the shape of a wide-topped knife. They were perforated for fastening and were worn suspended from the girdle.[81] The *kuei* was about 42 cm. to 66 cm. long with pointed top and the *hu* was about 52 cm. long, 6 cm. wide at the middle, and tapered at the ends to 5 cm.[82] They were described as made of green jade with a black mist or jades in other colors.[83] The narrow surface of these tablets seems to have been similar to that made of bamboo and wood carrying few lines of writing.

[78] *Ibid.*, p. 108.
[79] Legge, *Li Ki*, II, 12–13.
[80] *Ibid.*, I, 16.
[81] Wu Ta-ch'eng, *Ku-yü t'u-k'ao*, pp. 8–9, 17–18.
[82] Laufer, *op. cit.*, p. 115.
[83] Wu Ta-ch'eng, *op. cit.*, p. 17.

No satisfactory explanation has been given why few inscriptions on jade, either in writing or in engraving exist today, although a great number of plain and decorated jade objects are extant. We may infer, however, that the writing on the jade tablets was intended to be erased to make way for other notes; such writing was only temporary and not intended to be permanent. On the other hand, inscribing on jade probably needed special techniques and tools. One reference is made to Emperor Kuang-wu (r. A.D. 25–57), who decided to write with vermilion on jade tablets instead of engraving because the seal-makers available at the time were not capable of engraving jade.[84] Although competent engravers were later found for the job, this story indicates that engraving on jade was not so common as on other materials. For this reason, jade objects are generally considered more valuable for their artistic aspects rather than as historical documents. Inscriptions are sometimes also found on other hard and semi-precious stones, including rock crystal and agate, but their use was probably very late.

ORIGIN AND TECHNIQUE OF INKED SQUEEZES

The technique of taking inked impressions by squeezing[85] the surface of stone inscriptions is considered one of the important factors that eventually led to the invention of printing.[86] Although critics have suggested that the influence of the inked squeezes on printing may be exaggerated, the principle and purpose of these two processes are generally similar. They both obtain duplication on a piece of paper on the engraved objects, no matter whether it is from the surface of stone, metal, or wood.

The differences, however, lie in the process of engraving and in the technique of duplicating. The inscriptions on stone are always cut into the surface in the positive position, while the writings engraved for printing are cut in relief in the reverse position. Inked squeezes obtain the duplications by placing the paper on stone, bronze, or other materials, and squeezing with ink on the surface of the paper; but the method of printing from carved blocks is to apply the ink on the block and rub the back of

---

[84] *Hou-han-shu*, 17/7b.

[85] The process of taking impressions over a hard surface is usually called rubbing. But this technique of using a pad to strike on instead of to rub over the surface is rather a process of squeezing. Therefore, the term "squeezing" instead of rubbing is used throughout this writing.

[86] Carter, *op. cit.*, p. 19.

the paper, so that reversed writings will be printed in the positive position on the paper. The result is that, if the text is cut into the surface, in intaglio, the reproduction shows white text on black background, while printing, which is usually cut in relief, produces black text on white background.

Although the early technique of ink squeezing is unknown today, we assume that it was generally the same as that followed in modern practice. A sheet of thin, moistened paper is laid on the inscribed object with a soft brush to press the paper into every depression and crevice of the object. When the paper is dry, a stuffed pad of silk or cotton is dipped in ink and with this, the paper is struck lightly and evenly over the surface. When the inscription is engraved the depressed lines will not be touched by the ink and the process thus produces a white writing on a black background (Plates I, XI, XII, XIII). The paper is then peeled off and becomes a clear and exact duplication of the inscription. This is the process generally used for duplication of inscriptions on bone, shell, bronze, stone, clay, and other hard materials. Inscriptions contained inside bronze vessels sometimes cannot be reached except by the use of a pad or a brush with a long handle. A long inscription spreading over the inside of a vessel is sometimes difficult to squeeze but it can be managed with several separate pieces of paper.[87]

The origin of taking impressions from inscriptions cannot be definitely traced. The traditional opinion is that this technique goes back as far as the second century A.D., when duplications of Confucian classics on stone were made. This is based on the interpretation of the term *mo-hsieh* as used in the dynastic history to indicate the process of duplicating. This term, however, seems to mean "handwriting from a copy" rather than "make exact copies" by squeezing.[88] Moreover, squeezing from stone or other hard surfaces was only made possible when paper was perfected. The earlier specimens of paper of the second and third centuries discovered in northwestern China and Chinese Turkestan are thick and rough and do not seem suitable for taking impressions from inscriptions.

Although evidence concerning ink squeezing is found no earlier than the first part of the sixth century A.D., the technique is believed to have been first introduced before this. In the bibliographical section of the *History of the Sui Dynasty*, compiled by Wei Cheng and others in A.D. 629–32, a number of stone inscriptions are recorded as then preserved

---

[87] Jung Keng, *Shang Chou i-ch'i t'ung-t'ao*, I, 176–82.
[88] Cf. Carter, *op. cit.*, pp. 20, 23; notes 2 and 4.

in the imperial library of the Sui dynasty (581–618). These are listed as so many *chüan*, "rolls," and include one roll of the stone inscription made in Kuei-chi, Chekiang, in 211 B.C. by the First Emperor of Ch'in, 34 rolls of the remaining text of stone classics engraved in A.D. 175–183, and 17 rolls of those engraved in A.D. 240–248.[89] It is also mentioned that a number of such inscriptions, which had been kept in the imperial library of the Liang dynasty (502–556), had been lost or were incomplete in the Sui collection. That these reproductions on paper rolls were made by the process of inked squeezing is proved by a statement in the postscript to this section, which says "those squeezes made during previous dynasties are still preserved in the imperial collection."[90] This indicates that although the specimens of squeezings of the sixth and seventh centuries were preserved in the Sui dynasty, the method might have been inherited from earlier dynasties. Wang Kuo-wei believes that two of the stone classics of the Liang dynasty mentioned in the Sui bibliography were complete texts, which had been lost since the middle of the sixth century. Thus an inked squeeze of a complete version must have been made before that time.[91]

Taking inked impressions from stone inscriptions seems to have been an established practice under the T'ang dynasty. At least two official agencies in the T'ang government employed special officials, known as *t'a-shu-shou*, who were technicians in charge of squeezing inscriptions. According to an official administrative record of the T'ang dynasty, compiled under Imperial auspices in A.D. 722–738, three of these workers were employed in the Ch'ung Wen Kuan, an institution charged with the publication of classical texts and the training of learned scholars.[92] The *History of the T'ang Dynasty* says that six such workers were employed in 718 in the palace library, along with a group of scribes, paper-dyers, and brush-makers.[93]

The earliest specimens of squeezes from stone extant today include a copy of the *Diamond sutra* dating from the ninth century, which was found by Stein at Tun-huang.[94] Another squeeze, also from Tun-huang, a portion of the inscription from a stele of the Hua Tu Temple written by the famous calligrapher Ou-yang Hsün (A.D. 557–641), is cut and mounted

[89] *Sui shu*, 32/35a–b.

[90] *Ibid.*, 36b.

[91] Wang Kuo-wei, "Wei shih-ching k'ao," 8b, in *WCAIS*, ts'e 8.

[92] T'ang Hsüan-tsung, *Ta T'ang liu-tien*, 26/3a.

[93] *Chiu T'ang-shu*, 43/40a; *Hsin T'ang shu*, 47/8b.

[94] Carter, *op. cit.*, p. 21.

in sheets in book form.[95] Probably the earliest piece is the squeeze, dated
654, of a poem composed and written by the Emperor T'ai-tsung (A.D.
627–649) of the T'ang dynasty, which was found by Pelliot also at Tun-
huang.[96]

Specimens of writing by famous calligraphers cut on stone were later
transferred to wooden blocks, which were engraved with positive inscriptions but in intaglio form similar to those on stone, and squeezes
were made from them for use as models of calligraphy. The technique of
squeezing inscriptions from bronze and other objects was probably later
than that from stone. A Sung writer said that an imperial order was issued in A.D. 1051 to make ink squeezes from the bronze objects then kept
in the imperial collection.[97] If this record refers to the earliest application
of this technique to the bronze inscriptions, it was undoubtedly an imitation of the practice of making ink squeezes from the stone inscriptions.
The same technique is now applied to almost all kinds of inscriptions,
including those on bones and clay materials.

[95] Stein, *Serindia*, II, 918; IV, Plate 169.
[96] Carter, *op. cit.*, p. 23, note 5; Pelliot, *Les débuts de l'imprimerie en Chine*, pp. 23–24.
[97] Chai Ch'i-nien, *Chou shih*, 1/10b–11a.

V

DOCUMENTS OF BAMBOO AND WOOD

EVOLUTION OF BOOK MATERIALS

Ancient Chinese records as engraved on bone and stone, cast on bronze, or impressed on pottery and clay are hardly to be considered "books."[1] The direct ancestry of the Chinese book is believed to have been the tablets made of bamboo or wood which were connected by a string and used like a paged book of modern times. Bamboo and wood were not only the most popular materials for writing before paper was invented but also served probably a longer period in Chinese history than any other material as a medium of writing. Even after paper was invented in the second century A.D., bamboo and wood still survived for some three centuries in competition with the new material. The reason for their popularity was undoubtedly that they were native to China, as papyrus was to Egypt or palm-leaves to India, so that they could be supplied abundantly at lowest cost.

The origin of using bamboo or wood for writing in China is uncertain, but the system is evidently very old. Although no books made of bamboo or wood before the Warring States period (468–221 B.C.) are extant today, ancient inscriptions and literary records indicate that they were probably the earliest form of Chinese books. The character *ts'e* for book (see TableI, *6d*), which represents the picture of a bundle of tablets bound with two lines of cords, was already used in connection with sacrifice in the bone inscriptions of the Shang dynasty.[2] The same character and a related word *tien*, which depicts a book placed respectfully on a table, for

------

[1] The word "book" has been variously defined. Webster says it is "a collection of tablets, as of wood, ivory, or paper, strung or bound together." *Encyclopedia Britannica* emphasizes its literary aspect saying that "book is the name for any literary production of some bulk." *Columbia Encyclopaedia* comes to the conclusion that "the inscription cannot be considered as book even under the widest definition."

[2] Sun Hai-po, *Chia-ku-wen pien*, 2/27–28, 5/3; Chin Hsiang-heng, *Hsü chia-ku-wen pien*, 2/34–35; Creel, *Studies in Early Chinese Culture*, p. 38.

documents or archives, are found more frequently in bronze inscriptions of the Chou dynasty. They usually referred to official documents in which literary passages were written by scribes at the order of the king.[3] The system of conveying orders by means of written tablets was handed down to the Han and used as late as the fifth century A.D.[4]

A great amount of Chou literature describes the extensive use of bamboo and wooden tablets for written orders, records of sacrifice, and official documents. In the *Book of Poetry*, for example, a poem of the early Chou dynasty describes the return from an expedition of soldiers who wished that they could have come back earlier but who were "in awe of the orders in the [bamboo] tablets."[5] The *Book of Documents* records that two years after the conquest of the Shang dynasty (*ca.* 1120 B.C.), King Wu fell ill. The Duke of Chou prayed for the king, and "the Grand Historiographer by his order wrote on tablets his prayer."[6] When the Chou king conquered the Shang, he referred to a purportedly historical precedent, declaring that "the ancestors of the Shang had *ts'e* (books) and *tien* (documents) showing how Shang superseded the Hsia dynasty."[7] This statement implies that bamboo and wooden tablets were used as official documents as early as the beginning of the Shang dynasty.

Although no one has reached a conclusion on the exact age of this system, it has been generally agreed that the use of bamboo and wood preceded the use of silk. But there was no clear demarcation of time between the uses of bamboo, silk, and paper. It is a mistake to assume that the use of bamboo stopped when the use of silk or paper began. It has been suggested that the use of various writing materials in China may be divided into three periods: (1) bamboo and wood from the earliest times to the third or fourth century A.D.; (2) silk from the fifth or fourth century B.C. to the fifth or sixth century A.D.; and (3) paper from the second century A.D. to the present time.[8] These dates are generally correct; however, a few examples seem to suggest that bamboo and wood were carried over to a later date and that silk was introduced even earlier. Thus the uses of bamboo and silk overlapped by more than 1,000 years, those of silk and paper by 500 years, and those of bamboo and paper by 300 years.

[3] Hiraoka Takeo, "Chikusatsu to Shina kodai no kiroku," *Tōhō gakuho*. XIII (1943), 171–73.

[4] *Sui shu*, 9/3b, 12a.

[5] Legge, *She King*, p. 264.

[6] Legge, *Shoo King*, p. 353.

[7] *Ibid.*, p. 460.

[8] Ma Heng, "Chung-kuo shu-chieh chih-tu pien-ch'ien chih yen-chiu," *TSKHCK*, I (1926), 201–2.

Recent archeological discoveries of ancient documents have confirmed the assumption that the old-fashioned materials were only gradually replaced by new ones, and that the later the sites, the fewer the remains of the older materials. In the sites of Tun-huang and Chü-yen, where documents of the period from the first century B.C. to the second century A.D. were discovered, paper is extremely scarce. But at the Lou-lan site, where documents of the third to fourth century A.D. were found, the number of paper documents amounts to about 20 per cent of the number on wood.[9] At the site of Turfan, most of the documents from the fifth century A.D. were written on paper.[10] The increased proportion of paper indicates greater accessibility of the new material, especially since such locations as Lou-lan and Turfan were far distant from the places where paper was produced in China. During the initial stages, when paper was being introduced, the supply of new materials was probably limited, or they were too expensive for general use.

The records of the dynastic bibliographies also illustrate the changes of trend in the use of various kinds of materials.[11] The later the record, the more apparent is the decrease in the number of *p'ien*, a term for bamboo or wooden tablets, and the increase in *chüan*, a term generally used for silk or paper rolls. In the bibliographical section of the *History of the Former Han Dynasty* (206 B.C.–A.D. 24), about three-fourths of the books then extant are listed as *p'ien* and only one-fourth as *chüan*. The ratio, however, was about equal in the Later Han (A.D. 25–220), and rolls were more numerous than tablets in the period of the Three Kingdoms (A.D. 221–280). In the Chin dynasty (265–419) and after, when paper was extensively employed as a popular material for writing, books of bamboo and wooden tablets generally disappeared from the records, evidently supplanted by paper rolls.

BAMBOO TABLETS OF THE WARRING STATES PERIOD

Few books made of bamboo or wood prior to the Han dynasty exist today. Literary records, however, indicate that a large number of bamboo tablets dating back to the third century B.C. were discovered at the end of the third century A.D.,[12] having been buried underground for nearly

---

[9] Stein, *Serindia*, II, 674.

[10] Huang Wen-pi, *T'u-lu-fan k'ao-ku chi*, p. 2.

[11] Cf. Yang Chia-lo, *Ssu-k'u ch'üan-shu hsüeh-tien*, Part VI.a, p. 3–4.

[12] Ch'en Meng-chia, "Chi-chung chu-shu k'ao," *T'u-shu chi-k'an*, N.S. V, Nos. 2/3 (1944), 1–2.

six hundred years. It was recorded that in the year A.D. 280, a robber named P'i Chun broke into an old tomb of the Wei state at Chi-chün in the northern part of present Honan. He found there numerous tablets made of bamboo and written in black ink. Their recorded dimensions were two feet four inches long, with forty characters on each tablet, and they were bound with white silk cords.[13] This collection includes sixteen works totaling more than 100,000 words, bound in 75 bundles of tablets relating to history, geography, divination, short stories, and miscellaneous subjects. Most important among them is the *Chu-shu chi-nien*, or *Bamboo Annals*, which contains a chronology from the legendary period to 299 B.C., when this historical record was supposed to have been buried with the dead in the tomb.

After the discovery, these tablets were ordered by the Chin emperor Wu Ti (r. A.D. 265–289) to be kept in the imperial library; and a number of scholars, including Hsün Hsü and Shu Hsi, participated in the deciphering, collation, and critical study of the text. These documents were then copied on separate sheets of paper each two feet long, treated with a yellowish insecticidal substance. The original tablets were kept in the Chung Ching, or Central Library, and duplicates were deposited in three other libraries. Since the T'ang dynasty, most of these works have been lost. Only two were left in the Sung, and the *Bamboo Annals* was lost in the Yüan dynasty. The only one of them transmitted today is the *Mu-t'ien-tzu chuan*, which is a fictional narrative of the adventures of King Mu (r. 1001?–947? B.C.) of the Chou dynasty in his imaginary journey to the West.

Considering the number of words in each tablet and the total number of words reported in various records, we can estimate that more than 2,500 tablets must have been unearthed, although a number of tablets were destroyed by being used as torches by the diggers. This is the first and largest discovery of bamboo tablets ever recorded in history; they escaped the destruction of books in the Ch'in dynasty.

Another collection of bamboo books, dated even earlier than the one from the Wei tomb, is said to have been discovered in 479 in the tomb of a Ch'u emperor at Hsiang-yang in modern Hupeh. This consisted of some ten bamboo tablets two feet long and less than one inch wide, inscribed with the so-called "tadpole" characters and bound with blue silk cords.[14] If this record is true, the books possibly belonged to the period of 505–278 B.C., when the Ch'u state had its capital in that territory.

[13] *Mu-t'ien-tzu chuan*, Hsün Hsü's preface, p. 3a.
[14] Hsiao Tzu-hsien, *Nan-ch'i shu*, 21/2a–b.

The bamboo tablets mentioned in early records no longer survive today; those extant have been discovered during recent years. The tablets found in the northwestern regions of China are almost entirely made of wood and date from the Han dynasty or later. A number of tablets recently discovered at Ch'ang-sha and Hsin-yang are especially valuable because they are made of bamboo and date back as early as the Warring States period. Since 1936–37, a great many ancient tombs have been robbed or scientifically excavated in the suburbs of Ch'ang-sha, which was a site of the ancient Ch'u state from the eighth century B.C. to 223 B.C. It is reported that in one of these tombs, at Wu-li-p'ai, some 37 bamboo tablets were uncovered in 1952.[15] They vary in size, and the inscriptions are so blurred that they are illegible. Only a few can be recognized as enumerations of funeral objects.

In another tomb at Yang-t'ien-hu, some 43 bamboo tablets were found in 1953.[16] This group of tablets is the most important find so far, since they have been preserved in better condition, bearing clearer and unusual inscriptions, and are definitely dated around the fourth century B.C. These tablets are about 22 cm. long, 1.2 cm. wide, and 1 mm. thick, with sharp corners (Plate XV). Each tablet contains from two to 21 characters, inscribed in black ink on the back surface of the bamboo, while the skin on the front side is unscraped. The inscriptions are neither in the "great seal" form used in the Chou dynasty nor in the "small seal" form used in Ch'in, but rather resemble the style appearing on the bronzes of the Ch'u state, indicating a writing style in transition during the Warring States period. This appears to be a form of the so-called "tadpole" style, with heavy starting and fine ending of the strokes.

These tablets have all been preserved in perfect condition since all sides of the coffin, in which the tablets were found in the space between outer and inner chambers, were surrounded by a layer of preservative clay, a kind of lime burnt from clam-shells. The funeral deposits consisted of wood, lacquer, bronze, and pottery objects. These tablets are apparently lists of funeral deposits, primarily silk clothes and metal utensils, itemized with the names and quantity of articles which had been buried with the dead.[17] They appear to be the "Offering Tablets" mentioned in ancient literary records. The *Book of Etiquette and Ceremonial*

[15] Hsia Nai, "Ch'ang-sha chin-chiao ku mu fa chüeh chi-lüeh," *KHTP*, III (1953), No. 7; *Wen-wu ts'an-k'ao tzu-liao*, 1952, No. 2.

[16] Shih Shu-ch'ing, *Ch'ang-sha Yang-t'ien-hu ch'u-t'u ch'u-chien yen-chiu*, p. 2.

[17] *Ibid.*, pp. 6–16, 21 ff.; *Wen-wu ts'an k'ao tzu-liao*, 1954, No. 3; *Shodo zenshu*, I, 129–30, 214–15; Jao Tsung-i, *Ch'ang-sha ch'u-t'u Chan-kuo ch'u-chien ch'u-shih*.

PLATE XV
BAMBOO TABLETS OF THE WARRING STATES PERIOD

"Offering Tablets" with lists of funeral deposits (22 × 1.2 cm.)

thus describes the mourning ceremony of an ordinary officer of the Chou dynasty: "The bequest and the name of donor are written on a tablet, which may contain nine, seven, or five items."[18] During the ceremony, the Master of Ceremonies stood before the coffin and read the list of offerings on the tablets before they were buried with the deceased. The recent discoveries confirm what was described in the ancient documents.

The third group of tablets from Ch'ang-sha was discovered at Yang-chia-wan in 1954. It includes 73 tablets; all but 27 have inscriptions of one or two characters written in black ink. These tablets are about 13.5 cm. long and 6 mm. wide, and the inscriptions are all so blurred that they cannot be deciphered.[19] The writing style is said to be different from that on the tablets at Yang-t'ien-hu. Dated in the middle of the third century B.C., these tablets are a little later than the group previously discovered.

Another group of bamboo tablets was found in 1957 in a tomb at Ch'ang-t'ai-kuan, near Hsin-yang, Honan. It includes 28 tablets with 30 or 40 characters in archaic style on each. They also seem to be "Offering Tablets" belonging to the Ch'u state in the later part of the Warring States period.[20]

WOODEN TABLETS OF THE HAN AND CHIN DYNASTIES

The important sites from which the ancient tablets come are, besides Ch'ang-sha and Hsin-yang in the central part of China, Tun-huang, Chü-yen, and Wu-wei in the northwest and Lou-lan and Khotan in Eastern Turkestan. Among them, Ch'ang-sha yielded the oldest specimens of bamboo tablets belonging to the Warring States period, Chü-yen supplied the largest quantity and most important core of wooden tablets of the Han dynasty, and Lou-lan produced documents all of which belong to the Chin dynasty. The more than 12,000 pieces discovered since 1900 by archeologists of various nationalities cover a span of almost 1,000 years in Chinese history. They are not only important for the study of ancient history and institutions,[21] but also significant as the only surviving specimens of bamboo and wooden documents for possible examination of their physical properties.

During his first expedition to Central Asia in 1901, Aurel Stein, of the

[18] *I-li chu-su*, 39/5a; Cf. Steele, *The I-li*, II, 86.

[19] *Wen-wu ts'an-k'ao tzu-liao*, 1954, No. 12, pp. 29–30; Shih Shu-ch'ing, *op. cit.*, pp. 17–18.

[20] *Wen-wu ts'an-k'ao tzu-liao*, 1957, No. 9, pp. 21–32; plates.

[21] For a survey of recent studies on the Han tablets, see Hulsewé, "Han-time Documents," *TP*, XLV (1957), 1–50.

Indian Archeological Survey, first discovered at the Niya site in Khotan original ancient Chinese documents on wood.[22] About forty, probably from the Later Han period, were found in an ancient settlement of the Tarim Basin, north of Khotan, which was abandoned to the desert sands in the third century A.D.

Stein's largest number of finds, more than 1,000, was yielded by the ruins near Tun-huang, with a few from Chiu-ch'üan which adjoins Tun-huang on the east, during his second and third expeditions in 1906–8 and 1913–16 respectively.[23] Situated in the westernmost tip of the Kansu corridor, which was an important commercial and military route from China proper to Central Asia. Tun-huang was established in 111 B.C. as one of the district commanderies to guard against attack from the northern tribe called Huns. Most of the tablets from this site, dated from 98 B.C. to A.D. 153, are literary works, calendars, works on arithmetic, divination and astrology, messages and accounts of the garrisons stationed in the military posts, and miscellaneous records.[24]

Of particular interest among them are the fragments of a beginner's lexicon, *Chi-chiu chang*, composed in 48–33 B.C., a popular textbook of elementary instruction used in the Han dynasty (Plate XVI.A). Numerous portions of calendars had obviously been useful in the military establishments. Complete calendars have been recovered for the years 63, 59, 57, and 39 B.C. and A.D. 94 and 153.[25] The earliest one, for the year 63 B.C. (Plate XVI.C), is seventeen years earlier than the adoption of the Julian calendar in 46 B.C. There are also a great number of official dispatches and private communications which are useful for the study of military and civil administration of the commanderies, the organization of military stations, the signal system, and the security of stations by a courier system.

The largest single collection of original Han documents ever discovered was that found in the Chü-yen region in 1930 by the Scientific Expedition

[22] Stein, *Ancient Khotan*, Vol. I, 358–63; Vol. II, Plates CXII–CXIV.

[23] Stein, *Serindia*, Vol. I, Introduction; Vol. II, chap. xxii; *Ruins of Desert Cathay*, I, 393–402; "Preliminary Account," *Geographical Journal*, XLIII (1916), 97–130, 193–225.

[24] The tablets discovered during the first two expeditions are reproduced and deciphered in Edouard Chavannes, *Les documents chinois découverts par Aurel Stein dans les sables du Turkestan Oriental* (Oxford, 1913); also in Lo Chen-yü, *Liu-sha chui-chien* (3 vols.; Kyoto, 1915), and *Han Chin shu-ying* (1918). Those discovered in the third expedition are deciphered in Henri Maspero, *Les documents chinois de la troisième expédition de Sir Aurel Stein en Asie Centrale* (London, 1953); a summary of this work is given in Bruno Schindler, "Preliminary Account," *Asia Major*, N.S., I (1949), 216–64. Facsimiles from Stein's three expeditions were reproduced also in Chang Feng, *Han Chin hsi-ch'ui mu-chien hui-pien* (Shanghai, 1931).

[25] Chavannes, *Les documents chinois* p. xvii.

PLATE XVI

WOODEN TABLETS OF THE HAN DYNASTY

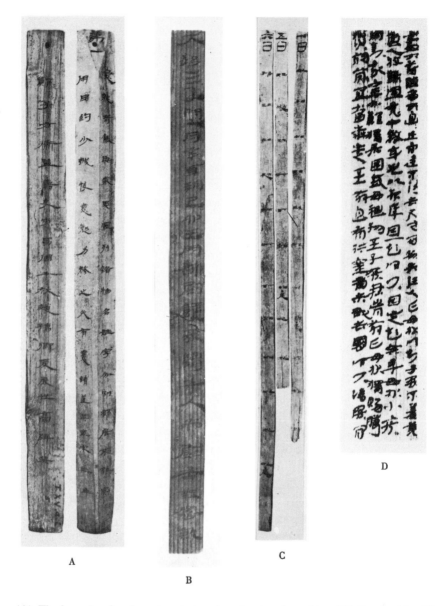

A   B   C   D

(A) Wooden prism for elementary instruction, showing three sides. (B) Dated tablet, 94 B.C. (C) Wooden calendar, 63 B.C. (D) Wooden tablet with four lines of writing.

to the Northwestern Provinces of China, known as the Sino-Swedish Expedition, under the leadership of Sven Hedin. Chü-yen is located in the northwestern part of Inner Mongolia where the Edsen-gol flows from the Kansu corridor. Situated on the lower reaches of the Edsen-gol and southwest of the dried eastern Chü-yen lake, the town of Chü-yen, known as Khara-khoto (Black City), was established about 104 B.C. as military and civil headquarters of the district commanderies between Tun-huang and Wu-wei, which form a triangle with Chü-yen. This region was fortified with watchtowers and beacons to guard the northern flank of the Kansu corridor.

This area was explored by P. K. Koslov of the Imperial Russian Geographical Society in 1908, by Stein in 1914, and again by Folke Bergman of the Sino-Swedish Expedition in 1930. From finds in a number of localities along the east bank of the Edsen-gol, this huge collection of about 10,000 inscribed tablets was gathered. The ruined fortress Mu-durbeljin alone yielded about 4,000 pieces, and in Taralingin-durbeljin and Ulan-durbeljin 1,500 pieces were excavated.[26] A large number of these tablets are dated, ranging from 102 B.C. to A.D. 30.[27]

These finds, like those made by Stein in Tun-huang, consist primarily of official dispatches to garrisons in the frontier outposts, documents and registers, letters, calendars, beginners' lexicons, laws and statutes, medical prescriptions, and miscellaneous records.[28] Most interesting is a bundle of 77 connected tablets, strung together by two lines of hemp threads at the ends (Plate XVII), confirming the system represented by the character *ts'e* as discussed before. The tablets are 23 cm. long and about 1.3 cm. wide, and the whole bundle spreads out about 122 cm. long. The text, written between A.D. 93 and 95, is an inventory of the weapons stored at the military outpost where it was discovered.[29] This is, in fact, the earliest complete Chinese "book" in existence.

Not far from Chü-yen, a group of 385 complete tablets and 225 fragments were unearthed at Wu-wei in 1959 by the Kansu Museum from a tomb dating from the Later Han period. Most of the tablets are made of

---

[26] Bergman, "Travels and Archeological Field-work in Mongolia and Sinkiang," *History of Expedition in Asia, 1927–1935,* IV, 146–48; Mori Shikazo, "Kyoen Kankan kenkyu josetsu," *Toyo-shi kenkyu,* XII (1953), 193–203; Yaneda Kenjiro, "Kyoen Kankan to sono kenkyu seika," *Kodai-gaku,* II (1953), 252–60; III (1954), 174–83.

[27] Lao Kan, "Chü-yen Han-chien k'ao-shih hsü-mu," *BIHP,* X (1948), 647–58.

[28] The transliteration and commentaries of this collection were made by Lao Kan, *Chü-yen Han-chien k'ao-shih* (6 vols., 1943–44); and a new edition, *Chü-yen Han-chien* (2 vols., 1957–60). The tablets are also reproduced with transliteration in *Chü-yen Han-chien chia-pien* (Peking, 1959).

[29] Lao Kan, *Chü-yen Han-chien k'ao-shih: shih-wen,* 3/27–30.

PLATE XVII

A HAN DOCUMENT ON WOODEN TABLETS

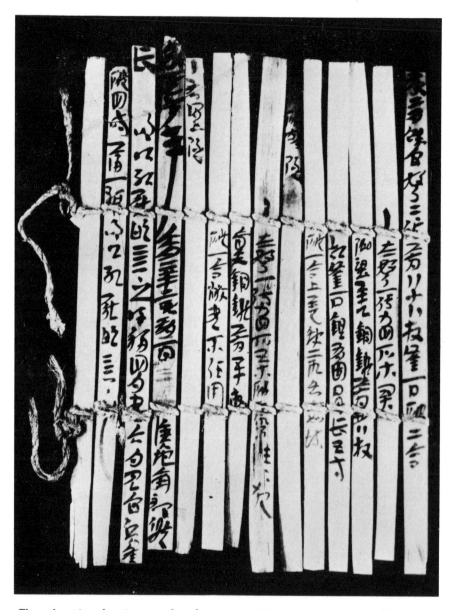

The end portion of an inventory list of weapons written in A.D. 93–95 on 77 tablets strung together by two lines of hemp threads. Each tablet is 23 × 1.3 cm., and the whole list spreads out 122 cm. long.

PLATE XVIII

LONG TABLETS FROM WU-WEI, LATER HAN DYNASTY

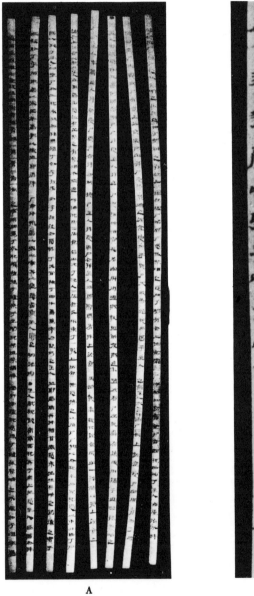

A   B

(A) Tablets of extra length. (B) Two tablets in actual width.

poplar and a few of bamboo. They are extraordinarily long, about 54 to 58 cm., and 1 cm wide, bearing as many as 60 to 80 characters on each tablet, some of which were written in simplified or variant forms of writing (Plate XVIII). The tablets are all numbered at the front and back, equivalent to the page numbers of a modern book. The document includes seven chapters of the *I-li*, or *Book of Etiquette and Ceremonial*. This group represents the longest size of individual tablets so far discovered.[30]

The documents unearthed at the ancient site of Lou-lan all belong to a later period. Lou-lan was a military colony founded on the northern bank of Lop-nor in the middle of the third century A.D., when the Emperor of the Chin dynasty resumed the policy of expansion into Central Asia which had been abandoned a century earlier. The earliest discoverer of this ancient site of Lou-lan was Sven Hedin, who made seven expeditions to Central Asia, beginning in 1894. At Lou-lan in 1903 he found many documents of wood, silk, and paper. They include 121 pieces of wooden tablets dated A.D. 266 and 269.[31] The Otani expedition of the Nishi-Honganji also explored this region between 1902 and 1914 and found some documents belonging to precisely the same period.[32] On Stein's third expedition in 1913–15, he discovered in this region 83 documents on wood, dating from A.D. 263 to 270.[33] They are primarily administrative and private documents, including one wooden "Letter Tablet," dated A.D. 266.[34]

PREPARATION OF BAMBOO AND WOOD FOR WRITING

Bamboo is a rapid-growing plant usually found in tropical and sub-tropical regions. In most parts of China, except the extreme northern regions, bamboo was extensively cultivated. Ancient records mentioned that bamboo formerly grew as far north as the states of Wei, Chin, Ch'in, and Ch'i, which correspond to the modern provinces of Honan, Shansi, Shensi, and Shantung along the Yellow River.[35] Probably the change of weather or deforestation drove the plant much farther south, though it is

[30] *K'ao-ku*, 1960, No. 5, pp. 10–12; plates.
[31] Conrady, *Die chinesischen Handschriften und sonstigen Kleinfunde Sven Hedin in Lou-lan*, pp. 117–40.
[32] Schindler, "Preliminary Account," *op. cit.*, p. 225.
[33] Maspero, *Les documents chinois*, p. 52.
[34] *Ibid.*, p. 77; No. 246.
[35] Cf. Legge, *She King*, pp. 91, 195, 303, etc.; *Ch'un ts'ew with Tso Chuen*, p. 281.

still found in some parts of the region. Its beautiful and luxuriant growth and varied usefulness are frequently referred to in ancient literature. A poem ascribed to the ninth century B.C. compares its elegant qualities with those of an accomplished prince:

> Look at those recesses in the banks of the Ch'i
> With their green bamboos, so fresh and luxuriant,
> There is our elegant and accomplished prince,
>
> . . . .
> How grave is he and dignified![36]

Almost every part of the bamboo is useful, especially the stem. Hollow and marked with joints or nodes, it is very hard but light and elastic. The external covering of the stem is remarkably siliceous and forms a sharp and durable cutting edge. Because of its various unique qualities, it was widely used in ancient China as material for building houses, suspension bridges, and rafts, and for making carriages and agricultural and domestic implements.[37] Its sharpness and elasticity make bamboo a good material for bows and arrows, and its hollow sections are ideal for musical instruments and brush-holders. Because of its light weight and smooth surface in comparison with other hard materials, bamboo was especially chosen by the Chinese people as the principal medium for writing before paper was extensively adopted.

Only a few species of wood are known to have been used for writing. Most of the tablets from the Tun-huang and Chü-yen regions are made of poplar and willow branches. These trees are widely cultivated throughout the northern part of China and some of the species, especially, are native to the oases of the desert region. Bamboo tablets, however, have been found very rarely in the northwestern region, because the plants were grown in China proper and were difficult to transport to the border area. Most of the wooden tablets Stein found in Tun-huang are made of white poplar and those the Academia Sinica found there include pines, willows, poplar, and Chinese tamarisk.[38] Woods belonging to these families are noted for their special qualities of whiteness, light weight, and easy absorption of ink. Native to the regions where these tablets were unearthed, they were naturally convenient for the use of writing.

Preparing bamboo tablets for writing was probably more complicated than preparing wood. The philosopher Wang Ch'ung, writing about A.D. 82, remarked that "wood is cut into large pieces of timber which are

---

[36] Legge, *She King*, p. 91.
[37] Ch'ü Tui-chih, "Ku-tai chih chu yü wen-hua," *Shih-hsüeh nien-pao*, I, No. 2 (1930), 117–22.
[38] Hsia Nai, "Hsin hu chih Tun-huang Han chien," *BIHP*, XIX (1948), 260–61; Appendix II.

separated into various boards and by using strength to smooth the surface, they are used for documents."[39] But for bamboo, writings were not made on the outer cuticle of the stem but rather on the under surface after the green skin was scraped off, although sometimes the inner side of the stem was also used for writing. The stem was first cut into cylinders of a certain length. These were then split into tablets of a certain width. The raw tablets, however, were not ready for writing until they had been treated and cured. This process was called *sha-ch'ing*, or "killing the green." After the external covering of green skin was scraped off, the tablets were dried over the fire to prevent quick decaying. The famous bibliographer Liu Hsiang (*ca.* 80–8 B.C.) noted that "*sha-ch'ing* is a process of making bamboo into tablets for writing. There is juice in fresh bamboo that causes decay and injuries by insects, so those who prepare bamboo tablets dry them over the fire."[40]

Old tablets could be used over again after the writing on the surface was removed. The process was known as *hsüeh-i* and the removed surface was called *shih*, which means "the slice as shaved from the wooden tablets" according to the *Shuo-wen*. When mistakes were made, the error could also be erased by scraping with a knife from the surface. Among Stein's discoveries at Tun-huang was a great mass of wooden shavings covered with Chinese characters, probably over a thousand in all.[41] These were chips from improvised tablets which had been used again and again for writing exercises. They were planed down with a knife each time to obtain a fresh surface. In 1944 the Academia Sinica also found shavings bearing inscriptions, which had evidently been cut off by a "book knife" from the tablets.[42] Tablets could thus be used many times in a process analogous to the production of vellum palimpsests.

SIZE AND FORMS OF ANCIENT TABLETS

Ancient documents on bamboo and on wood were generally different in format and in usage. Bamboo tablets were in the form of long and narrow strips of various lengths, written in one line of characters, and bound together with silk cords or leather thongs to form a volume like a modern paged book. Although wooden tablets were also made in long and narrow strips, they were sometimes square or rectangular in shape. These

[39] Wang Ch'ung, *Lun heng*, 12/10b.
[40] Ying Shao, *Feng-su t'ung-i*, p. 88.
[41] Stein, *Serindia*, II, 646.
[42] Hsia Nai, "Hsin hu chih Tun-huang Han-chien," *op. cit.*, pp. 235–36.

wooden boards formed a distinct unit, and they were usually not strung together. According to literary records, wooden tablets were primarily used for official documents, ordinances, short messages, and personal correspondence, whereas literary writings and books of considerable length were generally done on bamboo.

There seem to have been standard sizes for bamboo and wooden tablets used in ancient times. The standard varied according to the usage and the relative importance of the documents. The size of bamboo tablets for literary writings was fixed at two feet four inches, one foot two inches, and eight inches. According to Cheng Hsüan (127–200), the six classics were all written on tablets of two feet four inches. Those for the *Book of Filial Piety* were one foot two inches and for the *Confucian Analects*, eight inches.[43] The system seems to have been to use longer tablets for writing more respected literature and shorter ones for less important books, since the two latter works were not included in the corpus of canonical literature until the ninth century A.D. This theory is supported by the philosopher Wang Ch'ung (*ca.* 27–100), who says that "large tablets are used for classics and small ones for commentaries and historical records."[44] He also states that "the sayings of ancient sages were written on tablets of two feet four inches."

The discoveries in early literary records of ancient tablets gave similar data in regard to size. The tablets used for the *Mu-t'ien-tzu chuan*, written in the third century B.C., were described by Hsün Hsü as "two feet four inches according to the ancient measure fixed by myself,"[45] and those for the *K'ao-kung chi*, written earlier than the above work, are recorded in dynastic history as two feet, which equals two feet four inches according to the Han measure.[46] It appears that not only classics, but also other important works were written on tablets of two feet four inches.

The standard lengths of the wooden tablets used during the Han dynasty were from five inches to two feet. According to Ts'ai Yung (132–192), the imperial edicts were written on tablets of two feet and also on shorter ones of one foot.[47] The great mass of wooden tablets discovered by Stein near Tun-huang measured, in most cases, 23 cm. or 24 cm., which is equivalent to about one foot in Han times.[48] The standard size for wooden

[43] *Ch'un-ch'iu tso-chuan cheng-i*, Preface, 7a.

[44] Wang Ch'ung, *Lun heng*, 12/10b.

[45] *Mu-t'ien-tzu chuan*, Hsün Hsü's preface, 3a.

[46] Wang Kuo-wei, "Chien-tu chien-shu k'ao," 3a, in *WCAIS*, ts'e 26.

[47] Ts'ai Yung, *Tu-tuan* 1/4a.

[48] Stein, *Serindia*, II, 672.

stationery for ordinary use following Han was fixed at one foot. The term *ch'ih-tu*, or "one-foot tablet," for private correspondence originated from this system. The shortest tablets, five inches long, served as identification tickets for travel through the guarded passes.

According to Wang Kuo-wei, different kinds of wooden tablets vary not only in designation but in their relative lengths, ranging from three feet for an unpolished tablet, two feet for an official summons, one and one-half foot for an official dispatch, one foot for a private letter, and one-half foot for an identification ticket.[49] Thus the size of wooden tablets used for official and private documents in Han times was represented by multiples of five inches, and that of bamboo tablets by fractions of twenty-four inches. The reason for this difference was probably that the number six, and its multiples, was the standard unit used in the late Chou and Ch'in dynasties, while five was used in the Han dynasty.

According to the above discussion, tablets used in literary writings and other documents all seem to have been uniform in size for a certain kind of document. But there are contrary descriptions in the literature to the effect that the tablets used for a particular document were uneven and varied in their lengths. The *Shuo-wen* says that "the character *ts'e* for tablets, which means an order of the king to the feudal princes, derives from the picture of a bundle of long and short tablets."[50] No reference about this system of uneven sizes is found in pre-Ch'in literature.[51] But in the Han dynasty, when the three princes were granted their fiefs by Emperor Wu (r. 140–87 B.C.), the orders were written on tablets of uneven lengths.[52] Ts'ai Yung also reported that the system of imperial edicts was written on tablets of uneven size as well as those of one or two feet.[53] These records indicate that tablets of uneven lengths were used primarily for imperial orders of appointment, which were different from other kinds of official documents. Since the character *ts'e* was written with uneven strokes in bone and bronze inscriptions, this system must be very old and can be traced back to Shang and Chou times.

[49] Wang Kuo-wei, *op. cit.*, 8a–10b.

[50] Ting Fu-pao, *Shuo-wen chieh-tzu ku-lin*, p. 917

[51] The term *tuan ch'ang*, which means "short and long" or "defects or merits," was used to mean ancient diplomatic writings of the Warring States period. Wang Kuo-wei thought that the documents must have included some short and some long tablets, and that the term was accordingly applied to them. This theory, however, seems to be incorrect. Since this term should be interpreted as "defects and merits," for two sides of one fact, it represents the principle of diplomatic argumentation. See Wang, *op. cit.*, 5b–6a

[52] *Shih chi*, 60/8b. Notes by Ch'u Shao-sun.

[53] Ts'ai Yung, *Tu tuan*, 1/4a.

The width of the tablets, unlike the length, has not been exactly indicated in the literature. There is one note in the dynastic history that the tablets discovered in A.D. 479 were "several tenths of one inch wide."[54] The tablets discovered by Stein and recorded by Chavannes in *Les documents chinois* range from 8 mm. to 46 mm. wide, the majority being 10 mm. The inventory list discovered at Chü-yen was reported to be 13 mm. wide for each tablet. Those bamboo tablets recently discovered at Ch'ang-sha are reported to be 12 mm. wide in one group and 6 mm. in another. It seems that in most cases the width of the tablets was not more than 2 cm. But wooden boards for official documents sometimes had a much wider surface and could accommodate up to five or more lines of characters (Plate XVI.D).

COLUMNS AND STYLES OF WRITING

The number of columns and characters in each tablet also varied. Characters were usually written on one side in one column, but in some cases they were written on both sides or in two or more columns. Among the thirty tablets kept by the National Central Library, for example, it is reported that seven were written on both sides.[55] The number of characters ranges from eight to eighty, depending upon the length of the tablet and the size of the characters.

According to Cheng Hsüan (127–200), each tablet for the *Book of Documents* includes thirty characters.[56] It is assumed that tablets for other classics, including the *Spring and Autumn Annals*, which were all two feet four inches long, must have included the same number of characters. The *Tso chuan*, which is the commentary on the *Annals*, had eight characters in each tablet, according to Fu Ch'ien of the third century A.D.[57] It is obvious that the *Tso chuan* must have been written on tablets of eight inches, since it was less important than the text of the *Annals*. The bibliographical section of the *History of the Former Han Dynasty* noted that on some of the missing tablets of the *Book of Documents* there were twenty-five characters and on others, twenty-two.[58] Hsün Hsü

[54] Hsiao Tzu-hsien, *Nan-ch'i shu*, 21/2a.

[55] Su Ying-hui, "Chung-yang t'u-shu-kuan so-ts'ang Han-chien chung ti hsin-shih-liao," *TLTC*, III (1951), 23.

[56] *I-li chu-su*, 24/3b.

[57] *Ibid.*

[58] *Han shu*, 30/5a.

(231–289) said in his preface to the *Mu-t'ien-tzu chuan* that one tablet contained forty characters.[59]

Among the discoveries from Tun-huang, the beginner's lexicon was written with one paragraph containing 63 characters on each tablet. One tablet in the form of a prism was written on three sides with 21 characters in each column (Plate XVI.A), and another tablet had two columns of 32 and 31 characters, respectively. The bamboo tablets discovered at Ch'ang-sha have from two to 21 characters on each tablet of similar length. The recently discovered tablets at Wu-wei contain as many as 60 to 80 characters on each long tablet.[60] From the literary and archeological evidence, it seems correct to assume that no definite number of characters was set in each column of a tablet, but it rather depended upon the size of the characters and the length of the tablet.

Different styles of writing were used in the preparation of ancient tablets, depending not only upon the period when they were produced but also upon the relative importance of the documents. Ts'ai Yung (132–192) said that important documents were written on bamboo in the seal style, while a minor order was put on a wooden board in the clerical style.[61] Although the *k'ai* or model style has been popularly used since the late third century, some official appointments of the sixth century were still written in the seal style.[62] The tradition of using conventional form in writing important documents persisted for a long time. According to K'ung An-kuo (fl. 90 B.C.), the old text of the *Book of Documents* was copied from the ancient writing in the clerical style on the bamboo tablets.[63] It seems to be correct that the six classics of the Han dynasty were written in the popular clerical style.

In the middle of the first century B.C., there was developed a new style of writing, known as *chang ts'ao* which is actually a free version of the clerical style derived from the rapid execution of the strokes. It is believed that the term *chang* may have derived from the beginner's lexicon called *Chi-chiu chang*, which was written by Shih Yu during the period 48–33 B.C. This new style is found on the Tun-huang tablets dated 58 B.C., A.D. 48, and A.D. 68.[64] Some writings on earlier tablets and the inventory list of A.D. 93–95 from Chü-yen (Plate XVII) show a similar trend. This is the first step toward the development of the *hsing* or

[59] *Mu-t'ien-tzu chuan*, Hsün Hsü's preface, 3a.

[60] *K'ao-ku*, 1960, No. 5, p. 11.

[61] Ts'ai Yung, *Tu-tuan*, 1/4.

[62] *Sui shu*, 9/3a.

[63] *Shang-shu chu-su*, K'ung's preface, 13a.

[64] Lo Chen-yü, *Han Chin shu-ying*, Plate 1.

running style in the second century A.D. and the later *ts'ao* or rapid style in the fourth century A.D.

UNITS AND KINDS OF ANCIENT BOOKS

The units and kinds of ancient books vary according to the different materials used, the size and shapes of tablets, and the forms of binding. Ancient terms used to signify books, however, were not consistent in their application to different forms. This has resulted in confusion because the terms were sometimes used interchangeably in ancient literature.

There seem to have been some common differentiations between tablets made of bamboo and those of wood. Generally, those terms referring to tablets of bamboo bear a radical *chu* for bamboo, and those of wood a *mu* for wood or *p'ien* for a strip. A single tablet made of bamboo was called *chien*; it was generally written with one line of characters and read vertically from top to bottom. When more characters were required, they were written on several tablets bound with cords to form a unit called *ts'e*. When a writing of a certain length formed a literary unit like a chapter, it was called *p'ien*. While *ts'e* referred to a smaller and physical unit of a document, *p'ien* was used as a larger and literary unit which might include several *ts'e*.

Whether the term *chüan* for rolls was also used as a unit for books made of tablets is doubtful. It was generally considered to have been a unit used exclusively for silk and paper rolls. But from an actual examination of a bundle of 77 tablets discovered at Chü-yen, Lao Kan believes that "the tablets when piled up were called *ts'e* and when rolled up were called *chüan*."[65] A study by Ch'en P'an[66] attempts to find literary evidence to support this theory but, unfortunately, none of this evidence is earlier than the Han dynasty, when *chüan* was already extensively used for silk or paper rolls. Ch'en points out that in the bibliographical section of the *History of the Former Han Dynasty*, the modern text of the *Book of Documents* is mentioned in the introduction as 29 *p'ien*, but it is listed in the catalogue as 29 *chüan*.[67] In the preface to the old text of the *Book of Documents*, K'ung An-kuo (fl. 90 B.C.) said that this work, "including the

---

[65] Lao Kan, *Chü-yen han-chien k'ao-shih: k'ao cheng*, I, 74*b*.

[66] Ch'en P'an, "Hsien-Ch'in liang-Han chien-tu k'ao," *Hsüeh-shu chi-k'an*, I, No. 4 (1953), 12–13.

[67] *Han shu*, 30/3*b*, 4*b*.

preface, was 59 *p'ien*, in 46 *chüan*."[68] Ch'en says that these examples indicate that one or several *p'ien* could be rolled up into one *chüan*.

Since the Han bibliography lists books both in *p'ien* and *chüan*, these examples seem on the contrary to be evidence that books were made of two different kinds of materials and therefore entered as two different units. For if tablets were rolled up and called *chüan*, there was no reason to use the word *p'ien*. These two examples, according to my interpretation, mean that the old and modern texts of the *Book of Documents* were originally in 59 and 29 *p'ien* but were copied into 46 and 26 *chüan* (silk rolls). The unit *chüan* as listed in the catalogue meant the actual holdings of the imperial library, while the unit *p'ien* in the introduction referred to the original edition. Practically, however, tablets were much easier to roll up than to bind side by side. Even so, as in the inventory list of Chü-yen, the bundles of tablets are believed to have still been called *p'ien* instead of *chüan*.

Besides the *chien* and *ts'e* which were primarily used for literary writings, there were other kinds of documents made of bamboo used for particular purposes. There was the tally used for identification. According to the *Shuo-wen*, "the *fu*, which means 'to trust' and is divided into two halves to be fitted in exact agreement, was made of bamboo of six inches in the Han dynasty." The system described here is identical with what was discovered in the Tun-huang and Chü-yen regions. Some twenty-four short tablets were deciphered by Lao Kan as being used to certify official messages, for travel through guarded passes, and for identification of personal status in central and local governments.[69] Other materials, including wood, silk, jade, and metals, were used, but bamboo was more common for general purposes.

Another kind of tally was used as calculating rods for the higher forms of mathematics. It was shorter and narrower than the ordinary tablets used for writing. Tallies on which oracle verses were written were used for drawing lots in divination. Short tablets called *hu* were used as a medium of official communication between subordinates and the emperor; they were made of bamboo or other materials, slightly tapering to the ends. Short messages to be presented to the emperor were written on these. They were usually held before the breast at the audience.

Wooden tablets were used primarily as official documents and not intended for longer writings of literary compositions. A *fang* was a square board carrying a passage of not more than 100 characters written

[68] *Shang-shu chu-su*, K'ung's preface, 13a–b.

[69] Lao Kan, *op. cit.*, *shih-wen*, I, 81b–82b; *k'ao-cheng*, I, 32a–34a.

in five to nine lines, primarily for official registers or other documents. It was similar in use but different in shape or size from a *pan*, which was a rectangular board with a smooth and wide polished surface, and from a *tieh*, a thin and short board, or from a *tu*, a narrow board about one foot long primarily for official documents or private correspondence. These different kinds of wooden boards were all prepared from a raw wooden cylinder three feet long. They were generally used separately; but when a number were fastened together, they were called *cha*, a term equivalent to *ts'e* for bamboo tablets.

Wooden tablets were also prepared with more than two writing surfaces for use in elementary instruction or in practicing calligraphy. One prism fourteen inches long, discovered by Stein at Tun-huang, has the entire first paragraph of the *Chi-chiu chang*, a beginner's lexicon, in 63 characters divided equally among the three surfaces. The prism was originally one-half of a square pillar-shaped tablet which was divided diagonally into two pieces with three plain surfaces each. There is a perforation at the top of the prism, evidently for connecting it with the other prism in the opposite direction (Plate XVI.A). Another prism discovered at Chü-yen includes two parts of the *Chi-chiu chang* with 20 characters on each side and 60 to one chapter, which is identical with what was recorded in the bibliographical section of the *History of the Former Han Dynasty*.[70] Besides having more spaces than the ordinary tablets for beginner's practice, it also had the advantage of being stood on a table for reading and memorizing the characters upon one surface, with the others out of sight.[71]

SYSTEM OF BINDING AND SEALING

The individual tablet, corresponding to a folio, constituted the basic unit of an ancient book. The complete text of a literary composition was usually composed of a series of tablets, bound together with cords to keep them in proper order. The books were probably bound in two different forms. One was the roll form after the tablets were connected with a cord. Another was the accordion form in which the folios were placed face to face in a *ts'e*, from which the modern volume is derived.

Since most of the tablets discovered are disconnected, an experiment has been made to test the possibility of binding them into a complete

[70] *Han shu*, 30/15a.
[71] Lo Chen-yü, *Liu-sha chui-chien: k'ao-shih*, 2a–4b.

book. It has been suggested that the cord was doubled end to end with the first tablet placed in the bend, and an ordinary knot was tied. The second tablet was then laid with its notch against the knot between the two cords, which were then half-twisted. A third tablet was laid in the same way, and the process was continued until the last tablet, after which a knot was tied. The excess length of the cords could be used to tie the complete *ts'e* together when it was closed like an accordion.[72]

No tablets bound in the accordion form are extant today and no description of this system is found in ancient literature. A picture, however on a tomb tile dating from the third century B.C. shows a man holding a bamboo book, which seems to consist of six tablets piled up (see frontispiece). It seems that the tablets, after being connected by cords, could also be rolled up and stored in that form. The inventory list from Chü-yen, composed of 77 tablets, bound together with hemp cords (Plate XVII), was reported to be in roll form when discovered.[73]

The binding cords were made of silk, hemp, or leather. The bamboo tablets discovered in the Wei tomb in A.D. 280 were recorded as all bound with white silk cords, and those discovered in the Ch'u tomb in A.D. 479 had blue silk cords. The biography of Liu Hsiang (*ca.* 80–8 B.C.) mentions that "the work *Sun-tzu* was written on treated tablets and bound with bright silk cords."[74] The inventory list of weapons of the first century A.D. is bound with cords made of hemp. Traces of the same material are visible on the tablets discovered at Tun-huang. Whether other materials, such as leather thongs, were ever used for binding tablets is uncertain. The only mention of the use of leather thongs in ancient literature is the statement made by Ssu-ma Ch'ien (*ca.* 145–86 B.C.) that Confucius was fond of reading the *Book of Changes* and "the leather thongs had been broken three times,"[75] apparently by constant use.

Another use of cords in connection with the documents was for wrapping. Requisition tablets for 200 feet of "book cords" were discovered at Tun-huang and Chü-yen.[76] These were used to wrap the tablets, on which lines were clearly engraved for this purpose. The number of engraved lines on one side of the tablet varied from one to five, but examples found in Tun-huang all had three lines, each line wrapped once or twice with cords and then sealed with clay. Traces of cords impressed on ancient

[72] Stein, "Notes on Ancient Chinese Documents," *New China Review*, III (1921), 251–52.

[73] Lao Kan, *op. cit., k'ao-cheng*, I, 74*b*.

[74] *T'ai-p'ing yü-lan*, 606/2*a*.

[75] *Shih chi*, 47/23*b*.

[76] Lao Kan, *op. cit., k'ao-cheng*, I, 24*a–b*

tablets indicate that the direction of wrapping might be horizontal, vertical, or in the form of a cross, but was usually horizontal.

For sealing documents, a separate piece of wood called "sealing board" was bound with cords over the face of the written documents. Clay was spread over the cords and impressed with a seal which became an official signature of the sender of the document. The receiver's name and a brief description of the content of the document was usually written on the outside of the sealing board. The place for the seal impression was a square cut into the sealing board, known as "sealing teeth," to hold the clay (Plate VIII.C, upper). Many tablets discovered by Stein at Khotan indicate such a practice.[77]

The sealing board, however, could be applied to only one document. When a number of documents were dispatched, they were sealed in a bag made of cloth or silk in different colors to indicate the methods of delivery —red and white for urgent messages, green for imperial edicts, and black for ordinary documents.[78] A square bag with seamless ends, it opened in the center for the documents to be put in. The two ends of the bag were folded to cover the seam in the middle, and then wrapped with cords and impressed with the seal on clay. The methods of dispatch were usually indicated on the board. Messages were then passed from one station to another, carried by couriers or, for urgent business, delivered by special messengers on horseback.[79]

[77] Stein, *Ancient Khotan*, Plates XX, XXI, XXIV.
[78] Lao Kan, *op. cit., k'ao-cheng*, I, 75b.
[79] *Ibid.*, II, 3a–b.

VI

SILK AS WRITING MATERIAL

ORIGIN OF SERICULTURE

It is universally accepted that the cultivation of the silkworm and the reeling of its silk fibers is a Chinese discovery. Traditions have ascribed the invention of silk to a legendary emperor or empress of the third millennium B.C., but as yet no established evidence supports the legends. In 1926 an artificially cut cocoon of the *Bombyx mori* was discovered at a neolithic site at Hsi-yin in southern Shansi.[1] Spinning whorls made of stone or pottery have been unearthed at many other neolithic sites. These discoveries suggest that silk might already have existed even before historic times.

As early as the Shang dynasty, silk was certainly used in such a refined state as to indicate it had passed the experimental stages long before. Characters such as *ssu* (silk), *ch'an* (silkworm), *po* (silk fabrics), and *shang* (mulberry trees) are frequently found in oracle-bone inscriptions[2] (see Table I, 5d, 7b). Several remnants of silk fabrics on a bronze axe and urn found in the excavations at An-yang indicate that the Shang people had at their disposal the long, reeled, unthrown silk thread.[3] A silkworm carved of white jade, 3.15 cm. long, has been recently discovered at An-yang.[4] Other jade silkworms and remnants of silk fibers were found in an ancient tomb dated from the early Chou dynasty.[5]

Besides these archeological evidences, much of early Chou literature contains information on the cultivation, manufacture, and dyeing of silk

---

[1] Li Chi, *Hsi-yin-ts'un shih-ch'ien i-chi*, p. 20.

[2] Sun Hai-po, *Chia-ku-wen pien*, 7/19a, 13/1b–2a; Chin Hsiang-heng, *Hsü chia-ku-wen pien*, 6/8, 7/32, 13/3–4; Wen I-to, "Shih shang," *Wen I-to ch'üan-chi*, II, 565–72.

[3] Sylwan, "Silk from the Yin Dynasty," *BMFEA*, IX (1937), 119–26; *Investigation of Silk from Edsen-gol and Lop-nor*, p. 92; Plate 4.

[4] Ma Te-chih, "I-chiu-wu-san-nien An-yang Ta-ssu-k'ung-ts'un fa-chüeh pao-kao," *KKHP*, IX (1955), 65.

[5] Kuo Pao-chün, "Chün-hsien Hsin-ts'un ku ts'an-mu chih ch'ing-li," *TYKKPK*, I (1936), 200.

and indicates that sericulture was a domestic industry engaged in by women. The "Odes of Pin," a poem dated probably from the eighth or seventh century B.C., describes how the young women were busy all year round picking mulberry leaves, spinning, and dyeing silk fabrics in black, yellow, and red for the robes of the aristocrats.[6] Another poem, "Odes of Mang," says: "A simple-looking lad you are, carrying cloth to exchange for silk."[7] A bronze inscription, ascribed to the ninth or tenth century B.C., records also the use of silk for buying slaves.[8] Evidently silk was used not only as a material for clothing but also as a valuable medium of exchange and trade during the early Chou dynasty.

Recent discoveries of many silk fabrics at the site of Ch'ang-sha provide archeological evidence of the extensive use of plain silk in the Warring States period.[9] A number of silk textiles from the first century B.C. to the second century A.D., found at Lou-lan and other sites in the Edsen-gol and Lop-nor regions, bear sufficient witness not only to the manufacture of plain silk and several kinds of patterned silks but also to high quality and originality in design.[10] From the first century B.C., the product was carried over the old "Silk road" through the vast regions of Chinese Turkestan to western Asia and thence to Europe. Merchants from Phoenicia, Carthage, Syria, and other lands explored the sea routes to China in order to buy the precious fabric. The Roman Empire had extensive dealings in silk with China, and in the second century A.D. a pound of raw silk commanded more than its weight in gold.[11]

Silkworms and mulberry trees are raised throughout most of the temperate zone in China. The present area of domestic silk production lies between 20 and 30 degrees north, including the Yangtze Valley and regions south of it. But the silk-producing regions mentioned in ancient literature were all far north of the present general mulberry area. For example, the *Book of Poetry* makes frequent mention of silk in connection with the states along the Yellow River. The *Yü-kung*, or *Tribute of Yü*, also contains valuable information about the ancient silk-producing areas before or during the time when the book was written, probably in the middle Chou dynasty.[12] Among articles of tribute from various districts

---

[6] Legge, *She King*, pp. 228–29.

[7] *Ibid.*, p. 97; Wang Yü-ch'üan renders the word *pu*, cloth, as *pu* for spade money. Cf. his *Early Chinese Coinage*, p. 106.

[8] Creel, *Birth of China*, p. 88.

[9] Shang Ch'eng-tso, *Ch'ang-sha ku-wu wen-chien-chi*, p. 46a.

[10] Sylwan, *Investigation of Silk from Edsen-gol and Lop-nor*, p. 93.

[11] Hirth, *China and the Roman Orient*, p. 225, notes.

[12] Cf. Creel, *Studies of Early Chinese Culture*, pp. 98–99, notes.

of the country, silk was especially mentioned as produced in places corresponding to modern Shantung in north China.[13] Even in the Han dynasty, Shantung was still the most prosperous center of silk production and manufacture.[14] Writings on silk, of the first or second century A.D., from that location have been found at archeological sites in Chinese Turkestan. The center of silk production in north China shifted to the Yangtze Valley only after the eleventh century A.D., when both economic and cultural activities began to migrate from north to south.

Silkworms were probably used in their wild state before they were domesticated. Since wild silk today comes mainly from Shantung and other provinces along the Yellow River and as far north as Manchuria, it has been suspected that silk used in ancient China might have been produced by wild silkworms. It seems reasonable to believe that both wild and domestic silkworms existed in ancient times, but probably climatic changes drove domestic cultivation much farther south. Many scholars believe that the climate in the Yellow River valley was formerly much warmer than it is today.[15]

DATE OF THE USE OF SILK FOR WRITING

Most of the early literature and recent excavations indicate that silk was used as a material for clothing, musical strings, binding cords, or exchange medium. However, there seems no evidence to indicate that silk was used for writing prior to the Ch'un Ch'iu period. Chavannes thought that the earliest use of silk for writing dated back to the time of the First Emperor (r. 221–210 B.C.) of the Ch'in dynasty, when the brush-pen was supposed to have been invented. He contended that writing on silk was possible only with the brush and that there was no evidence of such writing prior to the third century B.C.[16] Recent discoveries and research, nevertheless, have proved that the brush was already used as early as the Shang dynasty, and actual documents have recently been excavated, which were written or drawn on silk as early as the fifth or fourth century B.C. From a survey of early literature, it may be concluded that the use of silk for writing originated no later than the sixth or seventh century B.C. and continued even after the third or fourth century A.D.

---

[13] Legge, *Shoo King*, pp. 99, 102, 107, 116, 119.

[14] Yao Pao-yu, *Chung-kuo ssu-chüan hsi-ch'uan shih*, p. 1.

[15] Hu Hou-hsüan, "Ch'i-hou pien-ch'ien yü Yin-tai ch'i-hou chi chien-t'ao," *CKHSSLT*, 2d ser., II, 20*b*.

[16] Chavannes, "Les livres chinois avant l'invention du papier," *op. cit.*, p. 8.

Recent discoveries of silk documents at the site of Ch'ang-sha, which will be discussed later, give indisputable evidence for the use of silk as a writing material during the Warring States period. Although no actual silk documents before this time are extant today, records in ancient literature seem to indicate that writing on silk was even earlier than the evidence produced by the recent discoveries. One early literary reference to writing on silk comes from the *Confucian Analects*, which says: "Tzu Chang (a disciple of Confucius) wrote the counsels [from his master] on the end of his sash,"[17] The *Rituals of Chou* says: "those who had performed meritorious services in the government were inscribed on the banners of the king."[18] Although sashes and banners were not primarily writing materials, these records at least indicate that materials made of silk were used for writing as early as the time of Confucius (551–479 B.C.).

When different materials for inscriptions were described by the philosopher Mo Ti (*ca.* 480–390 B.C.), he said that "the ancient sage-kings . . . recorded them on bamboo and silk."[19] Han Fei Tzu (*d.* 233 B.C.) also said that "the ancient kings left principles of government on bamboo and silk."[20] While these references were probably written during the Warring States period, the authors of these works all said that their ancestors had used silk for writing. Who these ancestors were and when they lived is not indicated.

One reference, however, does indicate the name of the ancestor. Duke Ching (r. 547–490 B.C.) of Ch'i once told Yen Ying (d. 493 B.C.), when giving him land after the precedent of his ancestor-king: "Formerly, my ancestor Duke Huan (r. 685–643 B.C.) gave Hu and Ku to Kuan Chung (d. 645 B.C.), covering seventeen districts, and this has been recorded on bamboo and silk."[21] While this conversation took place in about the fifth or sixth century B.C., it mentions an ancestor of the seventh century B.C.

Although writing on silk was mentioned in pre-Ch'in literature, its use seems to have been limited to important and sacred documents. From the time of the Han dynasty, however, it evidently became very common and popular. Not only does the Han bibliography, compiled in the first century A.D., record books written on silk rolls, but much of the Han literature frequently mentions this fact. Yang Hsiung (53 B.C.–A.D. 18), the poet and philosopher, who wrote a book on dialects, said that he usually carried with him a writing brush of three inches and a piece of silk of four

[17] Legge, *Confucian Analects*, p. 160.
[18] *Chou-li chu-su*, 30/2b.
[19] Mei Yi-pao, *Motse*, p. 167.
[20] *Han-fei-tzu*, 8/6b.
[21] *Yen-tzu ch'un-ch'iu*, 7/24a.

feet when he went to inquire about different dialects. He copied his findings on tablets with a stick of lead when he returned.[22] It is evident that silk was employed because it was much easier to carry than tablets. For this reason, silk became a common material for correspondence.

Many legends and stories relate the transmission of silk letters by means of fish and wild geese. An ancient poem says: "Calling my boy to cook the carp,/In its body was a silk letter of one foot."[23] Ch'en Sheng (d. 299 B.C.), a rebel of Ch'in who tried to establish his prestige by trickery, put into the bodies of fish silk documents written with cinnabar that "Ch'en Sheng should be emperor." When soldiers bought the fish for food, they read the messages with great surprise and took them as a sign that Ch'en Sheng's rebellion was commissioned by Heaven.[24] The *History of the Former Han Dynasty* records that several years after 86 B.C., the Han emperor sought the release of General Su Wu, who was then held captive by the Huns. The Tartars lied, saying that Su was dead. The negotiator made a counter feint, stating that "when the emperor was hunting in the imperial park, he received a letter written on silk and tied to the foot of a wild goose, saying that Su was living in a certain marshy place."[25] The release of Su Wu was finally gained by this pretended evidence of a silk letter. From such stories, "fish body" and "wild-goose feet" have since become recognized allusions in Chinese literature to a written communication.

Silk continued to be used as a writing material in the Chin dynasty (265–419) even though paper was already popular. It is recorded that a historiographer at the Chin court was asked to take charge of copying books, silk fabrics, brush and ink.[26] Hsün Hsü, official custodian of the Chin imperial library, compiled a catalogue in four divisions, known as the *Hsin-pu*, or *New Register*, including books in 29,945 *chüan*, "written on silk and wrapped with silk cloths."[27] As late as the T'ang dynasty (618–906), silk probably was still being used for writing. It is said that plain silk with red or black columns woven into the textile was manufactured in north China under the T'ang.[28] Although silk is used for painting even today, its use for writing evidently decreased after the third or fourth century. When Emperor Wu (r. 420–422) of the Sung dynasty came into

[22] Yen K'o-chün, *Ch'üan Han wen*, 52/9a, "Yang Hsiung's letter to Liu Hsin."
[23] Kuo Mao-ch'ien, *Yüeh-fu shih-chi*, 38/2a.
[24] *Han shu*, 31/2a.
[25] *Ibid.*, 54/20b.
[26] Su I-chien, *Wen-fang ssu-p'u*, 5/12b.
[27] *Sui-shu*, 32/4b.
[28] Li Chao, *T'ang kuo-shih pu*, hsia/18b.

power, he collected all the documents and books that could be found, to be preserved in the imperial library; but it possessed only 4,000 *chüan*, "written on blue paper and decorated with red rollers."[29]

DISCOVERIES OF BRUSH WRITING ON SILK

Remnants of silk materials bearing short and long inscriptions have been discovered in many sites in China as well as in some parts of Central Asia. They provide not only knowledge about the different kinds of materials and methods of weaving them but also evidence that actual writings were made with brush-pen and ink on silk fabrics. Since the turn of the twentieth century, archeologists have found fragments of silk in Eastern Turkestan along the "silk road" by which China communicated with the West. In 1901 Sven Hedin found silk fragments of various colors at Lou-lan, but none of them had inscriptions. During Stein's second expedition in 1908, he discovered at Tun-huang two well-preserved letters of silk belonging to the first half of the first century A.D.[30] They were both addressed by the same person, probably an officer of superior rank stationed at Ch'eng-lo on the northern border of Shansi, to another exile on the Tun-huang borders, complaining about the inconveniences and difficulties of communication between them. One letter is about 9 cm. square, and the other is about 15 cm. long and 6.5 cm. wide (Plate XIX.A). It could be conveniently inserted after folding into the silk envelope, which is about 6.7 cm. wide. Although they bear no date, these two silk letters were among other documents dated from A.D. 15 to 56, when true paper seems not to have been invented.

Another of Stein's discoveries near Tun-huang is a strip of plain undyed silk (Plate XIX.B). One side bears a seal impression with black ink, and the other a line of 28 characters which may be read as "one *p'i* of plain silk from K'ang-fu in the Kingdom of Jen-ch'eng; width, two feet two inches; length, forty feet; weight, twenty-five ounces; value, 618 [pieces of money]."[31] These few inscriptions furnish exact details of great historical importance. The size as inscribed here confirms the standard system recorded in ancient literature. Cheng Hsüan (127–200) in his commentary on the *Book of Etiquette and Ceremonial*, said: "Now

[29] *Sui shu*, 32/4b.

[30] Stein, *Serindia*, II, 726–63; Chavannes, *Les Documents chinois*, Nos, 398, 398A, 503.

[31] Stein, *Serindia*, II, 700–701; Chavannes, *Les Documents chinois*, No. 539; Lo Chen-yü, *Liu-sha chui-chien*, 2/43b.

PLATE XIX

BRUSH WRITINGS ON SILK

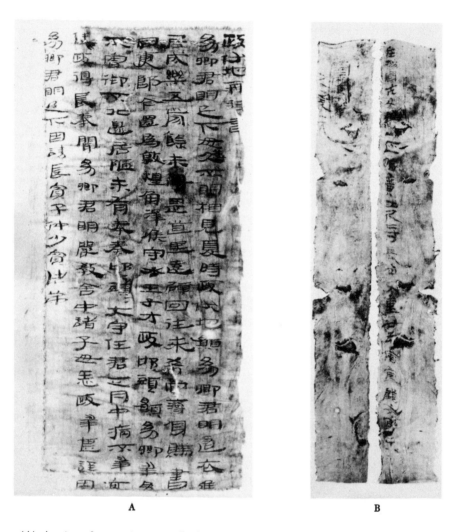

A
B

(A) A private letter written on silk, first century A.D. (15 × 6.5 cm.). (B) Writing on a silk strip, *ca.* A.D. 100 (31 cm. long), with a seal impression on the reverse side (left enlarged in Plate VIII.E).

official textiles are two feet two inches wide."[32] The *Huai-nan-tzu* says that "forty feet made one *p'i*,"[33] and the *Shuo-wen* also defines *p'i* as "forty feet." As late as A.D. 473, the government proclaimed a strict order to standardize the size as two feet two inches wide and forty feet long for one *p'i* of textile, following the old system.[34] While the price of other cloth was determined by its length and its thinness or coarseness, the price of silk was determined by its weight. The mention of Jen-ch'eng, which was established in A.D. 84 in the modern province of Shantung and is located in the district of Chi-ning, suggests that the silk dates from the end of the first century A.D. The *History of the Later Han Dynasty* says: "During the period of Shun Ti (r. 126–144), the barbarians rebelled several times, and Lord Ts'ung of Jen-ch'eng frequently contributed money and silk to aid the defense of the frontier."[35] This piece of silk could have been supplied by him from the silk-producing region.

Other interesting relics found near Tun-huang were two strips of fine undyed silk. One is 33 cm. long, and the other had a width of 49.5 cm. One end of this strip bears an inscription in Brahmi characters written with deep black ink. The inscription cannot be fully deciphered, but it indicates something about "[?] pieces [of fabric] 46 spans."[36] The use of Indian script proves that there was silk trade between ancient China and India and that traders were accustomed to use the Indian language during the early Christian era.

In the Lop-nor region, a number of silk pieces were found in ancient tombs by Folke Bergman in 1930. Among them a small silk strip, 26.5 cm. long, bears in the right hand corner a short ink inscription of ten words in Kharosthi language. The language employs an Indian alphabet which seems to have been used during the first centuries of our era down to the latter half of the third century A.D. According to Konow, the inscription may be translated "Sindhuaearya's roll, forty [feet long]."[37] On the other side of the strip, there are two Chinese characters, not very clear, which may be interpreted as *chin shih*, meaning "silk roll ten" or "ten silk rolls," according to Konow. He has dated this strip at the end of the second century A.D. Although the inscription is not as meaningful as the one Stein found at Tun-huang, it does help to substantiate the

[32] *I-li chu-su*, 13/17b.

[33] *Huai-nan-tzu*, 3/11b.

[34] *Wei shu*, 110/4b.

[35] *Hou-Han shu*, 72/17b.

[36] Stein, *Serindia*, II, 701–4.

[37] Konow, "Note on the Inscription on the Silk-strip No. 34:65," in Bergman, *Archeological Researches in Sinkiang*, Appendix I, pp. 231–34.

length of forty feet as the standard measure in the manufacture of silk in China.

SILK DOCUMENTS FROM CH'ANG-SHA

Since the 1930's, a large number of ancient objects associated with the Ch'u culture have been discovered at various sites in central China. The Ch'u culture was not entirely Chinese in origin but was increasingly under Chinese influence and was finally absorbed by the metropolitan northern culture. Among the pre-Ch'in relics that have come to light from Ch'ang-sha are two silk documents, one bearing long text and the other fine drawing, which represent the oldest specimens of brush writing and painting on silk extant today.

One document discovered during 1936–37 is a piece of silk, 30 cm. wide and 39 cm. high, written with brush-pen and black ink in the archaic style and surrounded by a border of strange, colored drawings accompanied by short writings (Plate XX). It was said that the silk document was contained in a lacquer box which was found in a deep tomb. The box was damaged, but the silk document inside was preserved in fair condition. The silk has since become so darkened as to be almost unreadable. The decipherment and studies of the text were all based on the reproductions currently copied by different hands.[38]

The main text of this document consists of two paragraphs, one of eight lines and the other of thirteen, with a total of about 600 characters remaining. Each paragraph is upside down in relation to the other. The pictures in red, blue, and brown surround the text on four sides and are associated with short writings in some 170 characters. Including characters now missing, this document is said to contain over 900 characters.[39] The readable parts of the text include names of Ch'u ancestors, passages in Ch'u dialects, and terms for the four seasons, five plants, five elements, and five directions, which are identical with those included in other ancient literature and contemporary inscriptions. All evidence indicates

---

[38] The original document was first obtained by Ts'ai Chi-hsiang, who reproduced the text and drawings in color by hand-copying and published it under the title *Wan-chou tseng-shu k'ao-cheng* about 1946. It was later reproduced in Chiang Hsüan-i, *Ch'ang-sha*, 1950, Vol. II, Plate 27; by Jao Tsung-i in the *JOS*, Vol. I (1950), following p. 84. Another hand-copied text is used by Ch'en P'an in *BIHP*, Vol. XXIV (1953), following p. 196; and by Tung Tso-pin in *TLTC*, X (1955), 174. Revised versions were made by Jao in his *Ch'ang-sha ch'u-t'u Chan-kuo tseng-shu hsin-shih* (1958) and by Noel Barnard in *Monumenta Serica*, Vol. XVII (1958), following p. 8. The various versions have some slight differences.

[39] Barnard, *op. cit.*, p. 4.

PLATE XX

SILK DOCUMENT FROM CH'ANG-SHA

A hand copy of an original document on silk, dating from the Warring States period. The main text contains two paragraphs, upside down in relation to each other; the strange figures in color are on four sides of the border with plants at four corners (39 × 30 cm.).

that this document belonged to the Ch'u state of the Warring States period.

The mention of many names of Ch'u ancestors provides archeological evidence for the study of ancient Chinese history. Among them, Yen Ti, a full brother of Huang Ti, or the Yellow Emperor, who is supposed to have lived in the third millennium B.C., Ch'ung, a grandson of the Yellow Emperor and a legendary officer in charge of the sacrifice to the gods; and Ti Chün, also called Ti Kao, a great grandson of the Yellow Emperor, are all significant in connection with the legendary emperor, Huang Ti, whose existence has not been proved by archeology. Besides these names there are those of Lu (Lu Chung), son of Wu Hui, and Lu's sister, Nü Kuei, who are both direct ancestors of the Ch'u people, according to ancient literature.[40]

The borders on the four sides consist of mysterious drawings of plants, birds, animals, human figures of strange appearance, and many things which cannot be fully recognized. Plants in different colors are located in the four corners of the document. According to the text, there should be five: blue, red, yellow, white, and black, with the yellow one at the center. Since there is nothing in the center, the yellow plant has probably faded away.[41] The twelve strange animals and human figures, equally distributed on four sides of the border, are said to be gods of the twelve months. Their names and duties and what should or should not be avoided during the month are described in the text accompanying the picture.[42]

The text and drawings in this document, although mysterious, seem generally to agree with the legends and traditions as recorded in ancient literature, especially the *Shan hai ching*, or *Classic of Mountains and Seas*. The content of the document in many respects reveals the mysticism of Ch'u civilization. It seems to indicate by the description of seasons, directions, plants, and five elements, that these were used by the Ch'u magicians for divination purposes. It was probably buried with the dead in order to secure blessings and protection from the ancestors and the deities.

Another silk piece was discovered in an ancient tomb at Ch'ang-sha in 1949. Measuring 20 by 28 cm., this rough-edged silk piece was contained in a lacquer coffin together with sacrificial pottery. Although the tomb was not scientifically excavated, it apparently belonged to the early part

---

[40] Jao Tsung-i, "Ch'ang-sha ch'u-mu shih-chan-sheng-wu t'u-chüan k'ao-shih," *JOS*, I (1954), 73–74; Tung Tso-pin, "Lun Ch'ang-sha ch'u-t'u chih tseng-shu," *op. cit.*, p. 177; Ch'en P'an, "Ch'ang-sha ku-mu chüan-chih ts'ai-hui chao-p'ien hsiao-chi," *BIHP*, XXIV (1953), 193.

[41] Jao Tsung-i, *op. cit.*, *JOS*, I, 80.

[42] *Wen-wu ts'an-k'ao tzu-liao*, 1960, No. 7, p. 68.

of the Warring States period.[43] Like other specimens mentioned above, the silk turned dark brown after it was unearthed. The main design is a picture showing a woman with wasp waist. Mo Tzu said: "Lord Ling (*ca.* 535 B.C.) of the state of Ch'u liked slender waists. And so all his subordinates limited themselves to a single meal [a day]. They tied their belt after exhaling, and could not stand up without leaning against the wall."[44] This picture illustrates the fashion in the Ch'u state.

The woman's hands are clasped as in prayer. Above her head are a bird and a strange animal. The bird has been identified as a phoenix and the animal as a *k'uei*, a kind of legendary monster with one leg and two horns.[45] Like the dragon, the *k'uei* is very common in ancient bronze designs. According to ancient literature, the phoenix is an emblem of life, marriage, or happiness, while the *k'uei* symbolizes death, famine, or evils. It is suggested that this picture is related to a kind of magic which was used in connection with practical life in ancient times. The fighting between the phoenix and the *k'uei* symbolizes the struggle between life and death and the woman looks like a witch who is praying that life will win over death.[46]

MATERIAL AND FORMAT OF SILK ROLLS

Silk is characterized by softness, light weight, durability, and absorbency. As a writing material it has many advantages over bamboo or wood. Being much lighter and less bulky, silk is easier to keep and carry. Its filaments have great tensile strength and are said to be almost as elastic as iron wire. It is insoluble but swells slightly in water and can be preserved longer than bamboo and wood. The discovery of silk documents in the region along the Yangtze Valley proves that silk can endure even in that damp climate. Having greater power of absorption, the silk surface takes up fluid ink much more easily than that of bamboo, and its whiteness makes a brighter background. All these qualities made it the best material available for writing before the invention of paper.

According to ancient literature, a great variety of material was made of silk fibers; there were more than sixty names for different textiles.[47]

---

[43] Kuo Mo-jo, "Kuan-yü wan Chou po-hua ti k'ao-cha," *Jen-min wen-hsüeh*, 1953, No. 11, pp. 113.

[44] Mei, *Motse*, pp. 83–84.

[45] Reproduced in Cheng Chen-to, *Wei-ta-ti i-shu ch'uan-t'ung t'u-lu*, 1st ser., Plate 12; *Ch'u wen-wu chan-lan t'u-lu*, p. 9.

[46] Kuo Mo-jo, *op. cit.*, 117–18.

[47] Wang Shih-to, "Shih po," in *Wang Mei-ts'un hsien-sheng chi*, 1/23a–25b.

Only a few, however, could be used for writing. The names of different silk textiles are usually defined in ancient literature by approximate synonyms which do not tell specifically what the quality is. In general, such technical details as fineness, coarseness, thinness, closeness, and whiteness of the textile have been the basis for the names of the plain fabric. Karlgren has discussed about fifteen terms for silk textiles,[48] using the *Shuo-wen* and other sources, but he has omitted such terms as *po*, *chüan*, and *tseng*, which are the names of the most important materials used for writing.

Silk textiles in general are called *po*, a word considered to have appeared in the oracle bone inscriptions. Plain white silk is called *su*, a general term for silk used especially for writing. This is made of raw silk fiber without design or dye. Another material made of raw silk is *chüan*, which is a thin and gauzy textile used for calligraphy and, especially, for painting. A similar material is *huan*, a gossamer white textile also made from raw silk. A finely woven silk with heavy threads, called *tseng*, was probably made from the product of wild silkworms and was thicker, darker, and more durable than the other kinds of plain silk materials. The document recently discovered from Ch'ang-sha is considered to have been written on *tseng*.

A textile similar to *tseng* is called *chien*; it was of double threads and yellowish in color. According to the *Shih-ming*, written about A.D. 200, the texture of *chien* was finer and closer than that of *chüan*, and it was waterproof. A closely woven fabric, it was more costly to produce than the ordinary *su*. The fragments discovered by Stein near Tun-huang bear inscriptions clearly indicating that they were *chien*. A statement including "three pieces of *chien*" inscribed on a wooden tablet was found in a Han tomb at Lo-lang, Korea.[49] The term *chien po* for a silk cloth has been used in general to represent silk material for writing.

Silk books must have been in the form of rolls, as indicated by the character *chüan* used in ancient literature. The bibliographical section of the *History of the Former Han Dynasty* includes books in rolls which must have been written on long pieces of silk or of material made of silk fiber and rolled up in the form of a scroll. A silk scroll with a red lacquer roller was said to have been found in an ancient Ch'u tomb at Ch'ang-sha.[50] But because the material became very fragile after it was exposed

---

[48] Karlgren, "Ancient Chinese Terms for Textiles," in Sylwan, *Investigation of Silk from Edsen-gol and Lop-nor*, pp. 170–74.

[49] Koizumi and Hamada, *Rakuro saikyozuka*, p. 12; Plate 39.

[50] Shang Ch'eng-tso, *Ch'ang-sha ku-wu wen-chien chi*, p. 46a.

to the air, it was impossible to open. Whether it carries any writing is unknown.

The length of a silk scroll depended upon the length of the text, and the silk could be cut according to the need. The standard length of plain silk was 40 feet, so the book could be extended up to that length without a seam. A seventh-century encyclopedia records that "ancient books were made of silk which was cut as needed according to the length of the text."[51] A silk book of the second century A.D. is described as having been written on "white silk ruled with red columns and wrapped in blue silk with title written in red."[52]

Silk scrolls could have been preserved in wrappers or covers to avoid damage in handling or transporting. Two specimens of painted lacquer scroll-holders were discovered in 1931 in the Han tomb at Lo-lang, Korea, dating from the second or third century A.D. The empty holder, decorated in polychrome on a black lacquer surface, is a half-cylindrical vessel with a small hole at each lateral end.[53] Other particulars of a silk roll can probably be observed from a paper roll which will be discussed in detail in the following chapter. Since the term *chih* for paper and *chüan* for roll are both inherited from silk or silk rolls, we can assume that the systems of both silk and paper rolls were analogous.

SPECIAL USEFULNESS OF SILK DOCUMENTS

The earliest known literary references to the use of silk as a writing material date from about the sixth century B.C. These references testify not only to the use of silk for writing but also frequently describe the peculiar nature of its use. The term *chu po* for bamboo and silk to indicate a written document has been in wide use only since the Warring States period. Since silk had a wider surface and was comparatively expensive, it was used only when bamboo and wood did not suit the special purposes.

Silk was usually employed as a material for final editions of books, while bamboo tablets were sometimes used for drafts. Although bamboo was also used for final editions, it was especially useful for preliminary texts because changes in writing could be made on it easily. It was also less costly than the absorbent silk. Ying Shao of the second century A.D. wrote: "Liu Hsiang has served the Emperor Hsiao-ch'eng (r. 32–7 B.C.)

---

[51] Hsü Chien, *Ch'u-hsüeh-chi*, 21/27a.
[52] *Hou-Han shu*, 60b/24a.
[53] Koizumi and Hamada, *op. cit.*, pp. 9, 46–47; Plate 5.

for more than twenty years in the custody and collection of books. They were first written on bamboo because writing could be changed easily by shaving the tablets. When texts were ready for copying, they were written on silk."[54] This applied, however, only to certain categories of books which were considered important enough to be carefully collated and copied for permanent preservation.

Ancient bibliographies illustrate this practice. Among the books recorded in the bibliographical section of the *History of the Former Han Dynasty*, about one-fourth of the total volumes were written on silk rolls. This includes a part of the classics and two entire sections on divination and medicine. Most of the others were on bamboo. Probably some of the works on classics from the pre-Ch'in period had been collated and transcribed on silk as final editions. As for books on divination and magical calculations, it seems to have been a tradition to record them also on silk. The *Rituals of Chou* relates that when the procedure of divination was over, the oracle inscriptions were written on tablets or silk for future checking.[55] A great amount of this kind of magical literature available in the Han dynasty is said to have been written on silk.[56] The newly discovered magical documents at Ch'ang-sha are drawn or written on silk materials.

Silk was particularly used for illustrations appended to books of bamboo tablets. As recorded in the Han bibliography, 790 *p'ien* of military works were written on tablets but 43 *chüan* were on silk for appended illustrations.[57] An individual work by Sun Wu (sixth century B.C.) includes eight rolls of illustrations, and another by Sun Pin (fourth century B.C.), four rolls. It is evident that the narrow strips of bamboo or wooden tablets were not suitable for drawing; only the unlimited length of silk cloth could provide a wide enough surface. The *Shan-hai ching*, or the *Classic of Mountains and Seas*, is said originally to have included illustrations of strange human beings and beasts appended to the first five chapters of this ancient geographical work.[58] Since they were lost in the sixth century B.C., new illustrations were substituted at a later date.

Ancient maps, especially, were drawn on silk because its surface was much wider than the wooden board which had earlier been used for them. It is said that in about A.D. 25 when Emperor Kuang-wu discussed strategy with his general Teng Yü in a city tower at Kuang-ho, the

---

[54] Cited in *T'ai-p'ing yü-lan*, 606/2a.

[55] *Chou-li chu-su*, 24/22b–23a.

[56] Ch'en P'an, "Hsien-Ch'in liang-Han po-shu k'ao," *BIHP*, XXIV (1953), 192–93.

[57] *Han shu*, 30/41a.

[58] Ho I-hsing, *Shan-hai-ching chien-su*, Postscript, 2b–3a.

Emperor pointed to an unrolled map.[59] Since it was carried with the army and read when unrolled, it must have been made of silk. Among the famous ancient maps, a general topographical drawing of the Empire in eleven rolls has been considered by a T'ang writer as the rarest item among the ancient collections of famous paintings.[60]

Silk seems to have been especially used for inscriptions for sacrifice to spirits and worship of ancestors. The *Kuo yü*, or *Discourses of the States*, mentions "two dragons to whom a prayer written on silk was shown."[61] The philosopher Mo Ti said: "Among the books of the ancient kings and the records of sages, testimonies to the existence of ghosts and spirits occur time and again even on a single foot of silk."[62] On several other occasions, he mentioned that the ancient sage-kings recorded their beliefs in spirits and ghosts on bamboo and silk to bequeath to their descendants. The *Huai-nan-tzu* also talks about spirits and ghosts, saying that "all things of this sort are fully recorded in books of bamboo and silk which are preserved in the official depositories."[63]

In the earlier period, silk seems to have been used primarily by kings and royal houses to record their sayings for transmission to posterity. Like those sage-kings mentioned by ancient philosophers, they employed silk along with bamboo for permanent records. Mo Ti has repeatedly referred to "writings on bamboo and silk" comparable to "engravings on bronzes and stone." The king of Yüeh was told in 476 B.C. that the virtues of kings and emperors and their fame should be preserved on bamboo and silk.[64] When the king talked to the economist Fan Li about agricultural problems, the latter suggested that the king follow the examples of ancient emperors, all of whom possessed the brilliance of farsighted prophecy, so that the people would not suffer from poverty even when there was a year of famine. The king said: "Fine! Record it on silk with cinnabar and preserve it as a state treasure."[65]

Silk was also used for permanent records of exceptional honors awarded to great statesmen and brilliant heroes of military achievements in the government. The *Rituals of Chou* said: "Those who have performed meritorious services in the government were inscribed on the silk banners

---

[59] *Hou-Han shu*, 46/2b.

[60] The map is called "Ho-t'u kua-ti-hsiang t'u" as recorded in Chang Yen-yüan, *Li-tai ming-hua chi*, 3/27a–32a.

[61] *Kuo-yü*, 16/7a.

[62] Mei Yi-pao, *Motse*, p. 167.

[63] *Huai-nan-tzu*, 13/20a–b.

[64] *Wu Yüeh ch'un-ch'iu*, 10/60b.

[65] *T'ai-p'ing yü-lan*, 707/3a.

of the king."[66] When general Su Wu (fl. 120–70 B.C.) returned from his captivity among the Huns, Li Ling, a military general who was also captured by the Huns, congratulated him by saying: "Now you are returning after having become famous among the Huns and demonstrated your victorious achievements for the Han court. No one could surpass you even among those who are recorded on bamboo and silk and painted on murals."[67] The famous statesman Teng Yü (A.D. 1–58), who aided Emperor Kuang-wu in establishing the Later Han dynasty, said: "I wish only to know that your majesty and virtue will influence the whole country, so that I could share a small part of your success and hand down my honor on bamboo and silk."[68] Such commemorative inscriptions were generally engraved on metal vessels or stone tablets but sometimes were also written on bamboo and silk.

[66] *Chou-li chu-su*, 30/2b.
[67] *Han shu*, 54/21a.
[68] *Hou-Han shu*, 46/3b.

VII

QUASI-PAPER AND PAPER MANUSCRIPTS

FROM SILK TO QUASI-PAPER

Before the invention of paper, Chinese books were generally written on bamboo, wood, or silk, as has been discussed earlier. These materials were, however, not the most ideal media for writing, "silk being expensive and bamboo heavy," as the dynastic history says.[1] To substitute for costly and bulky bamboo, a light but less expensive material was introduced. It has been generally supposed that paper was invented by Ts'ai Lun in A.D. 105, when his method of papermaking was formally reported to the throne. His raw materials were all vegetable fibers, including tree bark, hemp, rags, and fishing nets. There is evidence, however, that the Chinese people had tried to improve writing materials long before Ts'ai Lun. Although the raw materials used for the manufacture before Ts'ai seem to have been non-vegetable fibers, the paper made of such substances was definitely an important improvement over the expensive silk. If "paper" means a material made only of vegetable fibers,[2] the earlier form of quasi-paper may be considered as the first step toward the invention of true paper.

The word *chih*, which has been used to mean "paper" since its invention, is found in several places in the literary records with reference to events which happened as early as the first century B.C., but all these references are included in works written at a later date when true paper was certainly in extensive use. Whether *chih* before Ts'ai Lun's time was used to mean silk, paper, or quasi-paper is uncertain. For example, one record written in the fourth century A.D. relates to a story laid in 93 B.C. At that time Emperor Wu was sick, and the prince of Wei, who had a deformed nose, came to visit him. The imperial guard Chiang Ch'ung

---

[1] *Hou-Han shu*, 108/5a.

[2] Paper is generally defined, as in Webster's dictionary, as "a substance made in thin sheets or leaves from rags, straw, bark, wood, or other fibrous material, for various uses."

advised the prince: "The emperor dislikes your deformed nose; therefore you should cover your nose with a piece of *chih*."[3] The date of this incident seems to be the earliest to which the use of *chih* has been ascribed, but the late date of the record leaves the exact use of words uncertain.

An earlier source, written in the first century A.D., tells of a murder in 12 B.C., in connection with the Empress Chao. This account says that *ho-t'i* was used to wrap the poisonous medicine. According to the commentator Ying Shao (*ca.* 140–206), "*ho-t'i* means a small and thin piece of *chih*."[4] The use of the term *ho-t'i* seems to indicate the material was neither silk nor true paper.

About A.D. 76, the scholar Chia K'uei (31–101) was summoned to the court to select some twenty students of high intelligence to be instructed in the *Ch'un-ch'iu tso-chuan* at the White Tiger Hall. They were each given a copy of the classic written on tablets and *chih*.[5] This seems to indicate that the new material had already been developed enough to be used for writing the texts and commentaries of classics. It is recorded that when an imperial consort, née Teng, who was a lover of literature, was made empress in A.D. 102, "she disliked the precious and beautiful tributes from various countries but asked only for *chih* and ink-cakes."[6] These two references are both included in the dynastic history, written in the fifth century A.D., but neither of them indicates the nature of the substance from which *chih* was manufactured before the time of Ts'ai Lun.

There was a theory that the term *chih* was originally used as an alternative name for silk cloth for writing. Wang Yin (fl. A.D. 300), the author of the private *History of the Chin Dynasty*, said, quoting from a third century A.D. dictionary: "In ancient times writing was made on silk . . . which was called *fan chih*."[7] The *History of the Later Han Dynasty*, written by Fan Yeh in the fifth century A.D., also says: "In ancient times writings and inscriptions were generally made on tablets of bamboo or on pieces of silk called *chih*."[8] The later statement is evidently based on the former; but the word *fan*, which means a kind of silk cloth, was omitted. The character *chih*, which bears a silk radical on the left, undoubtedly indicates the nature of this material, but it was not necessarily silk cloth. Since silk used for writing was called in early literature *chien*, *po*, or *su*, the term *chih* probably meant something other than silk cloth.

---

[3] *San-fu ku-shih*, 9a.

[4] *Han shu*, 97b/13a.

[5] *Hou-Han shu*, 66/17a.

[6] *Ibid.*, 10a–19b.

[7] Wang Yin, *Chin shu*, quoted in *T'ai-p'ing yü-lan*, 605/7a.

[8] *Hou-Han shu*, 108/5a.

A statement by a writer of the second century A.D. seems to prove this point. Ying Shao mentions that in A.D. 25, when Emperor Kuang-wu restored the Han dynasty, he moved his capital from Ch'ang-an to Lo-yang, "carrying with him the classics written on silk, bamboo, and *chih* in 2,000 carts."[9] The mention of books made of silk and *chih* together indicates that *chih* was not identical with silk cloth.

Since paper is carefully recorded as being invented in A.D. 105 and no true paper before that date seems to have been discovered, we can only assume that the original form of *chih* before Ts'ai Lun was neither silk textile nor true paper but a kind of quasi-paper made of silk fibers. This assumption is suggested in the *Shuo-wen*, written about A.D. 100 by Hsü Shen, who defined *chih* as "a mat of refuse silk."[10] The commentator Tuan Yü-ts'ai (1735–1805) noted that the manufacture of paper originated from the process of pounding and stirring refuse silk in water, after which the wadded pulp was placed on a mat.[11] The treatment of refuse silk in water seems to have been an old and popular process, as the *Chuang-tzu* says : "There was a man of Sung who had a recipe for salve for chapped hands, and from generation to generation his family made their living by stirring refuse silk in water."[12] This process is known to have been used for making floss silk,[13] but it is very likely that an accidental placing of silk remnants on a mat might have suggested the idea of making a thin sheet of quasi-paper for writing.[14]

This assumption is further confirmed by Fu Ch'ien of the second century A.D., who defined *chih* as "a square piece of refuse silk."[15] Hsü Shen, the author of the *Shuo-wen*, was a student of Chia K'uei, the scholar who has been mentioned as using classics written on *chih*. If Hsü understood that *chih* was made of refuse silk, the *chih* used in the first century A.D. for writing must have been made of the same material. Although making *chih* of silk cocoons is not mentioned in early literature, a quasi-paper made of silk cocoons seems still to have existed in the fourth century A.D. The scholar Yü Ho of the sixth century A.D. said that

---

[9] Ying Shao, *Feng-su t'ung-i*, p. 99.

[10] Ting Fu-pao, *Shuo-wen chieh-tzu ku-lin*, p. 5901.

[11] *Ibid.*

[12] *Chuang-tzu*, 1/15b.

[13] Sung Ying-hsing, *T'ien-kung k'ai-wu*, p. 34. On the making of floss silk, the author wrote in 1634 that refuse silk or broken cocoons which could not be used to make silk thread were boiled in water with straw ashes. Cocoons were broken with the thumb and beaten with the fist. The good part became silk wadding, and the refuse was probably used for making quasi-paper.

[14] Ch'en P'an, "Yu ku-tai p'iao-hsü yin lun tsao-chih," *Annals of Academia Sinica*, I (1954), 257–65.

[15] Fu Ch'ien, *T'ung-su wen*, quoted in *T'ai-p'ing yü-lan*, 605/7a.

PLATE XXI
QUASI-PAPER

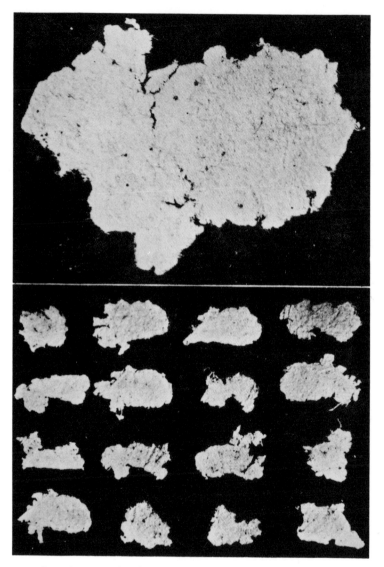

Fragments of quasi-paper with silk fiber discovered in Pa-ch'iao, Shensi, *ca.* first or second century B.C.

silk cocoon paper was used for writing by Wang Hsi-chih (321–379) and other famous calligraphers.[16]

A recent report indicates that some fragments of quasi-paper were discovered in Pa-ch'iao, Shensi, in a tomb dated not later than the period of Wu Ti (r. 140–87 B.C.) of the Han dynasty.[17] The specimens, including one large piece about 10 cm. square, are said to have been made of material similar to silk fiber (Plate XXI). They are yellow in color, thin, with textile lines on the surface. If the report is true, this will be an important piece of archeological evidence for the existence of quasi-paper before Ts'ai Lun. It seems reasonable that the quasi-paper made by mixing raw fibers from broken cocoons and textile fibers from refuse silk was much cheaper than woven silk. The invention and manufacture of paper of plant fibers in China must have originated and evolved from this process.

INVENTION OF TRUE PAPER

Although the word *chih* is found in literature earlier than A.D. 105, there is no controversy, from the available evidence, concerning Ts'ai Lun's connection with the invention of true paper. Some scholars believe that its invention was an evolutionary process and that many people probably experimented with various methods of paper making before the final result was achieved. It is possible that Ts'ai Lun's part was that of a sponsor or promoter who, as part of his official duty, reported to the throne the method he had observed. Or, since Ts'ai Lun is described as a man of talent who was in charge of government manufacture, it is also possible that he was actually the first to devise a satisfactory method for the use of cheap ingredients to manufacture a writing material to meet the increasing needs of the court and the various branches of government.

If literary records are correct, Ts'ai Lun was the inventor. The dynastic history and other sources agree in using the term *tsao-i*, "to initiate the idea," in attributing the method of paper-making to him. In about A.D. 102, three years before Ts'ai Lun's invention, Empress Teng, a woman of high intellectual tastes, asked that *chih* and ink cakes be collected as tribute from various countries. It seems very likely that the enthusiasm and needs of the court were influential in stimulating the inventiveness of Ts'ai Lun.

[16] Chang Yen-yüan, *Fa-shu yao-lu*, 2/10a; Ch'en Yüan-lung, *Ko-chih ching-yüan*, 37/8b–9a.
[17] *Wen-wu ts'an-k'ao tzu-liao*, 1957, No. 7, pp. 78–9, 81; illus.

Among such important Chinese inventions as the writing brush, ink, and printing, that of paper is most thoroughly documented in literature. Not only is the exact date given, but the materials, motives, and the life of the inventor are well recorded. The most detailed account is included in the *History of the Later Han Dynasty*, in which the biography of Ts'ai Lun contains almost 300 characters. It describes that he was first employed at the court as a eunuch, and later promoted to the *Shang-fang-ling*, an office charged with manufacture. It is apparent that the invention of paper was achieved during the time when Ts'ai held this office. The dynastic history further says:

> In ancient times writings and inscriptions were generally made on tablets of bamboo or on pieces of silk called *chih*. But silk being costly and bamboo heavy, they were not convenient to use. Ts'ai Lun then initiated the idea of making paper from the bark of trees, hemp, old rags, and fishing nets. He submitted the process to the emperor in the first year of Yüan-hsing [A.D. 105] and received praise for his ability. From this time, paper has been in use everywhere and is universally called the "paper of Lord Ts'ai."[18]

Although this work by Fan Yeh (398–445) includes the fullest information about the life and invention of Ts'ai Lun, it was written some three hundred years later. There are, however, earlier sources concerning the invention of paper by Ts'ai Lun upon which the account in the dynastic history was evidently based. The *Tung-kuan Han-chi*, an official history of A.D. 25–189 written by a group of contemporary historians, includes some 70 characters about Ts'ai Lun. It says:

> Ts'ai Lun, *tzu* Ching-chung, a native of Kuei-yang, served [at the court] as Chung-ch'ang-shih. He was a man of talent and learning, loyal and careful. When he was off duty, he usually shut himself up and refused to see visitors but exposed himself to nature. When he was charged with the office of Shang-fang, he initiated the idea of making paper from tree bark, old rags, and fishing nets. He submitted the process to the emperor in the first year of Yüan-hsing [A.D. 105] and received praise for his ability. From this time, paper has been in use and is universally called the "paper of Ts'ai Lun."[19]

The similarity of date and materials of papermaking in this brief but earlier source to the data in the dynastic history is obvious. Since this earlier work was lost and then reconstructed, it is probable that the above passage is an incomplete version of the original.

---

[18] *Hou-Han shu*, 108/5a–b. Cf. a fuller translation in Blanchet, *Essai sur l'histoire du papier*, pp. 13–14; Hunter, *Paper-making*, pp. 50–52; Carter, *op. cit.*, p. 5.

[19] *Tung-kuan Han-chi*, 20/2b.

Another source of earlier date is the work of Tung Pa, a scholar of the early third century A.D., who is quoted as saying: "The Eastern Capital has the 'paper of Lord Ts'ai,' which was the paper made by Ts'ai Lun. That made of used hemp was called hemp paper; of tree bark, mulberry paper; and of used nets, net paper."[20] This statement indicates that each one of the raw materials was used separately for a different kind of paper.

There does not seem as yet, however, to be adequate evidence to decide whether the materials used by Ts'ai Lun were mixed together or used separately. But in any case, the new material made of plant fibers was distinctly different from that made of silk fiber. Wang Yin of the third century A.D. mentioned that an old lexicon called *Ku-chin tzu-ku*, compiled by Chang Chieh in A.D. 232, changed the character *chih* with a silk radical into *chih* with a cloth radical after the invention by Ts'ai Lun. The lexicon said: "Although the sounds of the two words remain the same, their radicals are different. Hence it cannot be said that ancient paper is the same as modern paper."[21] This source does not clearly mention the quasi-paper made of refuse silk, but it suggests that the original form of the character *chih* was based on the use of silk material. When true paper was invented, it inherited the name although its substance was changed.

POPULARITY AND SPREAD OF PAPER

During the next few centuries after the invention of paper by Ts'ai Lun, the art of papermaking was advanced and popularized throughout the country. Among those who improved the art, Tso Po, *tzu* Tzu-i, who flourished at the end of the Han dynasty and was a native of Tung-hai of Shantung, was noted for his art of making fine paper.[22] Wei Tan (179–253), a famous inkmaker, said that a successful calligrapher must use "the brush of Chang Chih (*ca.* A.D. 200), the paper of Tso Po, and my ink."[23] When fine paper was compared with famous ink and writing brush, Hsiao Tzu-liang of the fifth century A.D. referred to "the paper of Tso Po, which was elegant and excellent, glossy and bright."[24] Apparently, the

---

[20] Tung Pa, *Yü-fu chih*, quoted in *T'ai-p'ing yü-lan*, 605/7a.
[21] Quoted in *T'ai-p'ing yü-lan*, 605/7a.
[22] Chang Huai-huan, *Shu tuan*, in *Shuo-fu* (1927 ed.), 92/4b.
[23] Chao Ch'i, *San-fu chüeh-lu*, 2/14a–b.
[24] Chang Huai-huan, *op. cit.*, 92/4b.

quality of paper during the later part of the second century A.D. must have been greatly improved, with variety of selection for artistic purposes. At the same time, the cost of manufacture was considerably reduced, so that henceforth paper became a popular material for writing. A scholar named Ts'ui Yüan (d. A.D. 143), writing to his friend Ko Yüan-fu, said: "I am sending you the works of Hsü Tzu in ten rolls. Being unable to afford a copy of silk, I provide only a paper copy."[25] This statement implies that silk was retained as a rare material, while paper became a popular medium of writing.

In the third or fourth century A.D., the use of paper had gradually supplanted that of bamboo tablets and partially that of silk. Books could therefore be more freely duplicated and distributed. The dynastic history says that Tso Ssu of the third century A.D. spent ten years in writing the "Poem of Three Capitals" which was so highly praised by his contemporaries that "the powerful and wealthy families competed with each other to copy this work until they raised the price of paper in Lo-yang."[26] In the fourth century, warlord Huan Hsüan (d. A.D. 404) ordered: "In ancient times paper was not available, so tablets were used, not because of their respectful nature. Now yellow paper should be substituted for tablets."[27]

Paper was not only a medium of popular communication, but its usefulness and aesthetic qualities became an interesting topic of praise in poems. The first writer about paper is the famous scholar Fu Hsien (234–294), who says:

> The material [paper] is beautiful and precious,
> Though cost is cheap yet quality is high . . .
> Stretching out when it opens and rolling up when put away,
> Able to contract or expand, hide or expose . . .
> To convey your affection to a distance of ten thousand miles away,
> With your refined thought written at one corner. [28]

Even after several centuries, paper was still a favored subject for writing by men of letters.

Throughout the centuries, paper became popular within the empire and spread over different parts of the world in all directions. As the dynastic history says: "From this time, paper has been in use everywhere." It traveled westward to Chinese Turkestan in the third century,

---

[25] Yü Shih-nan, *Pei-t'ang shu-ch'ao*, 104/5a.

[26] *Chin shu*, 92/8b.

[27] *T'ai-p'ing yü-lan*, 605/7b.

[28] Fu Hsien, "Chih fu," in Yen k'o-chün, *Ch'üan Chin wen*, 51/5a.

to Western Asia in the eighth century, to Egypt in the tenth century, and reached Europe in the twelfth century.[29] It also spread eastward to Korea in the fourth century, to Japan in the fifth century, and southward to India before the seventh century and to Indo-China even earlier.

When the eastward diffusion of Chinese culture was begun, Korea first acquired Chinese books and borrowed Chinese characters as their writing early in the fourth century A.D. Then the *Confucian Analects* and other books were introduced to Japan in 405 A.D. by a Korean scholar named Wani, who was invited to Japan as instructor to the Japanese heir-apparent. Since paper was extensively used in China at that time, these Chinese books must have been made of paper.[30] The craft of papermaking was, however, not introduced to Japan until A.D. 610, when the Korean monk Dokyo, who learned inkmaking and papermaking from China, went to Japan and suggested its manufacture to the court.[31]

The introduction of paper to India was probably not later than the seventh century. Paper manuscripts written in Sanskrit and dated in the seventh or eighth century, which have been discovered in Chinese Turkestan, indicate that communication between China and India through paper must have existed during that time. Chinese literary sources indicate that a Chinese monk named I-ching, who traveled to India between A.D. 671 and 694, wrote a bilingual lexicon in Chinese-Sanskrit, in which the word *kākali* for paper in the Sanskrit form was included.[32] Theories that paper was first introduced into India by the Mohammedans in the twelfth century are evidently not reliable.

The date of the introduction of paper to Indochina is probably earlier than that for India. Chi Han (d. A.D. 306) mentioned that some 30,000 rolls of "honey fragrance paper" were shipped to China in A.D. 284. This shipment, according to Hirth, was probably from Indochina.[33] Wang Chia of the fourth century said that *ts'e-li chih*, a kind of paper made of fern or lichens, was sent by Nan-yüeh (Indochina) as a tribute.[34] Although these sources are not confirmed by other evidence, there is a possibility that paper was introduced to Indochina at an earlier date because of her proximity to China proper.

---

[29] For a detailed account of its travel westward, see Carter, *op. cit.*, pp. 132–39.

[30] Naitō Torajirō, "Shi no wa," in *Tōyō bunka-shi kenkyū*, pp. 92–93.

[31] Nagasawa Kikuya, *Shoshigaku josetsu*, pp. 92–93.

[32] Chi Hsien-lin, "Chung-kuo chih ho tsao-chih-fa shu-ju Yin-tu ti shih-chien ho ti-tien wen-t'i," *Li-shih yen-chiu*, 1954, No. 4, p. 49.

[33] Hirth, *China and the Roman Orient*, pp. 274–75.

[34] Wang Chia, *Shih-i chi*, 9/7b.

THEORIES OF WESTERN ORIGIN OF PAPER

The fact of the Chinese invention of paper was not established in Western scholarship until the early years of this century. From the time of Marco Polo, Europeans had thought that the method of papermaking from rags was discovered only by the Germans or Italians in the thirteenth century.[35] Although the story of Ts'ai Lun and his use of rags was introduced to Europe through the Jesuit writings of the seventeenth or eighteenth century, it was not generally recognized until a later date. About 1690, Louis Le Comte, one of the earliest Jesuits who went to China, wrote that in France the paper of China was thought to be made of silk or cotton, but he did not mention its origin.[36] In the years around 1740, Jean Du Halde gave a more detailed account of its history: "A great mandarin of the palace . . . made use of the bark of different trees, and of old worn-out pieces of silk and hemp cloth by constant boiling of which matter he brought it to a liquid consistence, and reduced it to a sort of thin paste, of which he made different sorts of paper."[37] He mentioned the name of Ts'ai Lun but was mistaken in the date of A.D. 95.

A century later, Joseph Edkins, a missionary writer who lived in China in the middle of the nineteenth century, after discussing the use of paper and ink by the Greeks and Romans, said: "Why should it not then be suggested that both paper and ink were introduced to China from the West? Both these accomplishments of civilization were used in Europe several centuries before they were known in China. But the mechanical skill of the Chinese at once rendered them independent of foreign supply." He mentioned the Chinese work by Chi Han of the third century A.D. to support his argument that paper was "probably brought to China in return for silks from the trading posts near the Caspian Sea or by the sea route by Cochin China or Canton."[38] The original statement by Chi Han says:

> *Mi-hsiang chih*, or honey fragrance paper, is made of the bark and leaves of the honey fragrance tree; its color is grayish and it has spots giving it the appearance of fish-spawn. It is very fragrant, but strong and pliable; it may be soaked in water without spoiling. In

---

[35] Hoernle, "Who Was the Inventor of Rag-paper?," *JRAS* (1903), p. 663; Carter, *op. cit.*, p. 6.

[36] Le Comte, *Memoirs and Observations*, p. 191.

[37] DuHalde, *The General History of China*, II, 417–18.

[38] Edkins, "On the Origin of Paper Making in China," *Notes and Queries on China and Japan*, I, No. 6 (1867), 68.

the fifth year of T'ai-k'ang of the Chin dynasty (A.D. 284) Ta Ch'in[39] presented 30,000 rolls [to the Chinese emperor, who] bestowed 10,000 rolls on Tu Yü (222–284), the Grand General Guarding the Southern District and the Marquess of Tan-yang, commanding him to write thereon his works *Ch'un ch'iu shih li* and *Ching chuan chi chieh* to be submitted to the throne. But Tu Yü died before the paper had reached him; the latter was, therefore, ordered by Imperial command to be kept by his family.[40]

This statement, however, in no way implies that the Chinese invention was borrowed from the West. The so-called "honey fragrance paper," which is believed to have been made from garco wood (*Aquilaria agallocha, Roxb.*), was said to have been produced in Indochina and was by no means the papyrus of Egypt and Syria. Friedrich Hirth believed that this gift was possibly made by Alexandrian merchants who reached China via Ceylon and Indochina and purchased local produce from Indochina to serve as a present to the Chinese emperor in lieu of original home articles such as they had brought on previous missions.[41] Furthermore, this shipment, if it was indeed from the West, was made in the third century A.D., and the Chinese invention of paper was almost two centuries earlier, before any acquaintance with this fragrant paper.

The theory of a western origin of paper has been disproved by subsequent discoveries and scientific analyses. In 1877–78, a great many paper manuscripts dating from about A.D. 800 to 1388 were discovered in Egypt, together with other manuscripts written on papyrus and parchment. Microscopic analysis of the paper specimens showed that they were all made of rags. It was then believed that the Arabs of Samarkand were the inventors of paper made from linen rags. In 1904 when paper specimens discovered by Stein in Chinese Turkestan were analyzed, it was found that the main substance of these paper materials was the bark of the paper mulberry and rags were used as a substitute. In 1911, when paper of the first years of the fourth century, discovered by Stein during his second expedition, was analyzed, it was found that it was made of pure rags. These finds indicate that the Arabs were not the first to use rags in the production of paper.[42] In the years following Stein's discovery, more specimens uncovered in northwestern China proved to have been made even closer to the date of the invention, and the Chinese record of

---

[39] Ta Ch'in, as used in ancient records, refers to the Roman Empire or a part of its eastern provinces.

[40] Chi Han, *Nan-fang ts'ao-mu chuang*, 2/6a.

[41] Hirth, *China and the Roman Orient*, pp. 274–75.

[42] Hoernle, *op. cit.*, pp. 663–64; Carter, *op. cit.*, p. 7.

the invention of paper at the beginning of the second century A.D. has been finally confirmed by these archeological evidences.

Although the theory of the western origin of Chinese paper is now obsolete, some contemporary scholars, including Chinese, seem not yet to have been convinced of this fact.[43] They seem not to understand that, although the word "paper" is derived from "papyrus," the two are basically different. If it is granted that Chinese paper was evolved from the quasi-paper of silk fiber, as we have indicated, there is no probable relationship between the two kinds of materials. Papyrus was a natural product, sliced from the stem of the papyrus plant, while Chinese paper was manufactured by chemical processes, whether it was made of silk or plant fibers. If the fact that Chinese paper was evolved from the quasi-paper of silk fibers is understood, the confusion between paper and papyrus will be cleared and the assumption of a western origin of paper will be recognized as untenable.

DISCOVERIES OF EARLY PAPER SPECIMENS

Since the beginning of this century, tens of thousands of specimens of ancient paper and paper documents have been discovered at various sites in northwestern China, Central Asia, and Africa where the climate has been favourable for the preservation of this delicate material. They range in date from the earliest introduction of paper to its first use in printing. They have not only indicated exact routes and dates as this bearer of civilization traveled from China proper to other parts of the world but also provided us with valuable data concerning the composition and technique of ancient papers and ancient books in the roll form. As we have pointed out before, China was the center of paper manufacture before that technique was introduced to other parts of the world. The nearer the place to China proper, the earlier is the occurrence of paper as shown by the archeological evidence.

The earliest specimen of paper extant today is probably the one discovered near Chü-yen or Kharakhoto by members of the Academia Sinica in 1942.[44] The paper was found under the ruins of an ancient watchtower in Tsakhortei, south of Bayan Bogdo Mountain, where a

---

[43] Chien Po-tsan says: "paper existed in Athens and Alexandria four hundred years earlier than in China," see his *Chung-kuo shih-kang* (1947), II, 511; Jaroslav Cerny says: "it is a problem whether and to what extent the invention of paper in China about A.D. 100 was influenced by acquaintance with Egyptian papyrus," see his *Paper and Books in Ancient Egypt* (1952), p. 31, note 2.

[44] Lao Kan, "Lun Chung-kuo tsao-chih-shu chih yüan-shih," *BIHP*, XIX (1948), 496–98.

bundle of wooden tablets dated A.D. 93–95 and a single tablet dated A.D. 98 were discovered by Folke Bergman of the Sino-Swedish Expedition in 1930. The remnant of paper, twisted into a ball when discovered, bears not more than two dozen readable characters written in the free *li* style (Plate XXII). It was examined by a Chinese botanist, who reported that it was made of plant fiber and that the material is very coarse and thick with no sign of watermarks.[45] The paper bears no date; but it was first assumed, on circumstantial evidence, that this specimen must have been not later than A.D. 98, since one tablet bearing that date was discovered in the upper level. However, the fact that tablets bear the date of A.D. 93–98 does not mean that they were buried in that period. Lao Kan, who discovered this paper, suggests that the date when the paper was buried was possibly between A.D. 109 and 110, when the watchtowers along the western frontier were temporarily abandoned by the Chinese defenders because of the rebellion of the Hsi-ch'iang, a tribe of West China.[46] For this reason, this piece of paper is believed to have been contemporary with the time of Ts'ai Lun, when the manufacture of paper was only in the very initial stage.

Some later specimens were discovered by Aurel Stein near Tun-huang during his second expedition in 1907. Three pieces of paper inscribed with Chinese characters were reported as tissue-like, very thin and soft, and yellowish in color.[47] In another site near Tun-huang, a collection of paper documents written in Sogdian was discovered. This includes seven letters written by Sogdian merchants and sent home to Samarkand and Bokhara, in which postal difficulties, latest commodity prices, current exchange value of silver, and gossip about their friends were mentioned. They were folded up into neat little convolutes and some of them retained their original silk string fastening. These paper fragments were first attributed to the middle of the second century A.D., but a more recent study of their content indicates that they were all written between A.D. 312 and 313.[48]

In the Lou-lan region, Sven Hedin discovered in 1900 a number of paper documents. Some of them are very coarse gray material and others fine yellowish stationery. They include official documents, private business letters, and some ancient works. Most of them are not dated but a few bear the dates of A.D. 252, 265, and 310.[49] One important item is a frag-

---

[45] *Ibid.*, p. 497.

[46] Li Shu-hua, "Tsao-chih ti fa-ming chi-ch'i ch'uan-po," *TLTC*, X (1955), 54–55.

[47] Stein, *Serindia*, II, 674; Chavannes, *Documents Chinois*, nos. 706–8.

[48] Henning, "The Date of the Sogdian Ancient Letters," *BSOAS*, XII (1948), 601–15.

[49] Conrady, *Die chinesischen Handschriften und sonstigen Kleinfunde Sven Hedin in Lou-lan*, pp. 93, 99, 101; Plates 16:1–2, 20:1, 22:8.

PLATE XXII

PAPER SPECIMEN FROM CHÜ-YEN

Remnant of earliest known paper, discovered at Chü-yen, dated possibly from A.D. 109–110.

mentary manuscript copy of the *Chan-kuo ts'e*, or *Plots of the Warring States*, written on paper in the clerical style probably in the third century A.D. These specimens were also made of rags, possibly of hemp but mixed with a little animal and cotton fibers. In the same region, Stein found during his third expedition in 1914 some 711 fragments of paper belonging to the period of A.D. 263–280. The dates are similar to those of the material discovered by Hedin, with the same intervening gap.[50]

In the region of Turfan and Kao-ch'ang, the Prussian expedition of Albert Grünwedel and Von Le Coq from 1902 to 1914 discovered some old paper manuscripts, including one dated A.D. 399.[51] The Japanese expedition of the Nishi-Honganji headed by Tachibana Zuicho and Nomura Eizaburo also visited this site in 1909–10[52] and found many old paper manuscripts, including some dated from third or fourth century A.D. (Plate XXIII). The Chinese Northwest Scientific Expedition also worked in this area in 1928–30 and discovered a number of paper specimens and old manuscripts of classics all belonging to a later date, mostly of the seventh and eighth centuries. One manuscript, a Buddhist sutra, bears a postscript dated A.D. 436.[53] In general, the paper specimens discovered in this site are dated later but are much more numerous than those found in Tun-huang and Lou-lan.

In the site of Khotan, Stein found some paper specimens in Tibetan, Sanskrit, and the ancient Khotan language, which were dated in the eighth century A.D. At the same site, the dates of Chinese manuscripts written on pieces of thin paper all range between 781 and 790.[54] From the microscopic analysis of the Tibetan manuscript, it was learned that the paper was made from a raw fiber which is not native to Sinkiang and might have been imported from Tibet.[55] Unlike other papers found in the same region, they were not sized with gelatin but with a kind of starch. Stein also found at a monastery in Mazar-tagh near the Khotan River a book of accounts, in which the cost and quantity of papers are recorded: "One set of paper to be used for calendars cost 60 pieces of money."[56] It seems that the supply of paper was very plentiful and that it was not expensive under the early T'ang dynasty.

[50] Schindler, "Preliminary Account," *Asia Major*, N.S., I (1949), 225.

[51] Yao Shih-ao, "Chung-kuo tsao-chih-shu su-ju Ou-chou k'ao," *Fu-jen hsüeh-pao*, I (1928), 27–29.

[52] *Saiiki koko zufu*, Otani's preface.

[53] Huang Wen-pi, *T'u-lu-fan k'ao-ku chi*, p. 26; Plates 6–7.

[54] Stein, *Ancient Khotan*, I, 135, 271.

[55] *Ibid.*, 426.

[56] Chavannes, *Les documents chinois*, Nos. 969, 970, 971.

PLATE XXIII

EARLY PAPER MANUSCRIPT

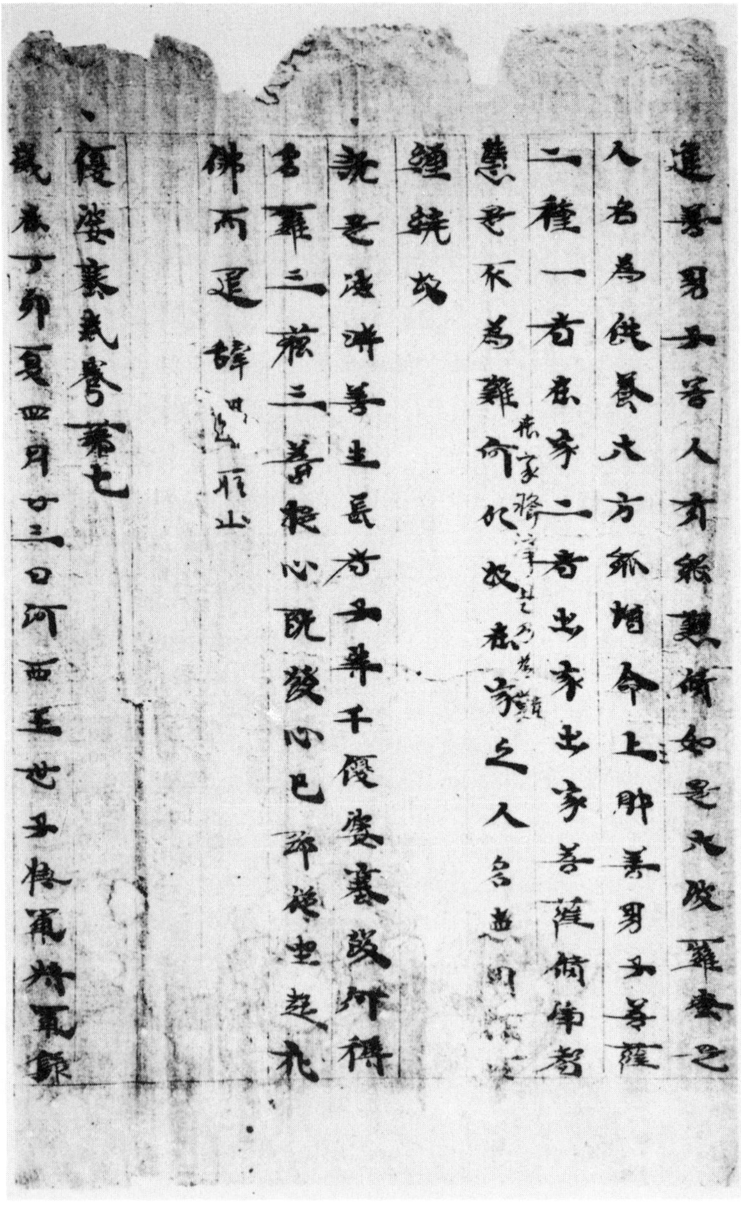

A Buddhist sutra, *ca.* fourth century A.D., found at Toyuk in Chinese Turkistan

PAPER MANUSCRIPTS FROM TUN-HUANG

The largest discovery of paper manuscripts was made by Stein in a walled-in monastery library at Tun-huang during his second expedition in 1907.[57] Tun-huang was established toward the end of the first century B.C. as one of the military posts to guard the northwestern frontier. It developed as an important center of communication between China and Central Asia during the following centuries. Under the Eastern Chin and Northern Wei dynasties (317–534), when Buddhism was espoused with particular enthusiasm, a series of stone caves decorated with sculptures and fresco paintings, known as the "Caves of the Thousand Buddhas," was started in A.D. 366; and the work continued for several centuries. The treasure of paper rolls was found in one of these caves, which was probably sealed up sometime after A.D. 1056, since no scroll bearing a date later than this is included in the collection.[58] It is believed that these books were removed from different monasteries to this cave for safety before an invasion of the Hsi Hsia.

Except for a few printed editions, this collection consists entirely of manuscripts. It includes a great variety of subject matter, with Buddhist sutras occupying the largest portion. There are also Confucian classics, Taoist works, writings of various philosophers, materials on history and phonology, poems, short stories, business contracts, calendars, and other official and private documents.[59] Most of these manuscripts are in Chinese, but some are in Sanskrit, Sogdian, Eastern Iranian, Uigur (Turkish), and especially Tibetan. A book of selections from the Old Testament in Hebrew is also included.

This collection of paper manuscripts includes more than 20,000 rolls, many of which are preserved in perfect condition. After the discovery by Stein, some 7,000 rolls were brought to the British Museum in London. Among them, 380 rolls are dated, ranging from A.D. 406 to 995.[60] Later the French sinologist Paul Pelliot went to Tun-huang and brought to the Bibliothèque Nationale in Paris some 3,000 rolls,[61] the latest date of which is of the period 995–996, appearing on the reverse side of a roll on

[57] Stein, Serindia, II, 801–25.

[58] Lao Kan, "Tun-huang chi Tun-huang ti hsin-shih-liao," *TLTC*, I, No. 3 (1950), 7–8.

[59] See Giles, *Descriptive Catalogue of the Chinese Manuscripts from Tunhuang* (1957).

[60] Giles, "Dated Chinese Manuscripts in the Stein Collection," *BSOAS*, VII (1933–35), 809–10.

[61] See Pelliot and Lu Hsiang, "Pa-li t'u-shu-kuan Tun-huang hsieh-pen shu-mu," *PPKK* VII (1933), 21–72; VIII (1934), 27–87; Pelliot's preliminary report, "Une bibliothèque médiévale retrouvée au Kan-sou," *BEFEO*, VIII (1908), 501–29, Stein, *Serindia II*, 826–29.

census data.[62] The Japanese also got some 400 rolls, and more than 2,000 rolls are now scattered in different private collections. The remaining portion of this collection was then requisitioned in 1910 by the Chinese government to be deposited in the National Library in Peking, totaling 9,871 rolls, with 43 rolls dated between A.D. 458 and 977.[63] The Peking collection is considered the largest, the Paris collection best in quality, and the London collection most perfect in physical condition. This discovery of paper manuscripts, although belonging to a later period as compared with other fragmentary specimens, not only includes many rare and unusual documents not extant elsewhere today, but its richness and completeness also provide important data about ancient paper books in the roll form (Plate XXIV).

METHODS OF ANCIENT PAPERMAKING

The procedure the ancient Chinese artisans followed in manufacturing paper is unknown today, but data gathered from the analysis of ancient paper specimens and records of papermaking written by later artisans are sufficient to form a general picture. The analytical study of the ancient papers discovered by Stein in Chinese Turkestan disclosed that they were made of a mixture of certain raw fibers with rags. The raw fibers proved to be those of mulberry, laurel, and China grass; and the rags were of flax, hemp, or China grass. Moreover, it was found that the main constituent of the paper was raw fibers, while the rags served as substitute.[64] These finds have confirmed what was mentioned in earlier records about the raw materials used for papermaking. The dynastic history tells us that the raw materials used by Ts'ai Lun were tree bark, hemp, rags, and fishing nets. They comprised two different classes of material, that is, the raw fibers of bark and hemp and the processed fibers of rags and fishing nets.

The research shows that bark, hemp, and rags were mixed together to form the pulp for paper. This conclusion, however, seems to contradict a traditional theory that each of the raw materials was used separately for a different kind of paper. In a third-century work by Tung Pa, it is recorded that paper "made of hemp was called hemp paper, of tree bark mulberry

---

[62] Carter, *op. cit.*, p. 63, note 1.

[63] Ch'en Yüan, *Tun-huang chieh-yü lu* lists 8,679 rolls; and Hu Ming-sheng has made a supplement including 1,192 rolls; see Hsü Kuo-lin, *Tun-huang shih-shih hsieh-ching t'i-chi*, preface, p. 1a.

[64] Hoernle, *op. cit.*, pp. 665 ff.

PLATE XXIV

A COMPLETE PAPER ROLL

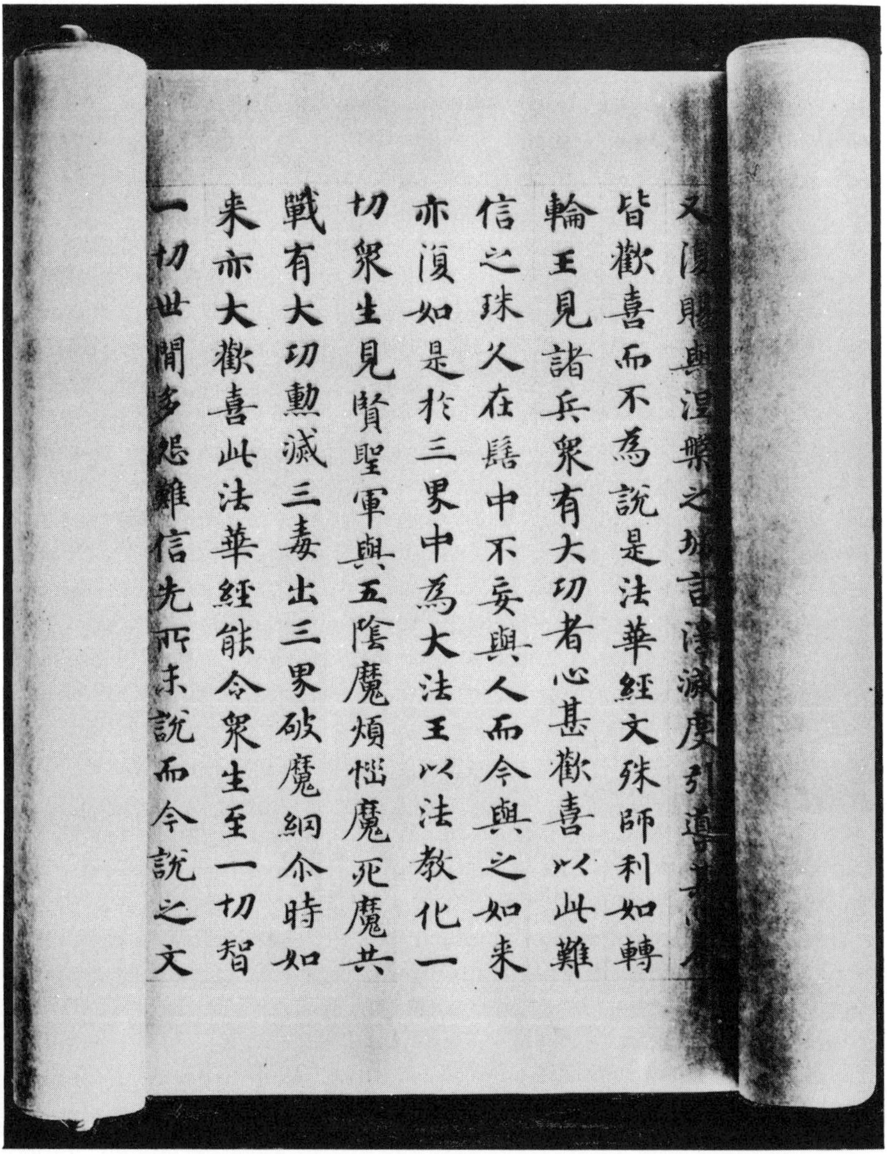

又復賜與涅槃之城言滅度引導

皆歡喜而不為說是法華經文殊師利如轉

輪王見諸兵眾有大功者心甚歡喜以此難

信之珠久在髻中不妄與人而令與之如来

亦復如是於三界中為大法王以法教化一

切眾生見賢聖軍與五陰魔煩惱魔死魔共

戰有大功勳滅三毒出三界破魔綱尒時如

来亦大歡喜此法華經能令眾生至一切智

一切世間多怨難信先所未說而今說之文

A fine specimen of paper book in the roll form, A.D. 774

paper, and of used nets net paper."[65] This difference seems not a controversial point, since the analytic examination was based on a later sample
while the Chinese record refers to the earlier process. Moreover, the
materials used in different periods may have varied according to different
circumstances. Paper could be made either from a mixture or from a
single material without technical difficulties. It is quite probable that
the constituents of the mixture may have varied in various districts
in China. According to Su I-chien (957–995), "paper was made of hemp in
Szechuan, bamboo in Kiangsu, mulberry-bark in the north, rattan in
Yen-ch'i, lichen in the south, and husks of grain in Chekiang."[66] This
statement means that these substances formed either the principal
or a peculiar constituent of the paper pulp of their respective
localities.

Aside from the raw materials, the focal point of the entire process of
papermaking is the invention of the mold. This is a screenlike mat on
which the macerated fibers are spread in a layer from which the water is
permitted to escape, leaving the interwoven fibers to form a sheet. The
earliest records give no details of the making or method of use of this mat,
which throughout later centuries has remained the most essential tool in
making paper by hand, and which is the principle upon which modern
paper machines are based. Dard Hunter suggests that the first mold was
nothing more than a square of coarsely woven cloth held in a bamboo
frame. This could have been successfully used in papermaking either by
dipping it perpendicularly into the water and bringing it up horizontally
under the macerated fibers or by holding it flat and pouring the mixture
upon the mold. The mold with the thin deposit of matted fibers was then
placed in the sun to dry. After the moisture had evaporated, the sheet was
easily stripped from the mold.[67]

The ancient method of papermaking was perhaps similar to that described in the *T'ien-kung kai-wu*, a technical work on manufacture written
by Sung Ying-hsing in 1634.[68] It says that for the manufacture of bamboo
paper the trunk is cut into pieces and steeped in water. After soaking
for more than one hundred days, the pieces are pounded to remove all the
coarse husk and green bark. The flaxlike soft mass is mixed with liquid
lime and boiled over fire for eight days and nights. Then the bamboo pulp
is washed in water and strained with the liquor of plant ashes. The

[65] Tung Pa, *Yü-fu chih*, quoted in *T'ai-p'ing yü-lan*, 605/7a.
[66] Su I-chien, *Wen-fang ssu-p'u*, 4/6b–7a.
[67] Cf. Hunter, *Paper-making*, pp. 78–79.
[68] Sung Ying-hsing, *T'ien-kung k'ai-wu*, pp. 217–19.

processes of boiling and straining are repeated until the bamboo fibers are completely soft. Then it is pounded in a mortar to produce a dough which is finally bleached by adding chemicals. The sheet is obtained by the use of a bamboo screen to retain the pulp into a mat, which is then inverted over a board. A number of these sheets are piled up and pressed to release the water. The sheets are then stripped off and dried on hot walls built of fire bricks heated by a fire behind them. For the making of bark paper, the bark of the paper mulberry or ordinary mulberry tree is used with the same processes except that bamboo or straw fibers are mixed in the pulp.

Bamboo, the most popular material for making paper in China, was, however, not used as raw material in the earliest times. No reliable reference to bamboo paper was made until the early ninth century, when Li Chao said that "bamboo paper was made in Shao-chou."[69] A work by Tuan Kung-lu (fl. 850) mentions the use of "bamboo-membrane paper," which was said to have been produced in Mu-chou of modern Chekiang.[70] Since the actual manufacture must have been earlier than the date of the records, it is assumed that bamboo was first used in making paper not later than the end of the eighth century. Since that time, bamboo paper has been very popular.

The use of raw cotton as a material for making paper in ancient times seems doubtful. Even modern paper manufacture abstains from the use of raw cotton as an impractical material. Although cotton was mentioned in Chinese records as early as the third or fourth century, it was not planted in the southern parts of China until the T'ang period nor in the Yangtze Valley until the Sung dynasty.

Although materials used for making paper before the seventh century were limited to hemp, mulberry, and rags, some sixty different varieties of ancient paper are kept in the British Museum. The earlier paper was made entirely of rags. Other papers of the fourth to the tenth century, made of paper mulberry or China grass, reached a high degree of excellence; but the quality decreased after the middle of the eighth century, probably because of the economic depression after the rebellion of An Lu-shan.[71] Most of the earlier specimens show that the processes of sizing to render the paper fit to be written on, and of loading to improve its quality, were already known to the Chinese paper makers.

[69] Li Chao, *T'ang kuo-shih pu*, 3/18b.
[70] Tuan Kung-lu, *Pei hu lu*, 3/7b.
[71] Giles, "Dated Chinese Manuscripts," *op. cit.*, 317.

PAPER-DYEING, REPAIR, AND PRESERVATION

Ancient papers were dyed in different colors and treated with a special substance for protection from quick deterioration and from injury by bookworms. The earliest colored paper was probably the *ho-t'i* mentioned in the Han dynastic history as a small piece of thin paper for wrapping. According to Meng K'ang of the third century A.D., it was a kind of "silk fabric dyed red for writing, as paper is dyed yellow today."[72] If this is correct, red was used as early as the first century B.C., and yellow must have been in vogue in the third century A.D. Hsün Hsü, the official curator of the imperial Chin library, said in his preface to one of the bamboo documents discovered in the Wei tomb that they were copied on separate sheets of paper and treated with a yellowish insecticidal substance.[73] This process seems to have been customary before paper was used for writing.

The dyeing of paper, which was called *jan-huang*, was fully discussed in the *Ch'i-min yao-shu*, a work on agriculture and handicraft written by Chia Ssu-hsieh of the fifth century A.D.[74] The process is described as dyeing the white paper with a yellowish liquid prepared from the *huang-nieh*, or Amur cork tree (*Phellodendron amurense*), the seeds of which have a toxic effect which protects the paper from injury by insects. The seeds are said to have been soaked in water to get the fresh juice, and the soaked seeds boiled after stamping. They were poured into a cloth bag and pressed for more juice. After stamping and boiling three times, the boiled juice was mixed with fresh juice and was then ready for use in dyeing. It is said that paper should be dyed a light color, since it will turn darker after a number of years. Paper was usually dyed before writing, but the effect was said to be better if dyeing was done after writing. In the case of a roll made of several pieces of paper, the edges which were pasted together were pressed with a hot iron to prevent separation after dyeing. Though this is the most detailed description of paper-dyeing, the practice seems to have been already in use not long after paper was invented.

This ancient description can be easily verified by the many paper manuscript rolls written in the fifth through the tenth centuries discovered in Tun-huang. Most of them have been dyed a yellowish color, and it is true that they have been preserved in very good condition and have not been damaged by bookworms.[75] After the Sung dynasty, when printing

[72] *Han shu*, 97b/13a.

[73] *Mu-t'ien- tzu chuan*, Hsün Hsü's preface, 3b.

[74] Chia Ssu-hsieh, *Ch'i-min yao-shu*, 3/15b; cf. interpretation by Shih Sheng-han, *Ch'i-min yao-shu chin-shih*, p. 213–14.

[75] Stein, *Serindia*, II, 809.

became popular and books were not so rare, paper was not so carefully protected as before. When the format was changed from rolls to flat binding, dyeing seems to have been difficult. Much Buddhist literature of the twelfth century, however, was still treated by the same process, since it retained the form of rolls.

Chia Ssu-hsieh said that a very thin piece of paper was used to repair torn pieces of paper. This adheres closely to the original paper so that one cannot see the repair unless he looks at it against the light. For preservation, it was suggested that paper rolls should be exposed to the light in a shaded place three times between the fifteenth day of the fifth month and the twentieth day of the seventh month, that is, during the summer season. Books should not be exposed directly under sunshine or during a cloudy day. Paper rolls should be left unrolled in hot weather. Otherwise, they are easily injured by bookworms.[76] Books preserved in this way are said to last for several hundred years.

SYSTEM OF PAPER ROLLS

Ancient books in the form of rolls can be observed among the preserved manuscripts of Tun-huang dated from A.D. 406 and traced in early records and bibliographies. Most of the manuscripts or the earlier forms of books referred to, however, are of paper, not silk. Since Chinese paper was a substitute for silk, the system of paper rolls undoubtedly originated from that of silk. The term *chih* for paper was borrowed from silk or quasi-paper, and *chüan* for rolls was originally a unit for a long roll of silk. Because of its elastic fibers, silk was easier to roll than to fold up. When paper was invented, the method of rolling books was handed down until the middle of the ninth century when paper began to be folded into a paged book. One Tun-huang manuscript is found to have been kept in 211 folded leaves[77] (Plate XXV).

The size of ancient paper seems to have been standardized for many centuries for the preparation of the rolls. Archeological discoveries indicate that the width of paper used from the fourth to the seventh century is about 24 cm., which equals about one foot according to the Han measure. The width of the paper closely approaches the standard height of wooden tablets, which measure about 24 cm. to 24.5 cm. in most cases among the

---

[76] Chia Ssu-hsieh, *op. cit.*, 3/15b-16a; shih sheng-han, *op. cit.*, p. 214.
[77] Giles, *Descriptive Catalogue*, No. 5591.

PLATE XXV
PAPER BOOK IN FOLDED LEAVES

A commentary on the *Lankavatara sutra*, written on 211 folded leaves of thick buff paper
to form a volume, T'ang dynasty (28 × 9 cm.).

Tun-huang discoveries.[78] From the size of the "one-foot tablet" used in the Han dynasty as the standard medium of private correspondence it appears highly probable that the width of paper at a later date was dictated by the same tradition. The length of the individual sheets ranges from 41 cm. to 48.5 cm.,[79] which equals about two feet by the ancient measure. This size seems to agree with that used in the third century A.D., when Hsün Hsü copied texts from the bamboo tablets on paper two feet long.[80] The separate sheets of paper were pasted together end to end as long as needed, and the length of the entire roll usually was nine to twelve meters; the longest one rolled out as many as thirty-two meters.[81]

Signatures or seals were put on the line where sheets were joined. Each roll forms a unit called *chüan*, and a book was of one or more *chüan* as required by the length of the text. The sheets were ruled off into narrow columns about the width of the bamboo or wooden tablets, suitable for writing one line of characters (Plate XXIII, XXIV). The number of columns on each sheet and of characters in each column does not seem definite. A later reference, however, mentions that the individual collection of the famous poet Li Shang-yin (813–53) was ruled into 16 columns and each column included 11 characters.[82]

Scrolls were usually fastened at the end to rollers of various materials and in different colors (Plate XXIII), sometimes with carved and inlaid knobs. It is mentioned that the scrolls written by the famous calligraphers Wang Hsi-chih and his son were fitted with rollers of coral for silk scrolls and gold, tortoise-shell, or sandal-wood for paper scrolls.[83] The *History of the Sui Dynasty* says that the books in the imperial libraries were differentiated by rarity according to the color of the rollers. Works of superior quality had rollers of red precious stone, of medium quality purple stone, and of lower quality painted wood.[84] The more valuable scrolls had their open end protected by an extension of silk gauze, brocade, or paper. Attached to this was a ribbon for tightening the scroll, the color of which sometimes denoted the class of literature.

Several scrolls were sometimes inclosed in a wrapper called "book-cloth." Certain wrappers were made of bamboo screen lined with white or dyed silk, gauze, or other cloth. Wrappers found with the Tun-huang

[78] Stein, *Serindia*, II, 671.

[79] *Ibid.*, 672, note 3a.

[80] *Mu-t'ien-tzu chuan*, Hsün Hsü's preface, 3a.

[81] Giles, *Descriptive Catalogue*, No 5587; cf. Stein, *Serindia*, II, 671–72.

[82] Ch'eng Ta-ch'ang, *Yen fan lu*, 7/8b.

[83] Chang Yen-yüan, *Fa-shu yao-lu*, 2/6a–b; 10a.

[84] *Sui shu*, 32/6b.

scrolls are decorated with extremely fine silk tapestry.[85] In shape and construction, the wrappers from Tun-huang show the closest agreement with a specimen dated A.D. 742, now preserved in the Shosoin collection of Japan. The number of rolls enclosed in one wrapper varied according to the size of the rolls. There were usually ten rolls in one wrapper; but sometimes the number was five, seven, eight, or twelve.[86] It is clear that books in the roll form, no matter how many rolls they contained, were usually protected by cloth wrappers made in different designs.

When rolls were wrapped and stored on shelves, they were difficult to locate if not properly identified. Labels marked with titles and the number of rolls were attached to the end of the book for identification of its content. These labels were commonly made of ivory in various colors— red, green, blue, and white to indicate the classes of classics, history, philosophy, and belles-lettres according to the traditional classification system in the imperial libraries.[87] This system seems to have been an indispensable part of early book-collecting. One very early extant specimen is a piece of ivory, 3 cm. long and 2 cm. wide, inscribed on both sides with the titles and number of rolls of the works by Wang I of the early second century (Plate XXVIII.C). According to the style of the inscription, this piece is dated from the fourth century.[88]

Paper rolls were usually written on one side but sometimes on both. The commentaries of classics are said to have been written on the back of the text and called "reverse notes," while exegeses of individual words or sentences, which were called "marginal notes," were usually written on the top or bottom margin and between the columns. The "collector's note" was written at the end of the paper roll where columns were usually reserved for this purpose.[89] Among the paper rolls found at Tun-huang, names of scribe, proofreader, reviser, dyer, and superintendent are sometimes postscribed at the end of the manuscript. The dates of copying and the number of pieces of paper used for the manuscript are occasionally noted. In several cases, it is indicated that 19 sheets of hemp paper were used in the preparation of the text of the *Lotus sutra*.[90]

The use of paper rolls continued until sometime in the T'ang dynasty (618–906), when scrolls were superseded by folded leaves (Plate XXV).

---

[85] Stein, *Serindia*, II, 900.

[86] Shimada Kan, *Ku-wen chiu-shu k'ao*, 1/20a.

[87] T'ang Hsüan-tsung, *T'ang liu-tien*, 9/10b.

[88] Chang Cheng-lang, "Wang I chi ya-ch'ien k'ao-cheng," *BIHP*, XIV (1949), 243.

[89] Shimada Kan, *op. cit.*, 1/22a.

[90] Giles, "Dated Chinese Manuscripts," *op. cit.*, 14–15; Nos. 671, 672.

From this time on, the format of Chinese books gradually changed, beginning with these folded sheets, known as "whirlwind" or "sutra" binding; followed by the "butterfly" binding with edges of leaves outward; then "wrapped-back" binding, with edges of the leaves folded inward and wrapped at the spine; and finally stitched binding, sewn at the back with silk thread in the fashion still in use today.

VIII

TOOLS AND VEHICLES OF WRITING

Chinese writing as a special form of art has been developed through the use and improvement of various tools and vehicles since ancient times. Paper, brush, ink, and ink-slab, the "four precious things of a scholar's study," have been the basic implements for committing thoughts to writing. How early these four things became a standard set is uncertain; but it is said that under the Later Han dynasty brush and ink were given to high officials every month, and in the Chin these four articles were used together at the court when the princes were crowned.[1] Some of these articles were elaborately made and luxuriously decorated so that their usefulness and artistic designs greatly inspired scholars and artists.

Wang Hsi-chih (321–379), a calligrapher renowned for many ages, commented: "Paper represents the troops arrayed for battle; the writing brush, sword and shield; ink represents the soldier's armour; the ink-slab, a city's wall and moat; while the writer's ability is the chief commander."[2] It was largely through the special characteristics of these implements that the traditional form of Chinese books and writing was preserved and developed.

DEVELOPMENT OF THE WRITING BRUSH

It has been a tradition for many centuries that paper was invented by Ts'ai Lun in the second century A.D. and the writing brush by Meng T'ien in the third century B.C. The invention by Ts'ai Lun is well documented in contemporary literature and evidenced by modern discoveries, but the association of the brush with Meng T'ien is not clear. Ssu-ma Ch'ien described Meng T'ien as a military general of the Ch'in dynasty,

---

[1] *T'ai-p'ing yü-lan*, 605/2b, 4b, 6a–b, 8b.

[2] Wang Hsi-chih, "Pi-shih lun," quoted in *Ku-chin t'u-shu chi-ch'eng*, Vol. 649, p. 45b.

who conquered his native state of Ch'i in 221 B.C. In 214 B.C., his army of 300,000 was commissioned for the conquest of the Huns and for the defense of the northern frontier by building the famous Great Wall. There is no mention of the writing brush, but Meng T'ien, having learned to write documentary literature, is said to have been promoted to be court historiographer after the unification of the empire in 221 B.C.[3]

A Sung scholar commented that the totalitarian rule of the Ch'in destroyed the records of achievements of past dynasties but boasted of inventions during their own reign.[4] Whether such claims of invention were made by the Ch'in rulers themselves, or when this tradition originated, cannot be traced; but ever since the third century A.D. scholars have questioned it. A certain Niu Heng asked: "There must have been writing brushes when writing began; why has Meng T'ien been called the inventor?"[5] Modern scholars seem to agree that Meng T'ien was not an inventor but may have been an improver. The historiographer's work of drafting, writing, or copying official documents perhaps led him to the improvement of the writing implements.

The theory of Meng T'ien's invention is derived from a statement which was probably first made by Chang Hua of the third century A.D., that "Meng Tien made the writing brush."[6] The controversy comes from the character *tsao*, which means either "to make" or "to create." If it is interpreted as "to make," it merely means that Meng T'ien *made* a special kind of brush. Ts'ui Pao (fl. 290–306) said that "the brush made by Meng T'ien was called *Ch'in pi*, a kind of brush used in the Ch'in state; its holder was made of dried wood and the brush of deer and goat hair, which was different from the rabbit hair and bamboo holder."[7] According to the *Shuo-wen*, the brush was called *yü* in Ch'u, *pu-li* in Wu, *fu* in Yen, and *pi* in Ch'in.[8] These characters probably indicate different pronunciations of the same term in southern, eastern, northern, and western China respectively, as dialectic variants of a basic form *bluet*.[9] They may have meant the same implement but of varying form and material. Ts'ui Pao's statement perhaps derived from this lexicon.

[3] *Shih chi*, 88/1b.

[4] Su I-chien, *Wen-fang ssu-p'u*, 1/2a.

[5] Ts'ui Pao, *Ku chin chu*, 3/8a.

[6] Chang Hua, *Po-wu chih*, quoted in *I-wen lei-chü*, 58/21b; *Pai-K'ung liu-t'ieh*, 14/28a; *T'ai-p'ing yü-lan*, 650/1a. This statement is, however, not included in the main text of many available editions but in the appendix of the *Chih-hai* edition, 7a.

[7] Ts'ui Pao, *Ku chin chu*, 3/8a. Other editions read *che-mu*, or "thorny wood," in this statement instead of *k'u-mu*, or "dried wood."

[8] Ting Fu-pao, *Shuo-wen chieh-tzu ku-lin*, 1271b, 1273a.

[9] Pelliot, "Les bronzes de la collection Eumorfopoulos," *TP*, XXVII (1930), 375–78.

Not only is the evidence of Meng T'ien's invention insufficient but literary and archeological testimony indicates that the brush had been used long before his time. The earliest lexicon, the *Erh-ya*, defines *pu-li* as writing brush.[10] The *Records of Ceremonial*, mentions that "a scribe should carry with him his *pi*, 'writing brush,' and a scholar the recorded words."[11] The *Chan-kuo ts'e* contains a story about the queen dowager of Ch'i. It is said that in 249 B.C., when she was sick and about to die, she advised her son, King Chien, who the most reliable minister was, and said: "Bring the writing brush and tablets to write down my words."[12] Not only do recent archeological discoveries show that characters were written on bamboo and silk with a brush, but an actual writing brush made of bamboo and goat hair, belonging to the Warring States period, has been found at Ch'ang-sha.

The use of the brush in the early Chou and Shang dynasties has been inferred by scholars because characters inscribed on Shang and Chou bronzes appear to be formed after brush-written patterns.[13] The oracle inscriptions of the Shang dynasty appear to have been first written with a brush on the surface and then carved into the bone. Several pieces of ox bone, dated roughly between 1400 and 1200 B.C., bear inscriptions which were not engraved but made by hair brush and ink.[14] The character *yü* for a writing brush in the bone or bronze inscriptions of the Shang dynasty clearly depicts a hand holding a brush either with hair full of ink or with spread-out dried hairs [15] (see Table I, 5*f*).

Some archeologists have even carried the account of the use of brushes back to prehistoric times when fine designs on painted pottery discovered at Neolithic sites in Yang-shao, Honan, were drawn with a brush.[16] This need not have been the same brush made of rabbit hair with bamboo holder which was used later, but it must have been a bunch of animal hair tied to a holder and used for writing or drawing with black fluid or other pigments. Brush writing, therefore, must be considered as a traditional method developed long before our knowledge about ancient writings.

FORMS OF THE BRUSH-PEN

The writing brush usually includes three main parts: holder, hair, and

[10] *Erh-ya chu-su*, 5/17a.

[11] Cf. Legge, *Li ki*, I, 91.

[12] *Chan-kuo ts'e*, 13/7a.

[13] Yetts, *George Eumorfopoulos Collection Catalogue*, I, 15–17.

[14] Tung Tso-pin, "Chia-ku-wen tuan-tai yen-chiu li," *op. cit.*, I, 417–18.

[15] Yetts, *op. cit.*, p. 16; Creel, *Studies in Early Chinese Culture*, p. 43.

[16] Liang Ssu-yung, "Hsiao-tun Lung-shan yü Yang-shao," *TYPLWC*, II, 555–68.

sheath. The holder was generally a bamboo tube, but it was not rare to use a wooden rod. The body of the brush was made of rabbit, deer, or goat hairs which were wrapped with silk or hemp string at one end, covered with lacquer to stiffen it, and inserted into the end of the holder. In order to protect the delicate hair, a sheath was used to cover the whole implement. The total length of the brush was about one foot according to ancient measure. In a poem on the writing brush, the scholar Ts'ai Yung (132–192) said:

> Cutting a bamboo to make a [brush] holder;
> Wrapped with silk string, covered with lacquer.[17]

The philosopher Wang Ch'ung (29–109) said that "the person with wisdom and ability could better serve in the court by his tongue of three inches and his writing brush of one foot."[18] Since the foot of the Han period was equivalent to about 23 cm., the size of the ancient brush as recorded in early literature seems in general agreement with modern archeological discoveries.

The earliest extant brush, belonging to the Warring States period, was discovered in 1954 in an ancient tomb at Ch'ang-sha.[19] The total length of this brush is 21 cm. and that of the sheath is 23.5 cm. Both the holder and the sheath are made of bamboo tubes, and the hair is said to be rabbit (Plate XXVI.A). A writing brush of the Han dynasty, found by Folke Bergman in 1932 at Mu-durbeljin near Chü-yen, is made of four vertical pieces of wood which are fastened into a rod with two hanks of hemp string. Thus the hair can be inserted into the end of the tabular rod and changed when necessary, like the pen point used in a modern penholder. The total length of this brush is 23.2 cm., including the hair outside of the holder[20] (Plate XXVI.B). The discovery of these two complete writing brushes has provided full data on the shape, size, and material of this ancient implement of writing, which is quite similar to what is used today. The inner portion of the brush was made of rabbit or deer hair and the outer portion of goat hair, as a stiff center covered with soft hair is most suitable for writing. Wang Ying (*ca.* A.D. 300) said: "Why is rabbit hair necessary in making the brush? Deer hair is also sharp and durable."[21] Ts'ui Pao of the third century A.D. said that the brush made by Meng T'ien was made of deer hair covered with goat hair.[22] The usual

---

[17] Ts'ai Yung, *Ts'ai-chung-lang chi*, 3/3b.

[18] Wang Ch'ung, *Lun heng*, 13/4b.

[19] *Wen-wu ts'an-k'ao tzu-liao*, 1954, No. 12, p. 8.

[20] Ma Heng, "Chi Han Chü-yen pi," *KHCK*, III, No. 1 (1932), 67–72.

[21] Hsü Chien, *Ch'u-hsüeh ch'i*, 21/27a.

[22] Ts'ui Pao, *Ku chin chu*, 3/8a.

PLATE XXVI

EARLY SPECIMENS OF WRITING BRUSHES

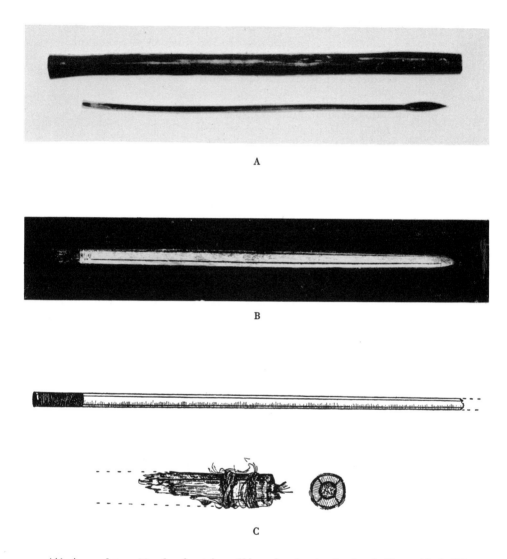

A

B

C

(A) A complete writing brush set from Ch'ang-sha, showing bamboo holder and hair (21 cm.) and bamboo sheath (23.5 cm.), Warring States period. (B) A complete writing brush from Chü-yen with split wooden holder and hair (23.2 cm.), Han dynasty. (C) Drawings of a fragment of wooden holder from Mu-durbeljin and a hair tip from Bukhentorei, near Chü-yen.

theory about the invention of the writing brush by Meng T'ien is that he probably initiated the substitution of wood for the bamboo holder and deer hair for rabbit hair.

The size of the hair point depends upon its use in writing different sizes of characters. The one from Ch'ang-sha measures 2.5 cm. and that from Chü-yen 1.4 cm. with the tip worn short. Several hair nibs, lacking the holder, were found in Chü-yen and in Korea. The one discovered in the tomb of Wang Kuang at Lo-lang, Korea, measures 2.9 cm. long, and one end of it is wrapped with a string.[23] The string was usually stiffened with black lacquer as an adhesive and so arranged that a fine point was available for writing. Fu Hsüan of the third century A.D. said that the hair was "wrapped with white hemp and fixed with black lacquer."[24] This is the traditional method of making the writing brush even today.

Many scholars believe that the brush is an advanced implement for writing and that before its use some more primitive tools must have been employed. The sharpened bamboo or wooden stylus is traditionally considered to have been the pioneer instrument used before the Ch'in dynasty.[25] Chao Hsi-ku of the fourteenth century said: "In very ancient times, writing was done with a bamboo stylus dipped in lacquer."[26] There is no indication, however, that Chinese writing was ever done with a stylus. On the contrary, the inscriptions discovered on tablets and other materials are all written with the brush or made after brush-written patterns.

During the expedition of Stein in 1900–1901, some reed and wooden pens, probably of the third century A.D. or later, were found at the Niya site near Khotan. The wooden pens are often merely thin twigs sharpened at one end and, in some cases, split up from the tip a short distance.[27] The length of these wooden pens is about 15 cm. to 23.5 cm., some have a knob made of horn at one end, and fitted with a polished conical top which is intended to serve as a burnisher. Since the noted T'ang poet Pai Chü-i (772–846) mentioned that "the Khotan people used wood for writing pens,"[28] it is possible that a wooden stylus could have been used for writing in some special districts at the same time as the widely accepted brush.

---

[23] Oba and Kayamoto, *Rakurō Ō Kō no haka*, p. 49.

[24] Fu Hsüan, *Fu-shun-ku chi*, 3/4b.

[25] Chavannes, "Les livres chinois avant l'invention du papier," *op. cit.*, p. 70; Li Shu-hua, "Chih fa-ming i-ch'ien Chung-kuo wen-tzu liu-ch'uan kung-chü,"*TLTC*, IX (1954), 170.

[26] Chao Hsi-ku, *Tung-t'ien ch'ing-lu*, quoted in *Ko-chih ching-yüan*, 37/20a.

[27] Stein, *Ancient Khotan*, I, 398, 403; Plate CV.

[28] Pai Chü-i and K'ung Ch'uan, *Pai K'ung liu-t'ieh*, 14/30a; *Hsin T'ang shu*, 221a–23a.

ORIGIN OF WRITING FLUID AND PIGMENTS

When a brush was employed for writing, there must have been some kind of fluid or pigments to write with. Hence, the term "brush and ink" has been used in Chinese literature to refer to the implement and vehicle of writing. The date of the first manufacture of true ink in China is unknown, but traditionally its invention was ascribed to a famous calligrapher and inkmaker named Wei Tan (179–253). Many scholars believe that, before this time, writings were inscribed on bamboo or wood by means of a pointed stylus dipped in a black varnish.[29] The arbitrary dating of the use of ink around the third century A.D. is apparently speculation and contrary to the testimony of both early literature and later archeological discoveries.

Wei Tan is described in Chinese sources as one of the earliest known inkmakers. He refused the ink bestowed on him by the emperor, preferring to use ink of his own making in order to produce better calligraphy.[30] Hsiao Tzu-liang, prince of the Southern Ch'i dynasty (479–501), commented that the ink made by Wei Tan was so black that "every drop was like lacquer."[31] Before this time, literary records indicate that ink was offered to the Han court at the beginning of the second century as tribute from various countries.[32] On some important occasions, ink was bestowed on princes, high officials and scholars by the favor of the emperor.[33] Even before the Han dynasty, the use of ink was not rare.

Mencius (372–289 B.C.) speaks of a carpenter's "string and ink"; ink was probably used for writing in his time.[34] The *Chuang tzu* mentions that when Prince Yüan of Sung desired to have a picture painted, all the scribes of the court stood up "licking their writing brushes and mixing their ink."[35] Chou She, the counselor of minister Chao Yang (d. 458 B.C.) of the Chin state, said to his master: "I wish I could be your critical subordinate, handling tablets with brush and ink and watching after you to record whatever faults you may have."[36] The *Kuan tzu*, a collected work attributed to Kuan Chung (d. 645 B.C.) but probably written at a later date, mentions that Duke Huan of Ch'i (r. 685–643 B.C.), in regard to

---

[29] Chavannes, *op. cit.*, p. 66; Laufer, *op. cit.*, p. 11.

[30] Lu Yu, *Mo shih*, 1/1a–b.

[31] *Ko-chih ching-yüan*, 37/21a.

[32] *Hou-Han shu*, 10a/19b.

[33] *T'ai-p'ing yü-lan*, 605/4b.

[34] Legge, *The Works of Mencius*, p. 474.

[35] *Chuang-tzu*, 7/36.

[36] Han Ying, *Han-shih wai-chuan*, 7/6a–b.

the improvement of his administration, "asked the officials to record his orders on a wooden board with ink and brush."[37]

While no reference to the use of black ink is found in literary records of the early Chou dynasty, archeological evidence indicates that some kind of writing fluid, black and red, was used on the oracle-bones of the Shang dynasty.[38] A potsherd of about the same period bears the character *ssu*, "to sacrifice," also written with black ink.[39] Chemical microanalysis of the specimens of oracle bone inscriptions indicates that the black is probably a carbon mixture of the nature of ink and that the red pigment is cinnabar.[40]

The use of red pigments for writing was also not rare in ancient times. They seem to have been applied on the more important official documents. The *Ta Tai li-chi*, written about 100 B.C., states that when King Wu (twelfth century B.C.) ascended the throne, he asked about the methods of ancient rule. Master Lü Shang replied: "They were preserved in cinnabar documents."[41] A king of the state of Yüeh (*ca.* fifth century B.C.) is said to have kept the official documents written with cinnabar as a state treasure.[42] In 550 B.C., Fan Hsüan-tzu had a slave named Fei Pao, one of those entered on the documents written with cinnabar. The slave asked that the document be burned as a reward for his success in killing the enemy general Tu Jung. It is recorded that Fan swore by the sun and agreed to do so.[43]

Although other pigments were also used in writing or drawing, as evidenced by the pictures on the silk document discovered at Ch'ang-sha, red ink was most commonly used. It was generally made of cinnabar and vermilion. Cinnabar is a natural product, known as *tan-sha* or *chu-sha* in ancient literature; and it was studied by the early alchemists as a medicine for prolonging life. Vermilion was produced from the mineral cinnabar by powdering and water flotation. It was also prepared by the direct combination of mercury and sulphur.

INK OF LAMPBLACK

Soot was used for the preparation of black ink probably at a very early period, since it was naturally produced in using fire. When fire was

[37] *Kuan-tzu*, 9/1b.
[38] Tung Tso-pin, "Chia-ku-wen tuan-tai yen-chiu li," *op. cit.*, I, 417–18.
[39] Creel, *Studies in Early Chinese Culture*, p. 45.
[40] Britton, "Oracle-bone Color Pigments," *HJAS*, II (1937), 1–3.
[41] *Ta Tai li-chi*, 6/1a.
[42] Quoted in *T'ai-p'ing yü-lan*, 707/3a.
[43] Legge, *Ch'un Ts'ew with the Tso Chuen*, p. 501.

controlled, lampblack, a finer soot, was collected. Lampblack was obtained by burning certain kinds of woods or liquid, including pine, tung oil, petroleum, and probably lacquer. The use of tung was rather late; it seems not to have been used until the tenth century when Li T'ing-kuei, a famous inkmaker, is believed to have used tung oil exclusively.[44] Soot made by burning crude petroleum was used in the eleventh century by Shen Kua, who said that this soot was even darker than that made of pine.[45]

Pine wood was probably the most popular material for obtaining lampblack, and pine soot is still the best material for making black or India ink today. It is certain that before the end of the second century A.D., pine wood was already used. This is testified to by the famous writer Ts'ao Chih (A.D. 192–224), whose poem opens with the line: "Ink is made of the soot of blue pine."[46]

No details about the manufacture of pine soot in those early days are available today. One later writer says that lampblack was obtained by burning the resin, and others the wood, of the pine tree.[47] Although we have an old recipe for the preparation of the ink, there is no mention of the source from which lampblack was obtained. The old recipe is included in the *Ch'i-min yao-shu*, a work on agriculture and manufacture written by Chia Ssu-hsieh of the fifth century A.D. The section called "Method of Mixing Ink" says:

> Fine and pure soot is to be pounded and strained in a jar through a sieve of thin silk. This process is to free the soot of any adhering vegetable substance so that it becomes like fine sand or dust. It is very light in weight, and great care should be taken to prevent it from being scattered around by not exposing it to the air after straining. To make one catty of ink, five ounces of the best glue must be dissolved in the juice of the bark of the *ch'in* tree which is called *fan-chi* wood in the southern part of the Yangtze Valley. The juice of this bark is green in color; it dissolves the glue and improves the color of the ink.
>
> Add five egg whites, one ounce of cinnabar, and the same amount of musk, after they have been separately treated and well strained. All these ingredients are mixed in an iron mortar; a paste, preferably dry rather than damp, is obtained after pounding thirty thousand times, or pounding more for a better quality.
>
> The best time for mixing ink is before the second and after the ninth month in a year. It will decay and produce a bad odor if the

[44] Wang Chi-chen, "Notes on Chinese Ink," *Metropolitan Museum Studies*, III (1930–31), 115.
[45] Shen K'uo, *Meng-ch'i pi-t'an*, 24/1a–b.
[46] Ting Yen, *Ts'ao-chi chüan-p'ing*, p. 58.
[47] Chiang Shao-shu, *Yün-shih chai pi-t'an*, 2/21a.

weather is too warm, or will be hard to dry and melt if too cold, which causes breakage when exposed to air. The weight of each piece of ink cake should not exceed two or three ounces. The secret of an ink is as described; to keep the pieces small rather than large.[48]

Although this recipe was first described in this fifth-century work, its author is believed to have been the famous inkmaker Wei Tan previously mentioned as the supposed inventor of Chinese ink. His name is not mentioned in this recipe but does appear in the preceding section on the making of the brush. The same recipe as quoted in the *T'ai-p'ing yü-lan*, an encyclopaedia compiled in 983 A.D., mentions Wei Tan as its author. It seems certain that this recipe must have been experimented with for many years before it was perfected in the second or third century A.D. It was still renowned at the end of the fifth century, and later methods are believed to have been copied or improved from this formula without remarkable differences.

Glue was also of importance in making ink of lampblack. It serves the purpose of uniting the fine particles of carbon and fixing the ink on paper permanently. Glue was usually manufactured from deer horn, cow hide, fish skin, or the waste of leather. The materials were soaked in water to soften them and then boiled with water and filtered through silk gauze or a cotton filter to obtain a clear liquid. The proportion of glue and lampblack for preparing a solid ink cake was probably kept a closely guarded secret by many inkmakers. It is mentioned in later literature as an equal weight of lampblack and glue, although this was varied by some makers.[49] In order to increase the intensity of the black color, other ingredients such as cinnabar were mixed in the paste. As disinfectants for preservation and for keeping the ink in permanent color, the bark of *ch'in* wood (*Fraxinus bungeana*, D.C. var. *Pubinervis wg.*), the skin of the pomegranate, blue vitriol, and the like were used. To camouflage the unpleasant odor of the glue, perfumes such as musk, camphor, or patchouly were sometimes added.

The form of the pre-Han ink is not clear today, but it was probably made in solid form from an early time, as the *Chuang tzu* mentions that ink was mixed before using. Under the Han and Chin dynasties, the unit of ink was described as *wan* and *mei*. One Han source records that "one large and one small *mei* of Yü-mei ink [made of pine from Yü-mei mountain] were given each month to the high officials in the court."[50] Chang

[48] Chia Ssu-hsieh, *Ch'i-min yao-shu*, 9/28; Shih sheng-han, *op. cit.*, p. 722.

[49] *Ko-chih ching-yüan*, 37/26–27.

[50] Quoted in *T'ai-p'ing yü-lan*, 605/4b.

Ch'ang of the Chin dynasty mentions that "four *wan* of fragrant ink were bestowed upon a prince when he was first crowned."[51] No one seems to understand clearly what the *wan* and *mei* looked like. Laufer explained the *wan* as "pills, pellets, and balls . . . to be easily swallowed."[52]

Although ink was later used as a kind of medicine, it is doubtful that such balls were originally made for "swallowing" in that early day. A mural painting discovered in 1953 in a Han tomb at Wang-tu in Western Hopei shows a scribe sitting on a low couch and before him is a round ink-slab with a conical piece of ink standing in the middle. A water container appears at the right side of the ink-slab (Plate XXVII). This picture seems to indicate clearly what the so-called *wan* was.[53]

During the first expedition to Chinese Turkestan, Stein reported that he found in the Endere ruins at Khotan "a cylindrical piece of hard Chinese ink drilled for a string at one end."[54] It is 2.3 cm. long with a diameter of about 1 cm. On another trip he also found a prismatic piece of ink which may perhaps come from the T'ang dynasty.[55] It seems to be the case that ink has been made in the form of round or flat cakes since the Han dynasty. Later on, ink was made into different shapes, decorated with pictures and calligraphy and colored with gold and other pigments, in order to suit artistic taste.

LACQUER AND MINERAL INK

Many Chinese and Western scholars have believed that the development of Chinese ink follows the order of lacquer, minerals, and lampblack. They contended that, according to the principle of evolution, natural products must have been used first and manufactured products later. Thus Chavannes thought that Chinese writing was first done with lacquer and later with ink.[56] Laufer added that under the Han dynasty ink was prepared from mineral products and from the third century A.D. onward was made from vegetable matters.[57] Carter believed also that lacquer was known in classical times and states that the invention of true ink from lampblack has been ascribed to Wei Tan.[58]

[51] *Ibid.*
[52] Wiborg, *Printing Ink*, pp. 22–23.
[53] *Wang-tu Han-mu pi-hua*, pp. 13–14; Plates 16, 17.
[54] Stein, *Ancient Khotan*, I, 438, 442; Plate CV.
[55] Stein, *Serindia*, I, 316.
[56] Chavannes, *op. cit.*, p. 66.
[57] Laufer, *op. cit.*, pp. 11, 13.
[58] Carter, *op. cit.*, (1925), p. 24; (rev. ed., 1955), p. 32, 35, note 1.

PLATE XXVII

A WRITING OUTFIT OF THE HAN DYNASTY

A mural painting of the Han dynasty from Wang-tu, Hopei, showing a scribe sitting before a round ink-slab with three legs and an ink stick standing on the palette. At the right is a cup of water for grinding ink.

These theories by various noted sinologists were undoubtedly influenced by some medieval or late Chinese sources. A thirteenth-century author, Chao Hsi-ku, wrote: "In very ancient times writings were made with a bamboo stylus dipped in lacquer; in mid-ancient times with a liquid obtained by rubbing a piece of stone ink, and not until the Wei and Chin dynasties (A.D. 221–419) were ink balls made by mixing the soot of lacquer and pine wood."[59] What this statement was based upon is unknown, but many later scholars have inherited this theory that lacquer was first used for writing. Wu Ch'iu-yen of the fourteenth century stated: "No brush and ink existed in antiquity; writings were made on bamboo tablets with a bamboo stylus dipped in lacquer."[60] T'ao Tsung-i of the fourteenth century and Chiang Shao-shu of the eighteenth century have made the similar statement that lacquer, stone ink, and lampblack are the order of development of Chinese ink.[61]

Whether lacquer was ever used as writing fluid is uncertain. There is no archeological evidence that ancient writings were ever made with lacquer. On the contrary, ancient writings on bones, bamboo, and silk, as discovered from time to time, were all made with ink of lampblack or of vermilion. In early literature, a few references to lacquer writing are found, all written in or after the fifth century A.D. Fan Yeh said that "Tu Lin (d. A.D. 47) had found at Hsi-chou one roll of the old text of the *Book of Documents*, written with lacquer."[62] He further mentioned the corruptions and controversies among the academic circles during the second century A.D. and "scholars even privately bribed with gold to change the lacquer writings of the official text of the classics so as to be in conformity with their own versions."[63]

Another reference to lacquer writing was made by Fang Hsüan-ling (578–648), who described that bamboo tablets of the third century B.C. discovered in A.D. 280 were "written with lacquer in the tadpole style."[64] These tablets, however, were recorded as "written in black ink,"[65] by Hsün Hsü, who was an eyewitness of the discovery and edited the documents in the imperial library. Furthermore, ink is defined in the *Shuo-wen* as "something used for writing," but there is no mention of such use in the definition under the character *ch'i* for "lacquer".

---

[59] *Ko-chih ching-yüan*, 37/20a.
[60] Wu Ch'iu-yen, *Hsüeh ku pien*, in *Shuo fu* (1927 ed.), 97/1a.
[61] T'ao Tsung-i, *Cho-keng lu*, 29/11; Chiang Shao-shu, *Yün-shih-chai pi-t'an*, first ser. 2/22–23.
[62] *Hou-Han shu*, 57/8a.
[63] *Ibid.*, 108/21b, 109a/3a.
[64] *Chin shu*, 51/25b.
[65] *Mu-t'ien-tzu chüan*, preface, 3a.

The dubious nature of the evidence has led some modern scholars to the opinion that lacquer was probably never used as a writing material. One suggested that the term "lacquer writing" merely means that the color of ink is as black as that of lacquer.[66] Another thought that since manufactured ink was popular in the Later Han dynasty, lacquer, being a natural product, would not still be used for writing.[67] Others consider that lacquer has no advantages over ink but has, on the contrary, decided disadvantages. It is difficult to write with after being mixed, and it dries slowly on the surface of bamboo or wood. As soon as silk and paper were invented, the brush proved most useful, and it is impossible to write in lacquer with a brush.[68]

The use of lacquer in writing, however, can have only two possibilities. First, as a natural product obtained easily from the sap of the lacquer tree, it may have been used parallel with other fluid material for writing. But it was certainly not so important as lampblack. Nor, judging from existing evidence, was it the original form of Chinese ink, as many scholars have believed. Secondly, the term "lacquer writing" may mean the use of soot manufactured by burning the sap of the lacquer tree, as is mentioned by many writers from the thirteenth century onward. Chao Hsi-ku and T'ao Tsung-i both said that "since the Wei and Chin dynasties, ink balls were made by mixing the smoke of lacquer and the soot of pine wood."[69] Some early recipes mention the use of dried lacquer as one of many ingredients to be mixed with pine soot[70] in order to increase the brightness of the color. In any case, lacquer seems to have been a minor substance if it was used in writing; and there is no evidence that it was used as a writing fluid earlier than lampblack.

Ink was probably also prepared from mineral substances as well as from lampblack. Many records, especially those written in the Chin dynasty, mention the use of *shih-mo*, or "stone ink." They generally relate the discovery of black minerals in the mountains located in present Kwangtung, Hupeh, Honan, Kiangsi, and other places. Ku Wei of the fourth century reported the stone ink of Huai-hua (in modern Kwangtung as "fine and good for writing."[71] Sheng Hung-chih of the fifth century mentioned a black mountain in Chu-yang (in modern Hupeh), "where rocks are all dark as ink."[72] Li Tao-yüan of the sixth century, noted

[66] Wang Kuo-wei, "Chien-tu chien-su k'ao," 8a, in *WCAIS*, ts'e 26.
[67] Ma Heng, "Chung-kuo shu-chieh chih-tu pien-ch'ien-chih yen-chiu," *op. cit.*, pp. 205–6.
[68] Wang Chi-chen, *op. cit.*, p. 119.
[69] *Ko-chih ching-yüan*, 37/20a.
[70] *Ibid.*, 37/25a.
[71] *T'ai-p'ing yü-lan*, 605/5b.
[72] *Ibid.*, 605/5a.

commentator on the *Water Classic,* said that Hsin-an and Yeh-tu (in modern Honan) all produced stone ink which could be used for writing.[73] Other sources mention similar black minerals in Lu-shan in modern Kiangsi.[74] Modern scholars believe that the so-called stone ink was probably either coal, graphite, or petroleum.[75] Since coal could not have produced an ink by rubbing on the palette, the so-called stone ink was probably graphite, which is a soft native carbon used for manufacturing "lead" pencils today. The locations in modern China where graphite is produced correspond closely to those described in the early literature mentioned above.[76]

MATERIALS AND FORMS OF INK-SLABS

Chinese ink was probably made in solid form from very early times. In order to obtain a liquid for writing, the solid ink was rubbed with water on a palette. How early the ink-slab was used in China is unknown, but since there were black and red pigments in the Shang dynasty, there might have been some kind of palette for mixing the fluid. We have, however, no literature concerning the ink-slab earlier than the first century A.D. nor any surviving ink-slab from the pre-Han period. Certain statements concerning the ancient use of the ink-slab made by later scholars are merely speculation, based upon insufficient evidence.[77] The earliest reliable information about the ink-slab comes from the lexicon *Shuo-wen,* written about A.D. 100, which defines the *yen,* or ink-slab, as "a polished stone."[78] The *Shih-ming* of about A.D. 200 says that "*yen* means rubbing."[79] It seems certain that the Chinese ink-slab of the Han period was made of stone and used for grinding ink.

The selection of stone for making the ink-slab has been a special art. Its quality, color, sound, texture and markings were especially considered by both the makers and the users.[80] It is easy to grind and produce ink on a fine stone, but a coarse one that is too absorbent dries the ink too quickly. Ink-slabs were of oblong, round, or other shapes, with wooden or lacquer

[73] Li Tao-yuan, *Shui-ching chu,* 10/9a; 15/9a.

[74] *Ko-chih ching yüan,* 37/29b–30a.

[75] Laufer, *op. cit.,* p. 13; Wang Chi-chen, *op. cit.,* p. 124.

[76] *Tz'u-hai* describes that *shih-mo,* or graphite, is produced in Kiangsi, Hunan, Kwangtung, Kiangsu, and Anhui.

[77] See passages quoted in *T'ai-p'ing yü-lan,* 605/6a; *Ko-chih ching-yüan,* 38/1–2.

[78] Ting Fu-pao, *Shuo-wen chieh-tzu ku-lin,* 4207b.

[79] Liu Hsi, *Shih-ming,* 6/45a.

[80] Cf. Van Gulik, *Mi Fu on Ink-stones,* pp. 22–23.

fittings. The surface of the palette usually included a water cavity at the end away from the user and an oval ink-grinding area at the center of the stone. Elaborate decorations or designs were sometimes made.

Besides stone, bricks and tiles were common materials for making ink-slabs. The bricks from the Han ruins of the Bronze Bird Terrace built by Ts'ao Ts'ao in A.D. 210 have been especially prized for their quality of not absorbing ink. An oblong ink-slab made of this brick is still preserved in the Palace Museum.[81] A round ink-slab made of a Han palace tile with an inscription has also survived.[82] They were not, however, actually used in the Han dynasty. Only a few pieces dating from the Han period and decorated with birds and animals, especially snakes, frogs, and turtles, are known to be extant.[83]

In 1934, a complete ink-slab set with accompanying case was discovered in a Han tomb in Korea dating from the second or third century A.D. It consists of two parts, an ink-slab and a rubbing piece, and a desk-shaped case or stand. The slab is an oblong slate; the rubber is a semi-circular, knoblike wooden piece. The two are placed on a black lacquered wooden board. The desk-shaped case has a drawer which is partitioned into six sections, large and small, for keeping liquid ink. On the surface of the case there are two pairs of bronze tubes for holding writing brushes. Besides this complete set, some detached or independent ink-slabs and rubbers have been found in other tombs in Lo-lang, Korea, and also in south Manchuria.[84]

Some special ink-slabs were occasionally made of such unusual materials as jade, crystal, silver, iron, bronze, shells, and perhaps bamboo and wood. The *Hsi-ching tsa-chi* says that the emperor used a jade ink-slab because the water on it would not freeze.[85] The crystal ink-slab was not used for grinding ink but for preserving the fluid prepared on other ink-slabs. The ink-slab made of iron from Khotan was said to have been bestowed by the Emperor Wu (r. 265–290) upon the scholar Chang Hua (232–300) when his writing of the *Po-wu chih* was completed.[86] Bronze ink-slabs with three legs and a cover are mentioned among the discoveries in an ancient tomb of unknown date during the Sung dynasty.[87]

---

[81] *Ku-kung chou-k'an*, No. 339 (1934), p. 4.

[82] *Ho-pei ti-i po-wu-yüan pan-yüeh-k'an*, No. 35 (1933), p. 1.

[83] Ferguson, *Li-tai chu-lu chi-chin mu*, p. 1111, lists seven items dating from the Han period as having been recorded and reproduced in various works.

[84] Koizumi and Hamada, *Rakurō saikyōzuka*, pp. 45–46.

[85] *Hsi-ching tsa-chi*, 1/1b.

[86] *T'ai-p'ing yü-lan*, 605/6a.

[87] Van Gulik, *Mi Fu on Ink-stones*, p. 54.

The tripod ink-slab was probably the form generally used in the Han dynasty, as shown on the mural from Wang-tu. A poem on an ink-slab made by Fan Ch'in is quoted as saying: "Balanced with three toes comparable to a tripod of Hsia bronze, symbolizing the mutual help of the constellations."[88] Su I-chien (958–996) believed that ancient ink-slabs were also made of wood, because Fu Hsüan (217–278), who wrote about the ink-slab, says: "Wood is prized for its softness; stone is good for its smoothness and hardness."[89] Here the wood mentioned by the writer was probably for making the cases or fittings, as it absorbs ink quickly and does not seem to be a good material for ink-slabs. There are many literary records concerning ink-slabs made of silver, shells, and other materials;[90] but their use was probably at a later date.

BOOK KNIFE AS ERASER

The book knife was an important tool for preparing bamboo and wood for writing and for deleting and correcting writings on the tablets. Pieces of bamboo and wood must have been sliced and cut into narrow tablets of definite length, and their surface was then smoothed ready for writing with brush and ink. When mistakes were made, the surface would be scraped off for correction and rewriting. When an old tablet was used over again, the used surface had to be removed in order to obtain a new one. For many of these processes a sharp tool was used, either an ordinary knife called *tao* or *hsüeh*, or a specially designed "book knife" known as *shu-tao*.[91]

There has been some confusion about the several different kinds of cutting tools in connection with their use in writing. For example, the Sung imperial catalogue of antique objects includes a short knife which was called the *tao-pi*, or knife pen, and described as being carried by people in the Han dynasty for deleting writings from tablets.[92] Juan Yüan, a Ch'ing scholar, named a short cutting knife, the *hsüeh*, which was described as similar to the *shu-tao*.[93] Another scholar even confused the *tao-pi* with the *ch'i-chüeh*, a crooked burin for engraving on stone and other hard materials, and with the *huo-tao*, or knife money.[94] Actually

[88] Su I-chien, *Wen-fang ssu-p'u*, 3/6a–b.

[89] *Ibid.*, 3/6a.

[90] *Ko-chih ching-yüan*, 38/20a–21b.

[91] For a detailed study of the "book knife," see Tsien, "Han-tai shu-tao k'ao," *BIHP*, Extra Volume, No. 4 (1961), pp. 997—1008.

[92] Wang Fu, *Hsüan-ho po-ku t'u-lu*, 27/40.

[93] Juan Yüan, *Chi-ku-chai chung-ting i-ch'i k'uan-shih*, 8/22b.

[94] Ma Ang, *Huo-pu wen-tzu k'ao*, 4/24b–25b.

all of these were different objects with different names, forms, and uses.

The words *tao*, knife, and *pi*, brush, were often used together as a designation for a scribe or an official of low rank but powerful in law enforcement. Ssu-ma Ch'ien mentioned that Hsiao Ho (d. 193 B.C.), the prime minister of the Former Han dynasty, was formerly a *tao-pi li*, a knife pen official, of the Ch'in.[95] Pan Ku said that the *tao* and *pi*, basket and chest (for holding tablets) are common things employed by ordinary officials.[96] Many writers since the T'ang dynasty have mistakenly believed that these two were one object used for engraving writings on tablets. Chia Kung-yen (fl. 650) said, "In ancient times when paper and brush were not used, the book knife was employed for engraving characters; and in the Han period, even when paper and brush were accessible, it was still used as a matter of tradition."[97] Even the modern dictionary *Tz'u-yüan* inherits this theory. It says: "Since ancient documents were made of bamboo or wood, a knife was used as pen and it was therefore called *tao-pi*, a 'knife-pen'."[98] Modern scholars however, have concluded that the *tao* was a knife for deleting and the *pi* was a brush for writing.[99] The knife was probably an indispensable tool which accompanied the writing brush, since erasing was always necessary.

Many literary references indicate that the *hsüeh* also was used for erasing writings from the tablets. Ssu-ma Ch'ien says that Confucius "used the *pi* when it was proper to write and the *hsüeh* when it was proper to delete."[100] The *Tso chuan* also mentions that in 546 B.C., when Tso Shih of the Sung state asked for a reward, the duke offered him sixty towns, but Tso refused to accept by scratching the statement off from the tablet and throwing it back.[101] On other occasions, the *hsüeh* is mentioned as having been used also for cutting oranges, melons, or wooden instruments.[102] It is apparent that both *tao* and *hsüeh* were common knives for cutting not only tablets but other objects too.

According to literature, the *tao* was a longer and wider knife with a straight blade attached to a ring-shaped end while the *hsüeh* was a shorter and narrower knife with a curved blade attached to a solid

---

[95] *Shih chi*, 53/6a.

[96] *Han shu*, 48/17a.

[97] *Chou-li chu-su*, 40/10a–b.

[98] *Tz'u-yüan* (one-volume ed., 1939), p. 188.

[99] Including Chavannes, Wang Kuo-wei, Ma Heng, Wang Chung-min, and Li shu-hua; see discussions in Tsien, *op. cit.*, p.1004.

[100] *Shih chi*, 47/26b.

[101] Legge, *Ch'un Tsew with Tso Chuen*, p. 531.

[102] See quotations from *Yen-tzu ch'un-ch'iu*, *Chou-li*, *Li chi*, *Chuang-tzu*, *Hsün-tzu*, *Mo-tzu*, and discussions in Tsien, *op. cit.*, p. 999.

handle.[103] The *K'ao-kung chi*, a chapter on ancient manufacture in the *Rituals of Chou*, says that artisans in metals manufactured the *hsüeh*, one foot long and one inch wide, with a curved blade bending 60 degrees. It is further described as made of an alloy with "two parts of tin in every five parts of copper."[104] This would produce a sharper and more elastic blade than other kinds of metal.

The earliest reference to associate the *hsüeh* with the *shu-tao* comes from Cheng Hsüan (127–200), who interpreted the *hsüeh* as "the *shu-tao* of today."[105] Cheng did not elaborate upon its use, but his contemporary Liu Hsi defined the term *shu-tao* in his lexicon as "a knife provided for deleting when writing was made on the bamboo and wooden tablets."[106] The *Tung-kuan Han-chi*, an official history of A.D. 25–180, mentions that the *shu-tao* was granted together with gold and other rare provisions to a prefect of Ch'en-liu by the emperor.[107] Ju Shun of the third century said: "The *shu-tao* with the design of a golden horse is now used for bestowing on the officials. The design consists of horses inlaid with gold on the ring."[108] The so-called "golden-horse book-knife" is further described in a poem by Li Yu (*ca.* 60–140), who wrote:

> It is skilfully smelted and tempered,
> Finished with a design of a golden horse;
> Polished and carved with yellow lines,
> And inscribed with the manufacturer's name.[109]

These descriptions are confirmed by recent discovery and other specimens surviving in several private collections. All these specimens are made of iron and bear inscriptions on one side and fine designs on the other. Both sides are decorated with gold inlaid in the blade and the ring handle. The designs consist of birds and animals. One specimen discovered in 1957 in a mountain tomb in T'ien- hui-shan, Ch'engtu, Szechuan, bears a picture of a flying phoenix in the center followed by two small ones (Plate XXVIII.B). Others bear designs of flying horses with wings.

The inscription tells the date and place of making, name of object and of the manufacturer (Plate XXVIII.A). One specimen in the former collection of Lo Chen-yü bears a long inscription of 28 characters in one line

[103] Sun I-jang, *Chou-li cheng-i*, 78/2*b*.
[104] *Chou-li chu-su*, 40/10*a*.
[105] *Ibid.*
[106] Liu Hsi, *Shih ming*, 7/52*b*.
[107] Quoted in *T'ai-p'ing yü-lan*, 345/3*a*.
[108] *Han shu*, 89/3*a*.
[109] Quoted in *T'ai-p'ing yü-lan*, 103/46; but the author of the poem is mistakenly given as Li Yüan. According to the *Hou-Han shu*, 110*a*/14*b*, Li Yu, a noted scholar, was a native of Kuang-han, where fine book knives are known to have been manufactured.

PLATE XXVIII

BOOK KNIVES AND LABEL

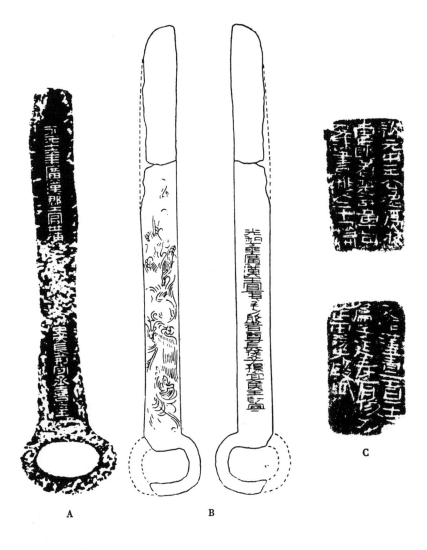

A   B   C

(A) An iron book knife inlaid with gold inscription for erasing writings on tablets, A.D. 104.
(B) A book knife from Ch'eng-tu, A.D. 184, showing flying phoenixes on one side and inscription on the other (18.5 × 1.5 cm.). (C) Inscriptions from both sides of an ivory book label, fourth century A.D.

on the blade. It may be read as "Made in the sixteenth year of Yung-yüan (A.D. 104) by Fung Wu, an official charged with the manufacture of book knives at Kuang-han prefecture (modern Kuang-han, near Ch'eng-tu, Szechuan). . . ."[110] The specimen from Ch'eng-tu bears an inscription which says: "Made in the seventh year of Kuang-ho (A.D. 184) by an official in charge of manufacturing at Kuang-han,"[111] followed by some good-will sayings similar to those in mirror inscriptions of the Later Han period. The mention of Kuang-han as the place of manufacture in all the inscriptions seems to agree with the record in the dynastic history, which describes Szechuan as the place of making book knives in the Former Han dynasty.[112] The recent discovery in Ch'eng-tu, Szechuan, confirms this fact. It was probably still the center of manufacture of book knives during the Later Han period.

[110] Lo Chen-yü, *Chen-sung-t'ang chi-ku i-wen*, 15/11a–12a; Huang Chün, *Heng-chai chin-shih shih-hsiao lu*, II, 6–7.

[111] *K'ao-ku hsüeh-pao*, 1958, No. 1, p. 101, Plate XII:4.

[112] *Han shu*, 89/2b–3a.

IX

CONCLUSION

TYPES OF WRITING MATERIALS

Early Chinese documents and books were recorded on a variety of materials. Some of them were hard and durable, others soft and perishable. The writings preserved on hard surfaces, including bones, shells, metal, stone, jade, pottery, and clay, are generally called inscriptions; while those on perishable materials, such as bamboo, wood, silk, and paper, are usually considered as "books." Although bamboo and wood have hard surfaces, they are perishable.

Apparently there were two major groups of materials used in early days for different kinds of communication. The perishable materials, which were more convenient and sometimes less expensive, were used extensively for government documents, historical records, literary compositions, personal correspondence, and other writings of daily use. The permanent materials, hard and durable, were used for making commemorative or other inscriptions of more lasting value. The former were intended primarily for horizontal communication among contemporaries and the latter for vertical communication across generations. The ancient Chinese seem to have preferred hard and permanent materials not only to communicate with the spirits or their ancestors but also to record messages for their sons and grandsons in posterity.

The demarcation between inscription and book, however, cannot be arbitrarily defined as being that between hard and soft or permanent and perishable materials, for monumental and commemorative records were sometimes kept on soft and perishable materials and literary writings or books were also inscribed on hard and durable surfaces.

TRANSMISSION OF ANCIENT LITERATURE

The written records surviving from ancient times consist of two different types of materials: archeological and literary. Archeological materials

179

have generally been unearthed from ancient ruins or found in hidden places, where they were originally made or preserved. The perishable materials have been discovered in various sites in or outside of China, where the weather or underground conditions were suitable for their preservation.

The literary materials, which preserve a greater number of the ancient texts, have generally been transmitted through transcription and mechanical reproduction, although their contents could have been retold from memory if the originals had been destroyed. The processes of transmission include inscribing on permanent materials, transcription by handwriting, reproduction by inked squeezes or by various methods of printing, and preservation in quotations from earlier sources. About 150 works, or one-fourth of the total number of books which are known to have existed in the first century A.D., have been transmitted by these processes. Even when the text was lost, the descriptions of books are sometimes included in historical bibliographies.

The ancient texts have been handed down through repeated destructions and restorations, revisions and reproductions, which have sometimes resulted in corruptions and interpolations in the original texts, through intentional changes or unintentional errors. Thus archeological materials, if genuine, preserve the exact original, while literary materials are less accurate but generally include more complete and longer texts than the former.

DATES OF INSCRIPTIONS

The earliest known writings in China are records of divination preserved on bones and shells, dating from the fourteenth century B.C. Inscriptions made during this period are also found on bronze, stone, jade, and pottery, but these are generally short and limited to a few characters. The use of bones and shells for writing existed for over two and one-half centuries but was practically discontinued after the fall of the Shang dynasty in the late twelfth century B.C.

Bronze inscriptions were then greatly developed as permanent records of political, social, and ceremonial affairs. They remained in use for over a millennium until sometime in the second or third century A.D. Since that time, stone has been extensively used not only for monumental inscriptions but also for the preservation of canonical texts of Confucian, Buddhist, and Taoist literatures. It is the only permanent material that has been used for inscriptions continuously from ancient times down to the present. Clay inscriptions, including those on pottery vessels, bricks, tiles, and sealing clay, flourished from the fifth or fourth century B.C. until the early fourth century A.D. They record primarily the names of persons and places, official titles, and good-luck sayings.

DEVELOPMENT OF THE CHINESE BOOK

Ancient inscriptions cast, engraved, or impressed on permanent materials are hardly to be considered "books." The direct ancestry of the Chinese book begins with strips and tablets made of bamboo or wood. These were bound together by two lines of cords and used in a manner similar to a modern paged book. The length of the strips was determined by the nature of the content, and the width was invariably narrow, bearing most often one vertical column of characters. Although no specimen of such books before the fifth or fourth century B.C. survives today, ancient literature tells us that the age of their flourishing was no later than that of bones and bronzes.

Silk was invented in China as early as Neolithic times, but no evidence has yet been found that it was used for writing until sometime in the seventh or sixth century B.C. Since bamboo was too bulky and silk too expensive to be wholly practical as a popular medium of communication, a kind of quasi-paper of silk fiber was used for a short period before true paper was invented in the early second century A.D. Thenceforth paper has been the most convenient and popular material for writing down to the present day. Paper books were first in the form of rolls, then of folded leaves, gradually evolved into wrapped and stitched volumes still in use today.

The old-fashioned materials, however, were not supplanted immediately by the new invention but were replaced gradually after its introduction. We have found that bamboo and wood survived for some three centuries and silk for five hundred years more in competition with paper after the new material was invented. Human conservatism was always in favor of the traditional practices which not only were more familiar to the users but also had some advantages over the new.

TECHNOLOGY OF WRITING AND DUPLICATION

Various methods and tools were employed for producing the early Chinese records. Certain hard and durable materials, such as bone and stone, were usually incised or engraved by means of a metal stylus or knife; while the perishable and soft materials, such as bamboo, wood, silk, and paper, were written on with the brush pen and ink of lampblack. Although the brush was also sometimes used to write on hard materials, such inscriptions are occasional and exceptional. Ink of lacquer and a stylus of bamboo or wood are said to have been used in ancient times, but the date of their actual existence is uncertain. The book knife is believed to have been used to remove mistakes in writing from bamboo or wooden tablets and not for inscribing on them.

Handwriting by brush pen or stylus was, however, not the only method for making Chinese records before the use of printing. Mechanical devices were sometimes employed for their production and duplication. Inscriptions on bronzes were generally cast from molds and those on clay were either made by molds or impressed with a stamp. Seals, which were either cast from metals or cut in stone or jade, were impressed on soft and sticky clay and later on silk and paper to make duplicate inscriptions.

The most interesting technique for the multiplication of writing before the invention of block printing was the process of taking inked impressions from stone or other inscriptions by squeezing paper over their surfaces. This method is in principle quite similar to that of printing, although the material on which the engravings are made and the result obtained from the surfaces are sometimes different. This technique, nevertheless, has been considered as the forerunner of mass production of early writings, and eventually led to the invention of block printing.

EVOLUTION OF CHINESE SCRIPT

The surviving records tell the story of the evolution of Chinese writing by which the ancient texts of different periods have been preserved. Although the general principles of construction of the Chinese written language have remained unchanged, the variation in number, shape, and position of strokes in writing has resulted in the formation of different styles from time to time.

These styles are sometimes named for the materials on which the characters are inscribed, such as the "shell-and-bone" and "bronze" scripts, or the forms or functions for which the script was used, such as the seal, clerical, running, model, and rapid styles. Almost all of the styles were introduced before the fourth century A.D., when the model style was standardized as the book script, which is still the most commonly used form of writing today.

In general, the writing style is evolutional from complex to simple construction, from irregular to stabilized forms, from formal to free lines, and from slow to rapid execution. Its evolution is parallel to the successive changes of materials, tools, and other vehicles of writing and to increasing frequency of communication, which demands a simpler and quicker medium for the expression of thought in writing.

INCREASE IN VOCABULARY

The evolution of Chinese writing is also reflected in the increasing number of characters used in the vocabulary and the methods used for multiplying them. The bone inscriptions contain over 2,500 characters and bronze inscriptions are known to have made use of around 3,000. These figures, however, do not represent the whole vocabulary used in Shang and Chou literature, because it is based merely on the inscriptions so far discovered. These were limited to the recording of certain particular matters on certain particular occasions. We know more definitely, however, that over 9,000 characters were used around A.D. 100, when the first Chinese etymological dictionary was compiled. This figure was doubled at the end of the fifth century, tripled around A.D. 1000, and increased to more than five times as many today. As one can see, the method used for the multiplication of characters is primarily based on the principles of phonetic combination and borrowing. The bone inscriptions contain mostly pictograms and ideograms but only a few phonograms. The last category was increased to a much greater proportion in the later vocabularies.

ORDER OF CHINESE WRITING

No matter what kind of material was used or what form of records was produced, Chinese writing has always been read vertically from top to bottom with the columns following from right to left, as is done today. Although some early inscriptions do not follow this order, it is believed that they were only exceptions.

The reason for this vertical arrangement is uncertain. It is suggested, however, that the predominantly downward strokes of the brush writing, the grain of bamboo and wood, and the narrow strips which allow only a single line of characters might have influenced such a movement. The habit of a right-handed scribe, who would lay the strips to his right in order as he finished them, might have resulted in a right-to-left arrangement of the columns.

There is no reason to suppose that the vertical arrangement of writing is backward or inefficient in reading. On the contrary, recent researches indicate that "vertical reading was found to be faster than horizontal reading by all investigators."[1] Psychologists have suggested that the manner in which the eyes open and the peculiar structure of the Chinese characters are possible reasons why vertical movement is preferable. Undoubtedly the materials and tools used in writing were also influential in this tradition.

FACTORS UNDERLYING THE DEVELOPMENT

The development of early Chinese documents and books was influenced by various social, political, economic, and intellectual forces. The religious beliefs of the ancient people encouraged the use of writing to communicate with the spirits. Divination, prayer, and sacrifice were all recorded in writing. Nevertheless, they reflect to a large extent the actual life of their times. Frequent communications among the feudal states and within the government structure increased the production of official and diplomatic documents and archives. Since the literate class before the time of Confucius consisted primarily of aristocrats, their leisure and wealth undoubtedly granted them such privileges as reading and writing.

With the social and intellectual changes that took place after the time of Confucius, private writers and book-collectors rose rapidly through the popularization of education. The triumph of Confucianism in government in the second century B.C. resulted in the restoration of ancient literature after repeated destructions by censors and wars. The centralized imperial library was established for the preservation, and library techniques were introduced for the control, of increasing numbers of books. Since this time ancient texts which survived have almost all been collated and edited by Confucian scholars.

With the spread of Buddhism in the third or fourth century A.D., a large amount of religious literature was imported; and for the first time foreign books were extensively translated and alien thought was introduced to Chinese scholarship and subsequently integrated into Chinese

[1] William S. Gray, *The Teaching of Reading and Writing: An International Survey* (Paris: Unesco, 1956), p. 50.

life in the following centuries. Taoist works also flourished contemporary with the increasing output of Buddhist writings. Although their quantity cannot compare with that of Confucian and Buddhist canons, they embody some material showing the development of early scientific thought.

The increasing demand for more religious literature stimulated the development of printing. This new device, however, did not end the production of books by hand. Nor did it change the general nature of their format, content, quality, or even quantity in creative writing. What it did was merely to increase the quantity of copies by facilitating duplication of the writing, so that communication by books became wider and easier. Nevertheless, human nature once again demonstrated its conservatism, for printing did not become popular until some three hundred years after its introduction in the early eighth century. Commemorative writings have always been inscribed on permanent materials, and manuscripts have since been more treasured than printed editions even down to our times.

TABLE

CHRONOLOGICAL DEVELOPMENT OF CHINESE

	DYNASTIES	CULTURE	INSCRIPTIONS
B.C. 1400 1300 1200	Shang [Yin] (1765?–1123? B.C.)	Agriculture Sericulture Ancestor worship Divination	Earliest writing on bones, shells, bronze, pottery, stone and jade
1100 1000 900 800	Western Chou (1122?–771 B.C.)	Feudalism Interstate communication Ritual vessels and weapons	Records on bronze
700 600 500 400 300	Eastern Chou (770–256 B.C.) Ch'un Ch'iu; or Spring and Autumn (722–481 B.C.) Chan Kuo; or Warring States (468–221 B.C.)	First law code Iron age Confucius Economic development Rise of philosophers	Stone drums Jade tablets Inscriptions on coins Inscribed curses on stone
200	Ch'in (221–207 B.C.)	Unification	Stone monuments
100 A.D.	Former Han (206 B.C.–A.D. 8) Wang Mang (9–23)	Civil service examination Imperial university Imperial library	Inscriptions on pottery, bricks, tiles and sealing clay
100 200	Later Han (25–220)	Introduction of Buddhism Study of classics	Mirror inscriptions Confucian classics on stone
300	3 Kingdoms (221–280)	Rise of Taoism	Stone classics in 3 styles
400	Chin (265–420)	Calligraphy as art	Grave tablets
500 600	Northern and Southern Dynasties (420–589)	Spread of Buddhism Stone sculptures	Cliff inscriptions Buddhist canons on stone
700	Sui (581–618)	Canal building	
	T'ang (618–906)	Commerce and industry Art and architecture Games	Taoist canons on stone

4

CULTURE, BOOKS, AND WRITING

PHYSICAL BOOKS	LITERATURE	IMPLEMENTS	VOCABULARY	STYLES	
					B.C. 1400
Documents on tablets		Brush Lampblack Cinnabar Turquoise	2,500	Shell-and- bone script	1300 1200
				Great seal	1100
	Book of Changes *Book of Documents* *Book of Poetry*				1000 900
			3,000		800
Writings on silk	*Spring and Autumn Annals* *State Discourses* *Book of Etiquettes*				700 600
Silk documents Bamboo documents	*Confucian Analects* *Tso Chronicle* Writings of phil. *Elegies of Ch'u*	Brush from Ch'ang-sha			500 400
					300
				Small seal	200
Quasi-paper Wooden calendar	Folk songs *Historical Record* Classified catalogue	Brush from Chü-yen	5,340	Clerical	100 A.D.
Wood inventory True paper	*History of F. Han* *Shuo-wen chieh-tzu*	Book knife Ink-slab set	9,353	*chang ts'ao* Running	100 200
			18,150		300
Wood documents Paper manuscripts	Taoist works Short stories	Ink by Wei-Tan Stone ink		Model Rapid	400
Inked squeezes Paper rolls	Buddhist sutras Parallel prose		22,726		500 600
					700
Block print	Poetical writings Commentaries		30,000		

GLOSSARY

List of Chinese characters for proper names, book titles, and special terms used in the text and not given in the Bibliography.

An-i 安邑
An Lu-shan 安祿山
An-yang 安陽
cha 札
Chan Kuo 戰國
ch'an 蠶
Chang Ch'ang 張敞
Chang Chieh 張楫
Chang Chih 張芝
Chang Hua 張華
chang ts'ao 章草
Ch'ang-an 長安
Ch'ang-lo t'ai-p'u 長樂太僕
Ch'ang-lo wei-yang 長樂未央
Ch'ang-sha 長沙
chao (omen) 兆 州 仦
Chao (state) 趙
Ch'en (town) 陳
Ch'en Chieh-ch'i 陳介祺
Ch'en Hsing 陳興
Ch'en Sheng 陳勝
Cheng Ch'iao 鄭樵
Cheng-chou 鄭州
Cheng Hsüan 鄭玄
ch'eng 丞
Chi 籍
Chi-chiu chang 急就章
Chi-chün 汲郡
Chi Han 嵇含
Chi-mo 即墨
Chi-ning 濟寧
Chi T'an 籍談
Ch'i (district) 齋
Ch'i (state) 岐

Ch'i-chüeh 剞 劂
Ch'i-lüeh 七略
Chia K'uei 賈逵
Chia Kung-yen 賈公彥
Chiang Ch'ung 江充
Chiao-shan 焦山
chieh 碣
Chieh-shih 碣石
chien (silk) 縑
chien (tablets; surname) 簡
Ch'ien (river) 汧
Ch'ien tzu wen 千字文
chih 紙; 帋
Chih-fou 芝罘
ch'ih-tu 尺牘
Chin (dynasty; state) 晋
chin (monetary unit) 釿
chin shih 巾十
Chin shu 晋書
Ch'in (dynasty; state) 秦
ch'in (tree) 梣
Ch'in-yang 沁陽
Ching-chung 敬仲
Ching Fang 京房
Ching-wan 靜琬
Chiu-ch'üan 酒泉
Chou (dynasty) 周
chou (writing) 籀
Chou Hsing-ssu 周興嗣
Chou She 周舍
chu 竹
Chu ch'u wen 詛楚文
chu po 竹帛
chu-sha 朱砂

188

Chu-shu chi-nien 竹書紀年

Chu Tsu 詛祝

Chu-yang 筑陽

Ch'u (state) 楚

chuan 篆

Ch'un Ch'iu 春秋

Chung-ch'ang-shih 中常侍

Chung Ku 終古

Ch'ung 重

Ch'ung Wen Kuan 崇文館

Chü-yen 居延

chüan (roll) 卷

chüan (silk) 絹

Chüeh-ch'iu 厥湫

Ch'üeh (Shang tribe) 崔

Chün-hsien 濬縣

Dharmaraksha 竺法護

Dokyo 曇徵

fan-chi (tree) 樊鷄

fan chih 幡紙

Fan Ch'in 繁欽

Fan Hsüan-tzu 范宣子

fang 方

Fang-shan 房山

Fei Ch'ang-fang 費長房

Fei Pao 斐豹

Feng-yü 風峪

fu 符

Fu Ch'ien 服虔

Fu Hsien 傅咸

Fu Hsüan 傅立

Fung Wu 馮武

Han (dynasty) 漢

Han (state) 韓

Han Chieh 韓珍

Han Fen Lou 涵芬樓

ho-t'i 赫蹏

Hsi-ch'iang 西羌

Hsi-yin 西陰

Hsia (dynasty) 夏

hsiang 鄉

Hsiang Chih 向摯

Hsiang-yang 襄陽

hsiao-chuan 小篆

Hsiao-t'un 小屯

Hsien-pi 鮮卑

Hsin-an 新安

Hsin-cheng 新鄭

Hsin-pu 新簿

Hsin-tien 辛店

Hsin Yu 辛有

Hsing-t'ai 邢台

Hsiung-nu 匈奴

Hsü (state) 許

Hsü-chou 徐州

Hsü Shen 許慎

Hsü Tzu 許子

hsüeh 削

hsüeh-i 削衣

Hsün Hsü 荀勗

hu 笏

Hua (Shang tribe) 畫

huan 紈

huang-nieh 黃蘗

Huang Ti 黃帝

Hui-hsien 輝縣

Hui Shih 惠施

Hui-ssu 慧思

Hun-yüan 渾源

Hung-chao 洪昭

huo-tao 貨刀

i 邑

I-ching 義淨

I-hsien 易縣

I-li 儀禮

I-shan 嶧山

jan-huang 染潢

Jen-ch'eng 任城

Juan Hsiao-hsü 阮孝緒

Jung 戎

k'ai 楷

K'ai-feng 開封

K'ang-fu 元父

Kao (town) 高

Kao-ch'ang 高昌

K'ao-kung chi 考工記

Ko Yüan-fu 萬元甫

K'o-yüan 可元

ku 觚

Ku-chin tzu-ku 古今字詁

Ku Piao 顧彪

Ku Wei 顧微

ku wen 古文

Kuan Chung 管仲

Kuan-tzu 管子

Kuang-han 廣漢

kuei (jade) 圭

kuei (vessel) 段

Kuei-chi 會稽

Kuei-yang 桂陽

k'uei 夔

Kung-hsien 鞏縣

Kung-sun Hung 公孫弘

kung tien 貢典

Kung-yang Kao 公羊高

K'ung An-kuo 孔安國

K'ung Ying-ta 孔穎達

Kuo-yü 國語

Lang-ya 琅琊

Li (town) 鬲

li (writing) 隸

Li chi 禮記

Li Ling 李陵

Li Shang-yin 李商隱

Li Ssu 李斯

Li Tao-yüan 酈道元

Li T'ing-kuei 李廷珪

Li Yu 李尤

Li Yüan 李元

Liang (dynasty; town) 梁

Lin-tzu 臨淄

Liu An 劉安

Liu Hsiang 劉向

Liu Hsin 劉歆

Liu Te 劉德

Lo-lang 樂浪

Lo-yang 洛陽

Lou-lan 樓蘭

Lu (state) 魯

Lu Chung 陸終

Lung-men 龍門

Lung-t'ing 龍亭

Lü Pu-wei 呂不韋

Lü Shang 呂尚

mei 枚

Meng K'ang 孟康

Meng T'ien 蒙恬

mi-hsiang chih 蜜香紙

miu-chuan 繆篆

Mo Tzu 墨子

mo-hsieh 摹寫

mo-yai 摩崖

mo-yin 摹印

mu 木

mu-chih 墓誌

Mu-chou 睦州

Nan Yüeh 南越

nei-shih 內史

Niu Heng 牛亨

Nü Kuei 女媧

o-mi-t'o-fo 阿彌陀佛

Ou-yang Fei 歐陽斐

Ou-yang Hsün 歐陽詢

Ou-yang Kao 歐陽高

pan 版

pan-liang 半兩

P'an Keng 盤庚

pao-huo 寶貨

pei 碑

pi 筆 聿 𦘒

Pi-shih lun 筆勢論

p'i 匹

P'i Chun 丕准

p'i-hsien Chin-kung 丕顯晉公

Pieh-lu 別錄

pien 編

p'ien (chapter) 篇

p'ien (strip) 片

po 帛
po-shih 博士
Po-wu chih 博物志
pu 卜 ㆒ ㆑ ㆓
p'u-shu 蒲書
Seng Yu 僧佑
sha-ch'ing 殺青
Shan hai ching 山海經
Shang (dynasty) 商
shang (tree) 桑
Shang-fang-ling 尚方令
Shang-lin 上林
Shang shu 尚書
Shang Ti 上帝
Shang Yang 商鞅
Shao-chou 韶州
Sheng Hung-chih 盛弘之
shih (scribe; surname) 史 肯
shih (slice) 柿
Shih ching 詩經
Shih Huang Ti 始皇帝
Shih-ming 釋名
shih-mo 石墨
Shih Yu 史游
Shou-ch'un 壽春
Shou-hsien 壽縣
shu 銖
Shu Hsi 束皙
shu-ssu 書肆
shu-tao 書刀
Sian 西安
Ssu-ma Hsiang-ju 司馬相如
Ssu-ma Kuang 司馬光
su 素
Su Ch'in 蘇秦
Su Wu 蘇武
Sui 隋
Sun Pin 孫臏
Sun Po-yen 孫伯翼
Sun-tzu 孫子
Sun Wu 孫武
Ta Ch'in 大秦

t'a-shu-shou 搨書手
Tai Te 戴德
T'ai-an 泰安
T'ai-shan 泰山
T'ai Shih 太史
tan-sha 丹砂
t'an 罎
T'ang 唐
T'ang Yung 唐邕
tao-pi li 刀筆吏
Tao-te ching 道德經
Teng Yü 鄧禹
Ti Chün 帝夋
Ti Hsin 帝辛
Ti I 帝乙
Ti Kao 帝嚳
tieh 牒
tien 典
ting 鼎
Ts'ai Lun 蔡倫
Ts'ai Yung 蔡邕
tsao-i 造意
Ts'ao Chih 曹植
Ts'ao Ts'ao 曹操
ts'e 冊;策
Ts'e-li chih 側理紙
tseng 繒
Tsinan 濟南
Tso chuan 左傳
Tso Po 左伯
Tso Ssu 左思
Tso Ts'e 作冊
Tsu-lai 祖來
Ts'ui Pao 崔豹
Ts'ui Yüan 崔瑗
tu 牘
Tu Lin 杜林
Tu Yü 杜預
T'u-fang 土方
tuan-ch'ang 短長
Tuan Yü-ts'ai 段玉裁
Tun-huang 敦煌

T'un-liu 屯留

Tung 董

Tung Cho 董卓

Tung-fang So 東方朔

Tung-kuan 東觀

Tung Pa 董巴

T'ung chih 通志

T'ung-chüeh (terrace) 銅雀

T'ung-su-wen 通俗文

T'ung-li 通理

tzu 字

Tzu-chih t'ung-chien 資治通鑑

Tzu-i 子邑

wan 丸

Wang Hsi-chih 王羲之

Wang I 王逸

Wang Kuan 王綰

Wang Kuang 王光

Wang Mang 王莽

Wang-tu 望都

Wani 王仁

Wei (river) 渭

Wei (state) 魏

Wei Chuang 韋莊

Wei Tan 韋誕

Wu-hsien 巫咸

Wu Hui 吳回

Wu-li-p'ai 五里牌

wu shu 五銖

Wu Ti 武帝

Wu Ting 武丁

Wu-wei 武威

Ya-t'o 亞駝

Yang-chia-wan 楊家灣

Yang-t'ien-hu 仰天湖

Yeh-tu 鄴都

Yen (state) 燕

Yen Shih-ku 顏師古

Yen Ti 炎帝

Yen Ying 晏嬰

yin 印

yin-yang 陰陽

Ying 郢

Ying Shao 應劭

Yü Ho 虞龢

Yü-kung 禹貢

Yü-mei 榆麋

Yüan An 袁安

Yüan Ch'ang 袁敞

Yüan Ting 元鼎

Yün-kang 雲崗

BIBLIOGRAPHY

ABBREVIATIONS USED IN THE NOTES AND BIBLIOGRAPHY

AYFCPK *An-yang fa-chüeh pao-kao* 安陽發掘報告 (Preliminary Reports of Excavations at An-yang), Peiping.

BEFEO *Bulletin de l'école française d'extrême-orient*, Hanoi and Saigon.

BMFEA *Bulletin of the Museum of Far Eastern Antiquities*, Stockholm.

BIHP *Kuo-li chung-yang yen-chiu-yuan li-shih yü-yen yen-chiu-so chi-k'an* 國立中央研究院歷史語言研究所集刊 (Bulletin of the Institute of History and Philology, Academia Sinica), Nanking and Taipei.

BSOAS *Bulletin of School of Oriental and African Studies*, London.

CKHSSLT *Chia-ku-hsüeh Shang-shih lun-ts'ung* 甲骨學商史論叢 (Collected Studies on Shell and Bone Inscriptions), Chengtu.

FEQ *Far Eastern Quarterly*, Ann Arbor, etc.

HJAS *Harvard Journal of Asiatic Studies*, Cambridge, Mass.

JA *Journal Asiatique*, Paris.

JAOS *Journal of the American Oriental Society*, New Haven.

JNCB-RAS *Journal of the North-China Branch of the Royal Asiatic Society*, Shanghai.

JOS *Journal of Oriental Studies*, Hongkong.

JRAS *Journal of the Royal Asiatic Society*, London.

KHCK *Kuo-hsüeh chi-k'an* 國學季刊 (Sinological Quarterly of the National University of Peking), Peiping.

KHCPTS *Kuo-hsüeh chi-pen ts'ung-shu* 國學基本叢書 (Basic Sinological Series), Shanghai.

KHTP *K'o-hsüeh t'ung-pao* 科學通報 (Bulletin of the National Academy of Sciences), Peking.

KKHP *Chung-kuo k'ao-ku hsüeh-pao* 中國考古學報 (Journal of Chinese Archeology), Nos. 2–4, Shanghai; changed to *K'ao-ku hsüeh-pao* (Journal of Archeology) since No. 5, Peking; see also *T'ien-yeh k'ao-ku pao-kao.*

PPKK *Kuo-li pei-p'ing t'u-shu-kuan kuan-k'an* 國立北平圖書館館刊 (Bulletin of the National Library of Peiping), Peiping.

SPPY *Ssu-pu pei-yao* 四部備要 (Essential Writings in Four Divisions), Shanghai.

SPTK *Ssu-pu ts'ung-k'an* 四部叢刊 (Collected Works in Four Divisions), Shanghai.

193

SSCCS　　　*Shih-san-ching chu-su* 十三經注疏 (Commentaries on Thirteen Classics), Nan-ch'ang.

TLTC　　　*Ta-lu tsa-chih* 大陸雜誌 (The Continent Magazine), Taipei.

TP　　　　*T'oung pao*, Leiden.

TSKHCK　　*T'u-shu-kuan-hsüeh chi-k'an* 圖書館學季刊 (Library Science Quarterly), Peiping.

TYKKPK　　*T'ien-yeh k'ao-ku pao-kao* 田野考古報告 (Report of Field Archeology), No. 1, Shanghai; continued as *Chung-kuo k'ao-ku hsüeh pao*.

TYPLWC　　*Ch'ing-chu Ts'ai Yüan-p'ei hsien-sheng liu-shih-wu sui lun-wen-chi* 慶祝蔡元培先生六十五歲論文集 (Studies Presented to Ts'ai Yüan-p'ei on His Sixty-fifth Birthday), Shanghai.

WCAIS　　　*Hai-ning Wang Ching-an hsien-sheng i-shu* 海寧王靜安先生遺書 (Collected Writings of Wang Kuo-wei), Shanghai.

WWTKTL　　*Wen-wu ts'an-k'ao tzu-liao* 文物參考資料 (Materials for the Study of Cultural Objects), Peking.

YCHP　　　*Yen-ching hsüeh-pao* 燕京學報 (Yenching Journal of Chinese Studies), Peiping.

BOOKS AND ARTICLES IN CHINESE, JAPANESE, AND WESTERN LANGUAGES

BARNARD, NOEL. "A Preliminary Study of the Ch'u Silk Manuscript: A New Reconstruction of the Text," *Monumenta Serica*, XVII (1958), 1–11.

BERGMAN, FOLKE. "Travels and Archeological Field-work in Mongolia and Sinkiang," in *History of the Expedition in Asia, 1927–1935*, Part IV (Sino-Swedish Expedition, Publication No. 26). Stockholm: Göteborg Elander, 1945.

BIEN MEI-NIEN. "On the Turtle Remains from the Archeological Site of An-yang, Honan," *Bulletin of the Geological Society of China*, Vol. XVII (1937), No. 1; Extract in W. C. White, *Bone Culture of Ancient China*, p. 51.

BLANCHET, AUGUSTIN. *Essai sur l'histoire du papier*. Paris: E. Leroux, 1900.

BLUM, ANDRE. *On the Origin of Paper*. Translated by HARRY MILLER LYDENBERG. New York: R. R. Bowker Co., 1934.

BODDE, DERK. *China's First Unifier: A Study of the Ch'in Dynasty as Seen in the Life of Li Ssu*. Leiden: E. J. Brill, 1938.

——— (trans.). *Statesman, Patriot, and General in Ancient China*. New Haven: American Oriental Society, 1940.

BOYER, AUGUSTE, M. *Kharosthi Inscriptions Discovered by Sir Aurel Stein in Chinese Turkestan*. Translated by E. J. RAPSON and A. E. SENART. 2 vols. London: Clarendon Press, 1920–27.

BRITTON, ROSWELL S. "Chinese Interstate Intercourse before 700 B.C.," *American Journal of International Law*, XXIX (October, 1935), 616–35.

——. "Oracle-bone Color Pigments," *HJAS*, II (1937), 1–3. With report on microchemical analysis of pigments by Professor A. A. BENEDETTI PICHLER.

BUSHELL, S. W. "The Stone Drums of the Chou Dynasty," *JNCB-RAS*, N. S., No. 8 (1874), pp. 133–79.

CARPENTER, H. C. H. "Preliminary Report on Chinese Bronzes," in *AYF CPK*, No. 4 (1933), 677–79.

CARTER, THOMAS FRANCIS. *The Invention of Printing in China and Its Spread Westward*. New York: Columbia University Press, 1925; 2d ed. rev. by L. C. GOODRICH. New York: Ronald Press, 1955.

CERNY, JAROSLAV. *Paper and Books in Ancient Egypt*. London: H. K. Lewis, 1952.

CHAI CH'I-NIEN 翟耆年 . *Chou shih* 籀史 (Notes on Bronze and Stone Inscriptions), in *Shou-shan-ko ts'ung-shu* 守山閣叢書 (1922).

Chan-kuo ts'e 戰國策 (Plots of the Warring States). Annotated by KAO YU 高誘 (ca. 168–212) and YAO HUNG 姚宏 (ca. 1100–1146). 6 ts'e. Shanghai: Chung Hua Book Co., 1927. *SPPY* ed.

CHANG CHENG-LANG 張政烺 "Wang I chi ya-ch'ien k'ao-cheng 王逸集牙籤考証" ("A Study of the Ivory Label of Wang I's Works"), *BIHP*, XIV (1949), 243–48.

CHANG FENG 張鳳. *Han Chin hsi-ch'ui mu-chien hui-pien* 漢晉西陲木簡彙編 (Wooden Tablets of the Han and Chin Dynasties Discovered in Chinese Turkestan during Aurel Stein's Three Expeditions). Shanghai, 1931.

CHANG HSIN-CH'ENG 張心澂 *Wei-shu t'ung-k'ao* 偽書通考 (A Study of Forged Books). 2 vols. Changsha: Commercial Press, 1939.

CHANG HUAI-HUAN 張懷瓘 *Shu tuan* 書斷 (Comments on Calligraphy and Calligraphers), in *Shuo fu* 説郛 (100 chüan ed., 1927), chüan 92.

CHANG KUO-KAN 張國淦 *Li-tai shih-ching k'ao* 歷代石經考 (A History of Stone Classics Engraved during Successive Dynasties). 3 ts'e. Peiping, 1930.

CHANG TE-CHÜN 張德鈞. "Kuan-yü tsao-chih tsai wo-kuo ti fa-chan ho ch'i-yüan ti wen-t'i 關於造紙在我國的發展和起源的問題" (On the Origin and Development of Paper in China), *KHTP*, 1955, No. 10, pp. 85–88.

CHANG YEN-YÜAN 張彥遠. *Fa-shu yao-lu* 法書要錄 (Catalogue of Famous Calligraphy), in *Ching-tai pi-shu* 津逮秘書 (1922).

——. *Li-tai ming-hua chi* 歷代名畫記 (Catalogue of Famous Paintings), in *Ching-tai pi-shu* (1922).

CH'ANG WEN-CHAI 暢文齋 and KU T'IEH-FU 顧鐵符. "Shansi Hung-chao-hsien Fang-tui-ts'un ch'u-t'u ti pu-ku 山西洪趙縣坊堆村出土的卜骨" (Oracle Bones Discovered in Fang-tui-ts'un, Hung-chao, Shansi), *WWTKTL*, 1956, No. 7, p. 27.

Ch'ang-sha fa-chüeh pao-kao 長沙發掘報告 (Report of the Excavation at Ch'ang-sha, Hunan). Peking: Science Press, 1957.

CHAO CH'I 趙岐 (d. 201). *San-fu chüeh-lu* 三輔決錄 (Miscellaneous Notes on the Han Capital), in *Erh-yu-t'ang t'sung-shu* 二酉堂叢書 (1821).

CHAO HSI-KU 趙希鵠 (ca. 1200). *Tung-t'ien ch'ing-lu* 洞天清錄, in *Shuo fu* (1647).

CHAO T'IEH-HAN 趙鐵寒. "Tu Hsi-p'ing shih-ching ts'an-pei chi 讀熹平石經殘碑記" (Notes on a Fragment of Stone Classics of the Second Century A.D.), *TLTC*, X, No. 5 (1955), 145–55.

CHAO WAN-LI 趙萬里. *Han Wei Nan-pei-ch'ao mu-chih chi-shih* 漢魏南北朝墓誌集釋 (Collected Inscriptions on Grave Tablets of the 2d–7th Centuries). 6 ts'e. Peking: Science Press, 1955.

CHAO YEN-WEI 趙彥衛. *Yün-lu man-ch'ao* 雲麓漫鈔, in *Pieh-hsia-chai ts'ung-shu* 別下齋叢書 (1856).

CHAVANNES, ÉDOUARD. *Les documents chinois découverts par Aurel Stein dans les sables du Turkestan Oriental*. Oxford: Imprimerie de l'Université, 1913.

———. "Les livres chinois avant l'invention du papier," *JA*, series 10, V (1905), 1–75.

———. *Mission archéologique dans la Chine septentrionale*. 2 vols. and plates. Paris: Ernest Leroux, 1909–15.

CH'EN MENG-CHIA 陳夢家. "Chi-chung chu-shu k'ao 汲冢竹書考" (A study of the Bamboo Tablets Discovered in the Wei Tomb in the Third Century A.D.), *T'u-shu chi-k'an* 圖書季刊, N.S., V, Nos. 2/3 (1944), 1–15.

———. *Hai-wai chung-kuo t'ung-ch'i t'u-lu* 海外中國銅器圖錄 "Chinese Bronzes in Foreign Collections"). 2 ts'e. Shanghai: Commercial Press, 1946. With a preface in English.

———. *Yin-hsü pu-t'zu tsung-shu* 殷虛卜辭綜述 (An Introduction to the Oracle Bone Inscriptions from the Shang Ruins). Peking: Science Press, 1956.

CH'EN P'AN 陳槃. "Ch'ang-sha ku-mu chüan-chih ts'ai-hui chao-p'ien hsiao-chi 長沙古墓絹質綵繪照片小記" (Notes on the Copy of the Silk Document from the Ancient Tomb of Ch'ang-sha), *BIHP*, XXIV (1953), 193–96.

———. "Hsien-Ch'in liang-Han chien-tu k'ao 先秦兩漢簡牘考" (A Study of the Tablets of the Pre-Han and Han Dynasties), *Hsüeh-shu chi-k'an* 學術季刊, I, No. 4 (June, 1953), 1–13.

———. "Hsien-Ch'in liang-Han po-shu k'ao 先秦兩漢帛書考" (A Study of the Silk Documents of the Pre-Han and Han Dynasties), *BIHP*, XXIV (1953), 185–96. With an appendix on the silk document from Ch'ang-sha.

———. "Man-t'an ti-chüan 漫談地莽" (On the Grave Deeds), *TLTC*, II, No. 6 (1951), 3, 12.

———. "Yu ku-tai p'iao-hsü yin lun tsao-chih 由古代漂絮因論造紙" (On the Invention of Paper from the Process of Stirring Refuse Silk), *Annals of Academia Sinica*, I (1954), 257–65.

CH'EN TENG-YÜAN 陳登元. *Ku-chin tien-chi chü-san k'ao* 古今典籍聚散考 (Collection and Dispersion of Chinese Books from Ancient Times to the Present). Shanghai: Commercial Press, 1936.

CH'EN YÜAN 陳垣. *Tun-huang chieh-yü lu* 敦煌劫餘錄 (Catalogue of Tun-huang

Rolls in the National Library of Peiping). 6 ts'e. Peiping: Institute of History and Philology, Academia Sinica, 1931.

CH'EN YÜAN-LUNG 陳元龍 (1652–1736). *Ko-chih ching-yüan* 格致鏡原 (An Encyclopedia of Scientific and Technical Origins). 24 ts'e. 1735.

CHENG CHEN-TO 鄭振鐸. "Building the New, Uncovering the Old," *China Reconstructs*, November–December, 1954, pp. 18–22.

———. *Wei-ta ti i-shu ch'uan-t'ung t'u-lu* 偉大的藝術傳統圖錄 (The Great Heritage of Chinese Art), first series. Shanghai: Shanghai Publishing Co., 1951–52.

CH'ENG TA-CH'ANG 程大昌 (1123–1195). *Yen fan lu* 演繁露, in *Hsüeh-ching t'ao-yüan* 學津討原 (Han Feng Lou ed.)

CHI HAN 嵇含 (d. 306). *Nan-fang ts'ao-mu chuang* 南方草木狀 (Flora of the Southern Regions), in *Han Wei ts'ung-shu* 漢魏叢書 (1925).

CHI HSIEN-LIN 李羨林. "Chung-kuo chih ho tsao-chih-fa shu-ju Yin-tu ti shih-chien ho ti-tien wen-t'i 中國紙和造紙法輸入印度的時間和地點問題" (On the Date and Place of the Introduction of Chinese Paper and Its Method of Manufacture to India), *Li-shih yen-chiu* 歷史研究, August, 1954, No. 4, pp. 25–52.

CHIA SSU-HSIEH 賈思勰 (5th century). *Ch'i-min yao-shu* 齊民要術 (Important Arts for the People's Welfare). 4 ts'e. Shanghai: Commercial Press, 1929. *SPTK* ed. See also under Shih Sheng-han.

CHIANG HSÜAN-I 蔣玄怡. *Ch'ang-sha: Ch'u min-tsu chi ch'i i-shu* 長沙: 楚民族及其藝術 ("Changsha: The Ch'u Tribe and Its Art"). Vol. I–II. Shanghai: Kunst-archaological Society, 1950.

CHIANG SHAO-SHU 美紹書. *Yün-shih-chai pi-t'an* 韻石齋筆談, in *Chih-pu-tsu-chai ts'ung-shu* 知不足齋鎹書 (1921), first series.

CHIANG-SU T'UNG-CHIH-CHÜ 江蘇通志局. *Chiang-su chin-shih chih* 江蘇金石志 (Bronze and Stone Inscriptions of Kiangsu Province). 26 ts'e. 1927.

CHIANG T'ING-HSI 蔣廷錫 (1669–1732) and others. *Ku chin t'u-shu chi-ch'eng* 古今圖書集成 (An Imperial Encyclopedia). 808 ts'e. Shanghai: Chung Hua Book Co., 1934.

CHIEN PO-TSAN 翦伯贊. *Chung-kuo shih-kang* 中國史綱 (Outline of Chinese History). Vols. I–II. Shanghai: Life Publishing Co., 1947.

CHIN HSIANG-HENG 金祥恆. *Hsü chia-ku-wen pien* 續甲骨文編 Supplement to Sun's Dictionary of Bone and Shell Inscriptions). 4 ts'e. Taipei, 1959.

Chin shu. See Fang Hsüan-ling.

Chiu T'ang shu. See Liu Hsü.

CHOU CHAO-HSIANG. "Pottery of the Chou Dynasty," *BMFEA*, I (1929), 29–37. Plates.

CHOU CH'UAN-JU 周傳儒. "The Study of Inscriptions on the Oracle Bones," *Philobiblon*, I, No. 1 (1946), 3–12.

CHOU I-LIANG 周一良. "Chih yü yin-shua-shu 紙與印刷術" (Paper and Printing), *Hsin-hua yüeh-pao* 新華月報, IV, No. 1 (May, 1951), 186–90.

Chou-li chu-shu 周禮注疏 (Commentaries on the Rituals of Chou). Annotated by CHENG HSÜAN 鄭玄 (127–200), LU TE-MING 陸德明 (fl. 620), and CHIA KUNG-YEN

賈公彥 (fl. 650) with critical notes by JUAN YÜAN 阮元 (1764–1849). Nanchang, 1887. *SSCCS* ed.

CHU I-TSUN 朱彝尊. *Ch'in-ting jih-hsia chiu-wen k'ao* 欽定日下舊聞考 (Archeological and Historical Descriptions of the Imperial Precincts in Peking and the Immediate Dependencies). Revised under imperial auspices by YÜ MIN-CHUNG 于敏中. 40 ts'e. 1774.

Ch'u wen-wu chan-lan t'u-lu 楚文物展覽圖錄 (Illustrated Catalogue of Exhibit of Cultural Objects of the Ch'u State). Peking: Peking Historical Museum, 1954.

Chuang-tzu 莊子; or, *Nan-hua chen-ching* 南華真經 (The Book of Master Chuang). Annotated by KUO HSIANG 郭象 (fl. 300) and LU TE-MING (fl. 620). Shanghai: Commercial Press, 1929. *SPTK* ed.

Ch'un-ch'iu tso-chuan cheng-i 春秋左傳正義 (Commentaries on the Tso Commentary of the Spring and Autumn Annals). By TU YÜ 杜預 (222–284), LU TE-MING (fl. 620), and K'UNG YING-TA (574–648). Nanchang, 1887. *SSCCS* ed.

Chü-yen Han-chien chia-pien 居延漢簡甲編 (Tablets of the Han Dynasty from Chü-yen, First Series). Peking: Science Press, 1959.

CH'Ü TUI-CHIH 瞿兌之. "Ku-tai chih chu yü wen-hua 古代之竹與文化 " (Bamboo and Ancient Chinese Civilization), *Shih-hsüeh nien-pao* 史學年報, I, No. 2 (1930), 117–22.

Ch'üan-kuo chi-pen chien-she kung-ch'eng chung ch'u-t'u wen-wu chan-lan t'u-lu 全國基本建設工程中出土文物展覽圖錄 (Illustrated Catalogue of an Exhibit of Cultural Objects Excavated during the Nation-wide Construction). 2 ts'e. Peking, 1955.

CLAPPERTON, ROBERT HENDERSON. *Paper: An Historical Account of Its Making by Hand from the Earliest Times Down to the Present Day.* Oxford: Clarendon Press, 1934.

CONRADY, AUGUST (ed.). *Die chinesischen Handschriften und sonstigen Kleinfunde Sven Hedins in Lou-lan.* Stockholm: Generalstabens Lithografiska Anstalt, 1920.

CREEL, HERRLEE GLESSNER. *The Birth of China: A Study of the Formative Period of Chinese Civilization.* New York: John Day, 1937.

———. "Bronze Inscriptions of the Western Chou Dynasty as Historical Documents," *JAOS*, LVI (1936), 335–49.

———. *Confucius: the Man and the Myth.* New York: John Day, 1949.

———. *Studies in Early Chinese Culture*, first series. Baltimore: Waverly Press, 1937.

DIRINGER, DAVID. *The Hand-produced Book.* New York: Philosophical Library, 1953.

DUBS, HOMER (trans.) *The History of the Former Han Dynasty.* Vols. I–III. Baltimore: Waverly Press, 1938–56. See also under Pan Ku.

DU HALDE, JEAN BAPTISTE (1674–1743). *The General History of China.* 4 vols. London: John Watts, 1736–41.

DUYVENDAK, J. J. L. (trans.) *The Book of Lord Shang.* London: Probsthain, 1928.

EDKINS, JOSEPH. "On the Origin of Paper Making in China," *Notes and Queries on China and Japan*, I, No. 6 (June, 1867), 67–68.

Erh-ya chu-su 爾雅注疏 (Commentaries on the Literary Expositor). Annotated by

Kuo P'o 郭璞(276–324) and Hsing Ping 邢昺(932–1010). Nanchang, 1887. *SSCCS* ed.

Erkes, Eduard. "The Use of Writing in Ancient China," *JAOS*, LXI (1941), 127–30.

An Exhibition of Chinese Antiquities from Ch'ang-sha Lent by Cox, March 26 to May 31, 1939 under the Auspices of the Associates in Fine Arts at Yale University. With "A Brief Guide to the Chinese Antiquities from Ch'angsha by John Cox."

Fan Yeh 范曄(398–445). *Hou-Han shu* 後漢書(History of the Later Han Dynasty). Shanghai: T'ung-wen Shu-chü, 1884.

Fang Hsüan-ling 房玄齡(578–648). *Chin shu* 晋書 (History of the Chin Dynasty). Shanghai: T'ung-wen Shu-chü, 1884.

Feng-ni ts'un-chen. See National University of Peking.

Feng Teng-fu 馮登府 (d. 1840). *Che-chiang chuan lu* 浙江磚錄 (Brick Inscriptions of Chekiang Province). 2 ts'e. 1836.

Ferguson, John C. *Li-tai chu-lu chi-chin mu* 歷代著錄吉金目(Catalogue of the Recorded Bronzes of Successive Dynasties). Shanghai: Commercial Press, 1939.

———. *Survey of Chinese Art.* Shanghai: Commercial Press, 1939.

Fu Chen-lun 傅振倫 "Ts'ai Ching-chung tsao-chih k'ao 蔡敬重造紙考 " (A Study of the Art of Paper-making by Ts'ai Lun), *Bulletin of the Library Association of China*, Vol. VIII (1933), No. 1.

Fu Hsüan 傅玄 (217–278). *Fu Shun-ku chi* 傅鶉觚集(Collected Writings of Fu Hsüan). 2 ts'e. 1876.

Fung Yu-lan 馮友蘭. *A Short History of Chinese Philosophy.* New York: Macmillan, 1953.

Giles, Lionel. "Dated Chinese Manuscripts in the Stein Collection," *BSOAS*, VII (1935), 809–36; VIII (1953), 1–26; IX (1937), 1–25; X (1940) 317–44; XI (1943), 148–73.

Goodrich, L. Carrington. "Paper: A Note on Its Origin," *Isis*, XLII, Part 2, No. 128 (June, 1951), 145.

———. *A Short History of the Chinese People.* Rev. ed. New York: Harper & Bros. 1951.

Han-fei-tzu 韓非子(The Book of Master Han Fei). Shanghai: Commercial Press, 1929. *SPTK* ed. Partially translated by W. K. Liao, *The Complete Works of Han Fei Tzu* (Vols. I–II; London: Probsthain, 1939–59).

Han-shih wai-chuan. See Han Ying.

Han shu. See Pan Ku.

Han Ying 韓嬰(2d century B.C.). *Han-shih wai-chuan* 韓詩外傳 Shanghai: Commercial Press, 1929. *SPTK* ed.

Hansford, Sidney Howard. *A Glossary of Chinese Art and Archeology.* London: China Society, 1954.

Henning, W. B. "The Date of the Sogdian Ancient Letters," *BSOAS*, XII (1948), 601–15.

Hiraoka Takeo 平岡武夫. "Chikusatsu to Shina kodai no kiroku 竹册上支那古代の記録" (Bamboo Tablets as Records of Ancient China), *Tōhō gakuho* (Kyoto), XIII (1943), 163–88.

HIRTH, FRIEDRICH. *China and the Roman Orient: Researches into Their Ancient and Medieval Relations as Represented in Old Chinese Records.* Shanghai and Hongkong: Kelly & Walsh, 1885.

———. "Die Erfindung des Papiers in China," *TP*, I (1890), 1–14.

Ho I-HSING 郝懿行 (1757–1825). *Shan-hai-ching chien su* 山海經箋疏 (Commentaries on the Classic of Mountains and Seas). 4 ts'e. 1881.

HOERNLE, A. F. RUDOLPH. "Who Was the Inventor of Rag-paper?" *JRAS* (1903), pp. 663–84.

Ho-pei ti-i po-wu-yüan pan-yüeh-k'an 河北第一博物院半月刊. No. 35, 1933.

Hou-Han shu. See Fan Yeh.

Hsi-ching tsa-chi 西京雜記 (Miscellaneous Records of the Western Capital). Attributed to LIU HSIN 劉歆 (d. A.D. 23) and compiled by KO HUNG 葛洪 (234–305). Shanghai: Commercial Press, 1929. *SPTK* ed.

HSIA NAI. "Arts and Crafts of 2300 Years Ago," *China Reconstructs*, January–February, 1954, pp. 31–35.

———. "Hsin-hu chih Tun-huang Han-chien 新獲之敦煌漢簡," *BIHP*, XIX (1948), 235–65.

———. "New Archeological Discoveries," *China Reconstructs*, July–August, 1952, No. 4, pp. 13–18.

HSIAO TZU-HSIEN 蕭子顯 (489–537). *Nan-ch'i shu* 南齊書 (History of the Southern Ch'i Dynasty, 479–502). Shanghai: T'ung-wen Shu-chü, 1884.

HSIEH CHAO-CHIH 謝肇淛. *Wu tsa-tsu* 五雜組. 16 ts'e. Ming Wan-li (1573–1620) ed.

Hsin T'ang shu. See Ou-yang Hsiu.

HSÜ CHIEN 徐堅 (659–729) and others. *Ch'u-hsüeh chi* 初學記 (Entry into Learning, a T'ang Encyclopedia). 12 ts'e. 1883.

HSÜ KUO-LIN 許國霖. *Tun-huang shih-shih hsieh-ching t'i-chi* 敦煌石室寫經題記 (Notes on Tun-huang Manuscripts). 2 ts'e. Shanghai: Commercial Press, 1937.

HU HOU-HSÜAN 胡厚宣. "Chia-ku-hsüeh hsü-lun 甲骨學緒論" (Introduction to the Study of Shell and Bone Inscriptions), *CKHSSLT*, second series (Chengtu: Ch'i-lu University, 1945), II, 1–11.

———. "Ch'i-hou pien-ch'ien yü Yin-tai ch'i-hou chih chien-t'ao 氣候變遷與殷代氣候之檢討" ("Climate Change and a Study of the Climate Conditions of the Yin Dynasty"), *CKHSSLT*, second series, II, 1–64.

———. *Wu-shih-nien chia-ku-hsüeh lun-chu mu* 五十年甲骨學論著目 (A Bibliography of the Study of Shell and Bone Inscriptions, 1899–1949). Shanghai: Chung Hua Book Co., 1952.

———. *Wu-shih-nien chia-ku-wen fa-hsien ti tsung-chieh* 五十年甲骨文發現的總結 (A summary of Fifty Years' Discoveries of Shell and Bone Inscriptions). Shanghai: Commercial Press, 1951.

———. "Wu-ting shih wu-chung chi-shih k'o-tz'u k'ao 武丁時五種記事刻辭考" (On the Five Types of Non-oracle Inscriptions of the Wu-ting Period), *CKHSSLT*, first series (Chengtu: Ch'i-lu University, 1944), III, 1–73.

——. *Yin-hsü fa-chüeh* 殷虛發掘 (Excavation of the Shang Ruins). Shanghai: Hsüeh-hsi Sheng-huo Ch'u-pan-she, 1955.

——. "Yin-tai pu-kuei chih lai-yüan 殷代卜龜之來源 " (Sources of Oracle Shells of the Shang Dynasty), *CKHSSLT*, first series, IV, 1–23.

Iuai-nan-tzu 淮南子 (Writings Collected by Liu An, the Prince of Huai-nan). Shanghai: Commercial Press, 1929. *SPTK* ed.

IUANG CHÜN 黃濬. *Heng-chai chi-chin shih-hsiao-lu* 衡齋吉金識小錄 (Miscellaneous Bronze Objects in the Huang Collection). 2 ts'e. Peiping: Tsun-ku Chai, 1937.

IUANG WEN-PI 黃文弼. *Kao-ch'ang chuan-chi* 高昌專集 (Collection of Brick Inscriptions from the Kao-ch'ang Kingdom). Peiping: Scientific Expedition to the Northwestern Regions, 1931.

——. *T'u-lu-fan k'ao-ku chi* 吐魯蕃考古記 (Archeology of Turfan). Peking: National Academy of Sciences, 1954.

Iui-hsien fa-chüeh pao-kao 輝縣發掘報告 (Report of the Excavation at Hui-hsien, Honan). Peking: Science Press, 1956.

IULSEWÉ, A. F. P. "Les insignes en deux parties (fou) sous la dynastie des T'ang (618–907)", *TP*, XLV (1957), 1–50.

IUMMEL, ARTHUR W. "The Development of the Book in China," *JAOS*, LXI (1941), 71–76.

IUNG I-HSÜAN 洪頤煊 (1765–1834). *P'ing Ching tu-pei chi* 平津讀碑記 (Stone Inscriptions from Peiping and Tientsin), in *Hsing-shu-ts'ao-t'ang ts'ung-shu* 行素草堂叢書 (1888), ts'e 25–28.

IUNTER, DARD. *Paper-making: The History and Technique of an Ancient Craft*. 2d ed. rev. and enl. New York: Alfred A. Knopf, 1947.

-li chu-su 儀禮注疏 (Commentaries on the Book of Etiquette and Ceremonial). Annotated by CHENG HSÜAN (127–200) and CHIA KUNG-YEN (fl. 650). Nanchang, 1887. *SSCCS* ed. See also Steele, John (trans).

-wen lei-chü. See Ou-yang Hsün.

IAO TSUNG-I 饒宗頤 *Ch'ang-sha ch'u-t'u Ch'u-chien ch'u-shih* 長沙出土楚簡初釋 (A Preliminary Study of the Inscriptions on the Bamboo Tablets Discovered at Ch'ang-sha). Kyoto, 1954. Mimeographed ed.

——. *Chan-kuo Ch'u-chien chien-cheng* 戰國楚簡箋証 (Study of the Inscriptions on the Bamboo Tablets from the Ch'u State of the Warring States Period.). Hongkong, 1955. A revision of the above.

——. "Ch'ang-sha Ch'u-mu shih-chan-sheng-wu t'u-chuan kao-shih 長沙楚墓時占神物圖卷考釋" (A Study of an Astrological Picture from a Ch'ang-sha Tomb of the Warring States Period), *JOS*, I (January, 1954), 69–84.

——. *Ch'ang-sha ch'u-t'u chan-kuo tseng-shu hsin-shih* 長沙出土戰國繒書新釋 ("A Study of the Ch'u Silk Document with a New Reconstruction of the Text"). Hongkong, 1958.

IUAN YÜAN 阮元. *Chi-ku-chai chung-ting i-ch'i k'uan-shih* 積古齋鐘鼎彝器欵識 (Inscriptions on Bronzes in the Juan Collection). 4 ts'e. 1804.

JUNG KENG 容庚. *Chin-wen pien* 金文編(Dictionary of Bronze Inscriptions of the Shang and Chou Dynasties). Rev. ed. 5 ts'e. Shanghai: Commercial Press, 1939.

———. *Chin-wen hsü-pien* 金文續編(Dictionary of Bronze Inscriptions of the Ch'in and Han Dynasties). 2 ts'e. Shanghai: Commercial Press, 1935.

———. "Ch'in-shih-huang k'o-shih k'ao 秦始皇刻石考 " (A Study of the Stone Inscriptions Engraved by the First Emperor of Ch'in), *YCHP*, XVII (1935), 125–71.

———. *Ku shih-k'o ling-shih* 古石刻零拾 (Studies of Some Early Stone Inscriptions). Peiping, 1934.

———. "Niao-shu k'ao 鳥書考" (A Study of the Bird Script), *YCHP*, XVI (1934), 195–203; Supplement, XVII (1935), 173–78.

———. *Shang Chou i-ch'i t'ung-k'ao* 商周彝器通考 (A General Treatise on the Sacrificial Bronzes of the Shang and Chou Dynasties). 2 vols. Peiping: Harvard-Yenching Institute, 1941.

KAO CH'Ü-HSÜN 高去尋. "Yin-tai ti i-mien t'ung-ching chi-ch'i hsiang-kuan chih wen-t'i 殷代的一面銅鏡及其相關之問題 " ("Problems of the Bronze Mirror Dis covered from a Shang Burial"), *BIHP*, XXIV (1958), 685–719.

K'ao-ku t'ung-hsün 考古通訊(Bulletin of Archeology). Peking, 1955–58. Continued as *K'ao-ku* since 1959.

KARLBECK, O. "Anyang Moulds," *BMFEA*, VII (1935), 39–60. Plates 1–VII.

KARLGREN, BERNHARD. "Ancient Chinese Terms for Textiles," in VIVI SYLWAN, *Investigation of Silk from Edsen-gol and Lop-nor* (Stockholm, 1949), pp. 170–74.

———. "Early Chinese Mirror Inscriptions," *BMFEA*, VI (1934), 9–79.

———. "New Studies on Chinese Bronzes," *BMFEA*, IX (1937), 1–118.

———. "On the Date of the Piao Bells," *BMFEA*, VI (1934), 137–49.

———. "On the Script of the Chou Dynasty," *BMFEA*, VIII (1936), 157–81.

———. "Some Early Chinese Bronze Masters," *BMFEA*, XVI (1944), 1–24.

———. "Yin and Chou in Chinese Bronzes," *BMFEA*, VIII (1936), 9–156. Plates I–LVIII.

KENYON, FREDERICK. *Ancient Books and Modern Discoveries*. Limited Deluxe Ed. Chicago: Caxton Club, 1927.

Ko-chih ching-yüan. See Ch'en Yüan-lung.

KOIZUMI AKIO 小泉顯夫 and HAMADA KŌSAKU 濱田耕作 *Rakurō saikyōzuka* 樂浪彩篋塚("The Tomb of Painted Basket and Other Two Tombs of Lo-lang"). Seoul: Society of the Study of Korean Antiquities, 1934.

KONOW, STEIN. "Note on the Inscription on the Silk-strip No. 34 : 65," in FOLKE BERGMAN, *Archeological Researches in Sinkiang* (Stockholm, 1945), Appendix I, pp. 231–34.

Ku ching t'u-shu chi-ch'eng. See Chiang T'ing-hsi.

Ku-kung chou-k'an 故宮週刊(Weekly Bulletin of the Palace Museum, Peiping). No. 339, 1934.

KU T'ING-LUNG 顧廷龍. *Ku t'ao-wen i-lu* 古匋文舜錄(Dictionary of Pottery Inscriptions). Peiping: National Research Institute of Peiping, 1936.

KU YEN-WU 顧炎武(1613–1682). *Chin-shih wen-tzu chi* 金石文字記 (Description of Bronze and Stone Inscriptions). 2 ts'e. n.d.

KUAN PAO-CH'IEN 關保謙 *I-ch'üeh shih-k'o piao* 伊闕石刻表 (Table of Stone Statues and Inscriptions of Lung-men, Honan). 2 ts'e. 1935.

Kuan tzu 管子 (The Book of Master Kuan). Annotated by FANG HSÜAN-LING 房玄齡 (578–648). Shanghai: Commercial Press, 1929. *SPTK* ed.

Kuang hung-ming chi. See Tao-hsüan.

KUO MAO-CH'IEN 郭茂倩(ed.). *Yüeh-fu shih-chi* 樂府詩集 (Collection of Ancient Songs and Ballads). Shanghai: Commercial Press, 1929. *SPTK*. ed.

KUO MO-JO 郭沫若. *Chin-wen ts'ung-k'ao* 金文叢考 (Miscellaneous Studies of Bronze Inscriptions). 4 ts'e. Tokyo: Bunkyudo Shoten, 1932.

————. *Ku-tai ming-k'o hui-k'ao* 古代銘刻彙考 (Studies of Ancient Inscriptions). 4 ts'e. Tokyo: Bunkyudo Shoten, 1933; Supplement, 1934.

————. "Kuan-yü wan-Chou po-hua ti k'ao-ch'a 關於晚周帛畫的考察" (A Study of the Silk Painting of the Late Chou Period), *Jen-min wen-hsüeh* 人民文學, XI (1953), 113–18; Supplement, XII (1953), 108.

————. *Liang-Chou chin-wen-tz'u ta-hsi* 兩周金文辭大系 (Bronze Inscriptions of the Western and Eastern Chou Dynasties). Tokyo: Bunkyudo Shoten, 1935. *T'u-lu* 圖錄 (Illustrations), 5 ts'e.; *K'ao-shih* 考釋 (Critical Studies), 3 ts'e.

————. *Pu-tz'u t'ung-tsuan* 卜辭通纂 (Studies of the Oracle-bone Inscriptions). 4 ts'e. Tokyo: Bunkyudo Shoten, 1933.

————. *Shih-ku-wen yen-chiu* 石鼓文研究 (A Study of the Inscriptions on the Stone Drums). Changsha: Commercial Press, 1940.

KUO PAO-CHÜN 郭寶鈞. "Chün-hsien Hsin-ts'un ku ts'an-mu chih ch'ing-li 濬縣辛村古殘墓之清理" ("Preliminary Report on the Excavations at Hsin-ts'un, Honan"), *TYKKPK*, I (1936), 167–200.

Kuo yü 國語 (Discourses of the States). Annotated by WEI CHAO 韋昭(197–278). Shanghai: Commercial Press, 1929. *SPTK* ed.

LAO KAN 勞榦. "Chien-tu chung so-chien ti pu po 簡牘中所見的布帛" (Cloth and Silk as Seen in the Inscriptions of Tablets), *Hsüeh-shu chi-k'an*, I, No. 1 (1952), 152–55.

————. *Chü-yen Han-chien k'ao-shih* 居延漢簡考釋 (Decipherment and Critical Studies of the Inscriptions on the Wooden Tablets from Chü-yen). Chungking: Academia Sinica, 1943–44. Ts'e 1–4, *shih-wen*; ts'e 5–6, *kao-chen*. Review by L. C. Goodrich in *FEQ*, XIII, No. 3 (1954), 350–52.

————. *Chü-yen Han-chien* 居延漢簡 ("Documents of the Han Dynasty on Wooden Slips from Edsin Gol"). 2 vols. Taipei: Academia Sinica, 1957–60. A revised edition of the above with plates.

————. "Lun Chung-kuo tsao-chih-shu ti yüan-shih 論中國造紙術的原始" ("The Invention of Paper in China"), *BIHP*, XIX (1948), 489–98.

————. "Shih tzu ti chieh-kou chi shih-kuan ti yüan-shih chih-wu 史字的結構及史

官的原始職務." (On the Formation of the Character *Shih* and the Original Duty of Scribes), *TLTC*, XIV, No. 3 (1957), 65–68.

———. "Tun-huang chi Tun-huang ti hsin shih-liao 敦煌及敦煌的新史料" (Tun-huang and New Historical Sources from Tun-huang), *TLTC*, I, No. 3 (1950), 6–10.

LATOURETTE, KENNETH SCOTT. *The Chinese: Their History and Culture.* 3d ed. New York: Macmillan, 1946.

LAUFER, BERTHOLD. *Jade: A Study in Chinese Archeology and Religion.* Chicago: Field Museum of Natural History, 1912.

———. *Paper and Printing in Ancient China.* Chicago: Caxton Club, 1931.

LE COMTE, LOUIS DANIEL. *Memoirs and Observations.* London: Tooke, 1697.

LEGGE, JAMES (trans.). *The Ch'un Ts'ew with the Tso Chuen.* London: Trübner, 1871.

———. *The Confucian Analects.* London: Trübner, 1861.

———. *The Li Ki.* Oxford: Clarendon Press, 1885. (The Sacred Books of China, Vols. III–IV.)

———. *The Life and Works of Mencius.* London: Trübner, 1875.

———. *The She King.* London: Trübner, 1871.

———. *The Shoo King;* or *The Book of Historical Documents.* London: Trübner, 1865.

LI CHAO 李肇 (fl. 806–820). *T'ang kuo-shih pu* 唐國史補 (Supplements to the History of the T'ang Dynasty), in *Ching-tai pi-shu* (1922).

LI CHI 李濟. *The Beginnings of Chinese Civilization.* Seattle: University of Washington Press, 1957.

———. "Chi Hsiao-t'un ch'u-t'u chih ch'ing-t'ung-ch'i 記小屯出土之青銅器" ("Studies of Hsiao-t'un Bronzes, Pt. I"), *KKHP*, III (1948), 1–99.

———. *Hsi-yin-ts'un shih-ch'ien i-chi* 西陰村史前遺跡 (Prehistoric Remains of Hsi-yin Village, Hsia-hsien, Shansi). Peking: Tsinghua University, 1927.

——— and others. *Ch'eng-tzu-yai* 城子崖 ("Ch'eng-tzu-yai: A Report of Excavations of the Protohistoric Site of Ch'eng-tzu-yai, Li-ch'eng-hsien, Shantung"). Nanking: Academia Sinica, 1935. Translated by KENNETH STARR. New Haven, Conn.: Yale University Press, 1956. (Yale Monograph of Anthropological Studies).

LI CH'IAO-P'ING 李喬苹. *The Chemical Arts of Old China.* Easton, Pa.: Journal of Chemical Education, 1948.

LI FANG 李昉 (925–996) and others. *T'ai-p'ing yü-lan* 太平御覽 (An Imperial Encyclopedia Compiled during the T'ai-p'ing Reign of the Sung Dynasty). Shanghai: Commercial Press, 1935. *SPTK* ed.

LI SHU-HUA 李書華. "Chih wei fa-ming i-ch'ien Chung-kuo wen-tzu liu-ch'uan kung-chü 紙未發明以前中國文字流傳工具" (Materials and Tools of Chinese Writing before the Invention of Paper), *TLTC*, IX, No. 6 (1954), 165–73.

———. "Tsao-chih ti fa-ming chi ch'i ch'uan-po 造紙的發明及其傳播" (The Invention and Spread of Paper), *TLTC*, X, No. 1 (1955), 1–6; No. 2, 53–60.

———. *The Spread of the Art of Paper-making and the Discoveries of Old Paper.* Taipei: National Historical Museum, 1958. Revision and reprint of the above with English text.

————. "Yin-chang yü mou-t'o ti ch'i-yüan 印章與摹搨的起源 ("Origin of the Seal and Ink-squeezing"), *BIHP*, XXVIII, Part I, (1956), 107–21.

————. "The Early Development of Seals and Rubbings", *Tsing Hua Journal of Chinese Studies*, N.S., I (1958), No. 3, 61–87. Revised version of the above in English.

LIANG SHANG-CH'UN 梁上椿. "Chung-kuo ku-ching ming-wen ts'ung-t'an 中國古鏡銘文叢譚" (Studies of Ancient Chinese Mirror Inscriptions), *TLTC*, II (1951), No. 3, 1–5; No. 4, 18–20; No. 5, 16–20.

————. "Sui T'ang shih ching chih yen-chiu 隋唐式鏡之研究" (Studies of Mirrors of the Sui and T'ang Dynasties), *TLTC*, VI, No. 6 (1953), 189–91.

LIANG SSU-YUNG 梁思永, "Hsiao-tun Lung-shan yü Yang-shao 小屯龍山與仰韶," *TYPLWC*, II, 555–68.

LIN YÜ-T'ANG. 林語堂 *A History of the Press and Public Opinion in China*. Chicago: University of Chicago Press, 1936.

LIU CHEN 劉珍 (fl. 107–125). *Tung-kuan Han chi* 東觀漢記 (An official History of the Later Han Dynasty). Shanghai: Chung Hua Book Co., n.d. *SPPY* ed.

LIU HSI 劉熙 (fl. 200). *Shih ming* 釋名 (Expositions of Names, a Dictionary). Shanghai: Commercial Press, 1929. *SPTK* ed.

LIU HSÜ 劉昫 (887–946) and others. *Chiu T'ang shu* 舊唐書 (Old History of the T'ang Dynasty, 618–906). Shanghai: T'ung-wen Shu-chü, 1884.

LIU T'I-CHIH 劉體智. *Hsiao-chiao-ching-ko chin-wen t'o-pen* 小校經閣金文拓本 (Bronze Inscriptions in the Liu Collection). 18 ts'e. 1935.

LIU YÜ-HSIA 劉嶼霞. "Yin-tai yeh-t'ung-shu chih yen-chiu 殷代冶銅術之研究" (A Study of Metallic Techniques of the Bronze of the Shang Dynasty), in *AYFCPK*, No. 4 (1933), pp. 681–96.

LO CHEN-YÜ 羅振玉. *Chen-sung-t'ang chi-ku i-wen* 貞松堂集古遺文 (Miscellaneous Inscriptions in the Lo Collection). 8 ts'e. 1931.

————. *Ch'in Han wa-tang wen-tzu* 秦漢瓦當文字 (Roof Tile Inscriptions of the Ch'in and Han Dynasties). 2 ts'e. 1914.

————. *Han Chin shu-ying* 漢晉書影 (Books of Han and Chin Dynasties). 1918.

————. *Ku ch'i-wu fan t'u-lu* 古器物范圖錄 (Illustrations of Ancient Molds). 1916.

————. *Ku ching t'u-lu* 古鏡圖錄 (Illustrations of Ancient Mirrors). 1916.

————. *Liu-sha chui-chien* 流沙墜簡 (Wooden Tablets from the Northwestern Desert). 3 ts'e. 1915.

————. *Yin-hsü shu-ch'i ching-hua* 殷虛書契菁華 (Choice of Bone Inscriptions). 1914.

————. *Yin-hsü shu-ch'i k'ao-shih* 殷虛書契考釋 (Critical Studies of Bone Inscriptions from the Shang Ruins). Rev. ed., 1927.

————. *Yin wen ts'un* 殷文存 (Collection of Shang Bronze Inscriptions). 1917. See also under Wang Ch'en.

LO FU-I 羅福頤 *Ku-nien wen-tzu cheng* 古鈢文字徵; *Han-yin wen-tzu cheng* 漢印文字徵 (Dictionary of Pre-Han and Han Seal Inscriptions). 8 ts'e. 1930.

————. "T'an Ch'ang-sha fa-hsien ti Chan-kuo chu-chien 談長沙發現的戰國竹

簡 ” (On the Bamboo Tablets of the Warring States Period Discovered at Ch'ang-sha), *WWTKTL*, 1954, No. 9, pp. 87–90.

Lo Ken-tse 羅根澤. "Chan-kuo ch'ien wu ssu-chia chu-tso shuo 戰國前無私家著作說 ” (Absence of Books by Individual Writers before the Warring States Period), *Ku-shih pien* 古史辨, IV (1933), 9–14, 29–61.

Loehr, Max. *Chinese Bronze Age Weapons*. Ann Arbor: University of Michigan Press, 1956.

Lu Yu 陸友 (14th century). *Mu shih* 墨史 (History of Ink), in *Chih-pu-tsu-chai ts'ung-shu* (1921).

Lun heng. See Wang Ch'ung.

Lü-shih ch'un-ch'iu 呂氏春秋　(Spring and Autumn of Master Lü), attributed to Lü Pu-wei 呂不韋　(290–235 b.c.). Shanghai: Commercial Press, 1929. *SPTK* ed.

Ma ang 馬昂. *Huo-pu wen-tzu k'ao* 貨布文字考 (A Study of Numismatic Inscriptions). 2 ts'e. 1924.

Ma Heng 馬衡. "Chi Han Chü-yen pi 記漢居延筆 ” (On the Brush-pen from Chü-yen), *KHCK*, III (1932), 67–72.

————. "Chung-kuo shu-chi chih-tu yen-chiu 中國書籍制度研究 ” ("A Brief Sketch of the Evolution of the Chinese Book"), *TSKHCK*, I, No. 2 (1926), 199–213.

————. *Han shih-ching chi-ts'un* 漢石經集存 (Collected Inscriptions of Han Stone Classics). 2 ts'e. Peking: Science Press, 1957.

————. "Han shih-ching kai-shu 漢石經概述 ” (A Treatise on the Stone Classics of the Han Dynasty), *KKHP*, No. 10 (1955), pp. 1–9.

————. "Shih-k'o 石刻 ” (A Treatise on Stone Inscriptions),　*K'ao-ku t'ung-hsün* 考古通訊 , 1956, No, 1, 49–56.

————. "Shih-ku wei Ch'in k'o-shih k'ao 石鼓為秦刻石考 ” ("In Defense of the Theory that the 'Stone Drum' Inscriptions Were Made by the Ch'in State"), *KHCK*, I (1923), 17–23.

————. "Ts'ung shih-yen shang k'uei-chien Han shih-ching chih i-pan 從實驗上窺見漢石經之一班 ” (Han Stone Classics as Seen from Original Objects), *TYPLWC* I (1933), 65–72.

Ma Hsü-lun 馬叙倫. "Shih-ku wei Ch'in-wen-kung shih wu k'ao 石鼓為秦文公時物考 "(Stone Drums as Objects Made during the Period of Duke Wen, 765–716 b.c.), *PPKK*, VII, No. 2 (1933), 1–3.

Ma Te-chih 馬得志 and others. "I-chiu-wu-san-nien An-yang Ta-ssu-k'ung-ts'un fa-chüeh pao-kao 一九五三年安陽大司空村發掘報告” (Report of the Excavation of Ta-ssu-k'ung Village, Anyang, in 1953), *KKHP*, IX (1955), 25–90.

Ma Tuan-lin 馬端臨 (fl. 1254–1322). *Wen-hsien t'ung-k'ao* 文獻通考 (An Encyclopedia of Institutions). 2 vols. Shanghai: Commercial Press, 1936. *Wan-yu wen-k'u* ed.

Maspero, Henri, *Les documents chinois de la troisième expédition de Sir Aurel Stein en Asie Centrale*. London: British Museum, 1953. Introduction translated by L. C. Goodrich, *BIHP*, XXVIII (1956), 197–218.

Mei Yi-pao 梅貽寶 (trans.). *The Ethical and Political Works of Motse*. London: Probsthain, 1929.

Miao Ch'üan-sun 繆荃孫(1844–1919). *Shun-t'ien-fu chih* 順天府志(Local History of Shun-t'ien Prefecture, Chih-li Province). 64 ts'e. 1885.

Mori Shikazō 森鹿三. "Kyoen Kankan kenkyū josetsu 居延漢簡研究序説 " ("Introduction to the Studies of the Etsin-gol MSS. Discovered by Sven Hedin in Chinese Turkestan"), *Tōyō-shi kenkyū*, XII, No. 3 (1953), 193–203.

Mu-t'ien-tzu chuan 穆天子傳 (Account of the Travels of King Mu). Annotated by Kuo P'o 郭璞(276–324). Shanghai: Commercial Press, 1929. *SPTK* ed.

Nagasawa Kikuya 長澤規矩也. *Shoshigaku josetsu* 書誌學序説(Introduction to Bibliography). Tokyo: Yoshikawa Kōbunkan, 1960.

Naitō Toranjirō 内藤虎次郎. "Shi no wa 紙の話" (Talks on Paper), in *Tōyō bunkashi kenkyū* (Tokyo), 1933, 75–84.

Nan-ch'i shu. See Hsiao Tzu-hsien.

Nan-hua chen-ching. See Chuang-tzu.

National University of Peking. *Feng-ni ts'un-chen* 封泥存真(Inscribed Sealing Clay in the Collection of the National University of Peking). Shanghai: Commercial Press, 1934.

Oba Tsunekichi 小場恒吉 and Kayamoto Kamejirō 榧本龜次郎.*Rakurō Ō Kō no haka* 樂浪王光墓(The Tomb of Wang Kuang of Lo-lang). Seoul: Society of the Study of Korean Antiquities, 1935.

Ou-yang Hsiu 歐陽修(1007–1072). *Chi ku lu* 集古錄(Catalogue of Antique Inscriptions), in *Hsing-su-ts'ao-t'ang ts'ung-shu* (1887), ts'e 1–3.

———. *Hsin T'ang shu* 新唐書 (New History of the T'ang Dynasty). Shanghai: T'ung-wen Shu-chü, 1884.

Ou-yang Hsün 歐陽詢(557–641). *I-wen lei-chü* 藝文類聚 (Classified Encyclopedia of Literary Records). 32 ts'e. 1879.

Pai Chü-i 白居易 and K'ung Ch'uan 孔傳. *Pai K'ung liu-t'ien* 白孔六帖(Pai's Classified Encyclopedia Enlarged by K'ung). 32 ts'e. Ming Chia-ching (1522–66) ed.

Pan Ku 班固(32–92). *Han shu* 漢書 (History of the Former Han Dynasty). Shanghai: T'ung-wen Shu-chü, 1884. For translation see Homer Dubs.

Pelliot, Paul. "Une bibliothèque mediévale retrouvée au Kan-sou," *BEFEO*, VIII (1908), 501–29.

———. "Les bronzes de la collection Eumorfopoulos publiés par M. W. P. Yetts, I et II," *TP*, XXVII (1930), 359–406.

———. *Les débuts de l'imprimerie en Chine.* Paris: Imprimerie Nationale, 1953.

——— and Lu Hsiang 陸翔. "Pa-li t'u-shu-kuan Tun-huang hsieh-pen shu-mu 巴黎 圖書館敦煌寫本書目" (A Catalogue of Tun-huang MSS. Preserved in the Bibliothèque Nationale, Paris), *PPKK*, VII, No. 6 (1933), 21–72; VIII, No. 1 (1934), 27–87.

Pi Yüan 畢沅(1730–1797) and Juan Yüan 阮元(1764–1849). *Shan-tso chin-shih chih* 山左金石志 (Bronze and Stone Inscriptions from Hopei Province). 12 ts'e. 1797.

Ping Chih 秉志. "Ho-nan An-yang chih kuei-k'o 河南安陽之龜殼 " (Turtle Shells from Anyang, Honan), *AYFCPK*, No. 3 (1931), pp. 443–46.

*Saiiki kōko zufu*西域考古圖譜(Illustrations of the Archeological Explorations in Northwest Regions). Preface by OTANI KOZUI大谷光瑞. 2 pts. Tokyo: Kokka-sha, 1915.

San-fu chüeh-lu. See Chao Ch'i.

San-fu ku-shih 三輔故事 (Anecdotes Concerning the Han Capital), edited by Chang Chu 張澍(1781–1848), in *Erh-yu-t'ang ts'ung-shu* (1821).

SCHINDLER, B. "Preliminary Account of the Work of Henri Maspero Concerning the Chinese Documents on Wood and Paper Discovered by Sir Aurel Stein on His Third Expedition in Central Asia," *Asia Major*, N.S., I (1949), 216–64.

Shan-hai-ching chien-su. See Ho I-hsing.

SHANG CH'ENG-TSU 商承祚. *Ch'ang-sha ku-wu wen-chien-chi*長沙古物聞見記(An Account of the Antique Objects Discovered at Ch'angsha). 2 ts'e. Chengtu: University of Nanking, 1939.

————. *Shih-k'o chuan-wen pien*石刻篆文編(A Collection of Seal Script in Stone Inscriptions). 2 ts'e. Peking: Science Press, 1957.

————. *Yin-ch'i i-ts'un*殷契佚存(Some Bone Inscriptions of the Shang Dynasty from Private Collections). 2 ts'e. Nanking: University of Nanking, 1933.

Shang-shu cheng-i 尚書正義 (Commentaries on the Book of Documents). Annotated by K'ung An-kuo (fl. 91 B.C.), Lu Te-ming (fl. A.D. 620), and K'ung Ying-ta (A.D. 574–649). Nanchang, 1887. *SSCCS* ed. For translation see James Legge, *The Shoo King.*

SHAO PO邵博. "Shao-shih wen-chien hou-chi邵氏聞見後記," in *Hsüeh-ching t'ao-yüan*, series 18.

SHEN K'UO沈括(1032–1096). *Meng-ch'i pi-t'an*夢溪筆談(Miscellaneous Jottings). Shanghai: Commercial Press, 1934. *SPTK* ed.

SHIH CHANG-JU石璋如. "Ku-pu yü kuei-pu t'an-yüan骨卜與龜卜探源" (Origin of Divination with Bones and Shells), *TLTC*, VIII, No. 9 (1954), 265–69.

————. "Shang Chou i-ch'i ming-wen pu-wei li-lüeh 商周彝器銘文部位 例略" (A Study of the Location of Bronze Inscriptions of the Shang and Chou Dynasties), *TLTC*, VIII, No. 5 (1954), 129–34.

————. "Ti-ch'i-tz'u yin-hsü fa-chüeh弟七次殷墟發掘"(The Seventh Excavation of the Shang Ruins), *AYFCPK*, IV (1933), 709–28.

————. "Yin-hsü tsui-chin chih chung-yao fa-hsien殷墟最近之重要發現" (Recent Important Discoveries from the Shang Ruins), *KKHP*, II (1947), 1–81.

Shih chi. See Ssu-ma Ch'ien.

Shih ming. See Liu Hsi.

SHIH SHENG-HAN石聲漢. *Ch'i-min yao-shu chin-shih* 齊民要術今釋(New Commentaries on the *Ch'i-min yao-shu*). 4 vols. Peking: Science Press, 1957–58. See also Chia Ssu-hsieh.

SHIH SHU-CH'ING 史樹青. *Ch'ang-sha Yang-t'ien-hu ch'u-t'u Ch'u chien yen-chiu* 長沙仰天湖出土楚簡研究(A Study of the Bamboo Tablets from the Ch'u State Discovered at Yang-t'ien-hu, Ch'angsha, Hunan). Shanghai: Ch'ün Lien She, 1955.

SHIMADA KAN島田翰. *Ku-wen chiu-shu k'ao* 古文舊書考 (A Study of Ancient Chinese Books). 5 ts'e. Peking, 1927.

Shodō zenshū 書道全集 (Collection of Chinese and Japanese Calligraphy). Ed. by SHIMONAKA YASABURŌ下中彌三郎and others. Vols. I–VIII (Shang to T'ang dynasties). Tokyo: Heido-sha, 1954–60.

*Shui-ching chu*水經注(Commentary on the Waterways Classic). Annotated by LI TAO-YÜAN 酈道元(d. 527). Shanghai: Commercial Press, 1929. *SPTK* ed.

Shuo fu. See T'ao Tsung-i.

SSU-MA CH'IEN司馬遷(*ca.* 145–86 B.C.). *Shih chi*史記(The Records of the Grand Historiographer). Shanghai: T'ung-wen Shu-chü, 1884. Partially translated by ÉDOUARD CHAVANNES, *Les mémoires historiques de Se-ma Ts'ien*. 5 vols. Paris, 1900. BURTON WATSON, *Records of the Grand Historian of China*. 2 vols. New York: Columbia University Press, 1961.

STEELE, JOHN (trans.). *The I-li*; or, *Book of Etiquette and Ceremonial*. London: Probsthain, 1917.

STEIN, MARK AUREL. *Ancient Khotan*: *Detailed Report of Archeological Exploration in Chinese Turkestan*. 2 vols. Oxford: Clarendon Press, 1907.

———. "Notes on Ancient Chinese Documents Discovered along the Han Frontier Wall in the Desert of Tun-huang," *New China Review*, III (1921), 243—53.

———. *Serindia*: *Detailed Report of Explorations in Central Asia and Westernmost China*. 4 vols. Oxford: Clarendon Press, 1921.

SU I-CHIEN蘇易簡(953–996). *Wen-fang ssu-p'u* 文房四譜(Collected Studies of the Four Articles for Writing in a Scholar's Studio), in *Shih-wan-chüan-lou ts'ung-shu* 十萬卷樓叢書(1879).

SU YING-HUI蘇瑩輝. "Chung-yang-t'u-shu-kuan so-ts'ang Han-chien chung ti hsin shih-liao中央圖書館所藏漢簡中的新史料 " (New Historical Sources in the Wooden Tablets of the Han Dynasty in the Collection of the National Central Library), *TLTC*, III, No. 1 (1951), 23–25.

Sui-shu. See Wei Cheng.

SULLIVAN, MICHAEL. "Pictorial Art and the Attitude toward Nature in Ancient China," *Bulletin of College Art Association of America*, Vol. XXXVI, No. 1 (March, 1954). Fig. 1 on silk scroll from Ch'ang-sha.

SUN HAI-PO孫海波. *Chia-ku-wen pien*甲骨文編 (A Dictionary of Shell and Bone Inscriptions). 5 ts'e. Peiping: Harvard-Yenching Institute, 1934. See also under Chin Hsiang-heng.

SUN I-JANG孫詒讓(1848–1908). *Chou-li cheng-i* 周禮正義 (Commentary on the Rituals of the Chou). Shanghai: Chung Hua Book Co., 1934. *SPPY* ed.

SUN PAO-T'IEN孫葆田and others. *Shantung t'ung-chih* 山東通志 (Gazetteer of Shantung Province). 128 ts'e. 1915.

SUN SHIH-PAI孫師白 (ed.). *Chi-mu ts'ang-t'ao*季木藏匋(Inscribed Pottery in the Collection of Chou Chi-mu). 4 ts'e. Shanghai, 1943.

Sung Ying-hsing 宋應星 (fl. 1600). *T'ien-kung k'ai-wu* 天工開物 (Exploitation of Works of Nature). Shanghai: Commercial Press, 1937. *KHCPTS* ed.

Sylwan, Vivi. *Investigation of Silk from Edsen-gol and Lop-nor*. Stockholm, 1949. (Sino-Swedish Expedition, Publication No. 32.)

———. "Silk from the Yin Dynasty," *BMFEA*, IX (1937), 119–26.

Ta Tai li-chi 大戴禮記 (Collected Ritual of Tai the Elder). Shanghai: Commercial Press, 1929. *SPTK* ed.

T'ai-p'ing yü-lan. See Li Fang.

Takada Tadachika 高田忠周. *Kuchu hen* 古籀篇 (A Study of Ancient Writings). 68 ts'e. Tokyo, 1925.

T'ang Hsüan-tsung 唐玄宗 (685–762). *Ta T'ang liu-tien* 大唐六典 (Codes and Regulations of the Six Boards of the T'ang Dynasty). 8 ts'e. Japanese ed., 1836.

T'ang Lan 唐蘭. "Huo pai-ssu k'ao 獲白兕考" On the Capture of a White Rhinoceros), *Shih-hsüeh nien-pao* 史學年報, I, No. 4 (1932), 119–24.

———. *Ku-wen-tzu-hsüeh tao-lun* 古文字學導論 (Introduction to Chinese Paleography). 2 ts'e. Peiping, 1935.

———. "Shih-ku-wen k'o yü Ch'in Ling-kung k'ao 石鼓文刻于秦靈公考" (A Study of the Stone Drums Inscribed in 422 b.c.), *TLTC*, V, No. 7 (1952), 228–29; supplement, No. 12, pp. 398–400.

Tao-hsüan 道宣 (597–667). *Kuang hung-ming chi* 廣弘明集 (Collection of Buddhist Writings). Shanghai: Commercial Press, 1929. *SPTK* ed.

T'ao Tsung-i 陶宗儀 (*ca.* 1320–1399). *Cho-keng lu* 輟耕錄, in *Ching-tai pi-shu* (1922).

———. *Shuo fu* 説郛 (A Collection of Miscellaneous Writings). 160 ts'e. 1647; 40 ts'e. 100 chuan ed., 1927.

Tchang, Mathias. *Synchronismes chinois*. Shanghai: Imprimerie de la Mission catholique, 1905.

Teng Ssu-yü 鄧嗣禹 and Biggerstaff, Knight. *An Annotated Bibliography of Selected Chinese Reference Works*. Rev. ed. Cambridge: Harvard University Press, 1950.

Ting Fu-pao 丁福保. *Ku-ch'ien ta-tz'u-tien* 古錢大辭典 (Encyclopedia of Ancient Chinese Coinage). 12 ts'e. Shanghai: Medical Bookstore, 1938; supplement, 1939.

———. *Shuo-wen chieh-tzu ku-lin* 説文解字詁林 (Collection of Commentaries on the Old Lexicon). 66 ts'e. Shanghai: Medical Bookstore, 1930.

Ts'ai Chi-hsiang 蔡季襄. *Wan Chou tseng-shu k'ao-cheng* 晚周繒書考證 (A Study of the Silk Document of the Late Chou Period). Shanghai, 1946?

Ts'ai Yung 蔡邕 (132–192). *Ts'ai Chung-lang chi* 蔡中郎集 (Collected Writings of Ts'ai Yung). Shanghai: Chung Hua Book Co., n.d. *SPPY* ed.

———. *Tu-tuan* 獨斷, in *Han Wei ts'ung-shu* 漢魏叢書 (1925).

Tsien Tsuen-hsuin 錢存訓. "A History of Bibliographical Classification in China," *The Library Quarterly*, XXII (1952), 307–24.

———. "Han-tai shu-tao k'ao 漢代書刀考" (A Study of the Book-knife of the Han Dynasty), *BIHP*, Extra Volume, No. 4 (1961), pp. 997–1008.

Ts'UI PAO 崔 豹 (fl. 290–306). *Ku chin chu* 古 今 註 (Commentary on Things Old and New). Shanghai: Commercial Press, 1936. *SPTK* ed.

TUAN KUNG-LU 段 公 路 (fl. 850). *Pei-hu lu* 北 户 錄, in *Hu-pei hsien-cheng i-shu* 湖 北 先 正 遺 書 (1923).

Tung-kuan Han-chi. See Liu Chen.

TUNG PA 董 巴 (3d century A.D.). *Yü-fu chih* 輿 服 志, quoted in *T'ai-p'ing yü-lan*, 605/7a.

TUNG TSO-PIN 董 作 賓 *Chia-ku-hsüeh wu-shih-nien* 甲 骨 學 五 十 年 (Fifty Years of the Study of Bone and Shell Inscriptions). Taipei: Yi-wen Press, 1955.

———. "Chia-ku-wen tuan-tai yen-chiu li 甲 骨 文 斷 代 研 究 例]" (On the Dating of Shell and Bone Inscriptions). *TYPLWC*, I, 323–418.

———. "Ch'in-yang yü-chien 沁 陽 玉 簡" (On the Jade Tablets from Ch'in-yang, Honan), *TLTC*, X, No. 4 (1955), 107–8.

———. "Ch'un-ch'iu Chin pu-ku wen-tzu k'ao 春 秋 晉 卜 骨 文 字 考" (A Study of a Bone Inscription of the Chin State of the Ch'un Ch'iu Period), *TLTC*, XIII, No. 9 (1956), 271–74.

———. "Chung-kuo wen-tzu ti ch'i-yüan 中 國 文 字 的 起 源" (Origin of the Chinese Writing), *TLTC*, V, No. 10 (1952), 348–58.

———. *An Interpretation of the Ancient Chinese Civilization.* Taipei: Chinese Association for United Nations, 1952.

———. "Lun Ch'ang-sha ch'u-t'u chih tseng-shu 論 長 沙 出 土 之 繒 書" (On the Silk Document Unearthed at Ch'ang-sha), *TLTC*, X, No. 6 (1955), 173–76.

———. "Shang-tai kuei-pu chih t'ui-ts'e 商 代 龜 卜 之 推 測]" (An Assumption of the Use of Tortoise Shell in Divination of the Shang Dynasty), *AYFCPK*, No. 1 (1929), pp. 59–130.

———. "Ten Examples of Early Tortoise-shell Inscriptions," *HJAS*, XI (1948), 119–29.

———. *Yin-hsü wen-tzu* 殷 虛 文 字 (Inscriptions from the Shang Ruins). Part I, *Chia-pien*. Shanghai: Commercial Press, 1948. Part II, *I-pien*. Taipei: Academia Sinica, 1949–53.

———. *Yin-li-p'u* 殷 曆 譜 (A Study of the Shang Chronology). 4 ts'e. Li-chuang, Szechuan: Academia Sinica, 1945.

———. "Yin-tai ti niao-shu 殷 代 的 鳥 書" (Bird Script of the Shang Dynasty), *TLTC*, VI, No. 11 (1953), 345–47.

TUNG YU 董 逌 (fl. 1127). *Kuang-ch'uan shu-pa* 廣 川 書 跋 (Postscripts on Famous Calligraphy), in *Ching-tai pi-shu* (1922), ts'e 20–21.

Tz'u-yüan 辭 源 (The Chinese Encyclopedic Dictionary). One-volume ed. Shanghai: Commercial Press, 1939.

VAN GULIK, R. H. *Mi Fu on Ink-stones.* Peiping: Henri Vetch, 1938.

VAUDESCAL, LE COMMANDANT. "Les pierres gravées du Che King Chan et le Yün Kiu Sseu," *JA*, 1914, pp. 374–459.

WANG CH'ANG 王 昶 (1725–1807). *Chin-shih ts'ui-pien* 金 石 萃 編 (Collection of Bronze and Stone Inscriptions). 64 ts'e. 1805.

WANG CHEN-TO 王振鐸. *Han-tai k'uang-chuan chi-lu* 漢代礦磚集錄 (Collection of Tomb Bricks of the Han Dynasty). Peiping: Archeological Society, 1935.

WANG CH'EN 王長. *Hsü Yin wen-ts'un* 續殷文存 (Supplementary Collection of Shang Bronze Inscriptions). 2 ts'e. Peiping: Archeological Society, 1935.

WANG CHI-CHEN. "Notes on Chinese Ink," *Metropolitan Museum Studies*, III, Part I (1930), 114–33.

WANG CHIA 王嘉 (4th century). *Shih-i chi* 拾遺記, in *Han Wei ts-ung-shu* (1925), ts'e. 32

WANG CHUNG-MIN 王重民. *Lao-tzu k'ao* 老子考 (A Bibliography on Lao-tzu). Peiping: Library Association of China, 1927.

———. "Shuo chuang-huang 說裝潢" (On Paper-dyeing), *TSKHCK*, V (1931), 39–41.

———. "Tao-pi k'ao 刀筆考" (On the Book-knife), *TSKHCK*, III (1929), 131–32.

WANG CH'UNG 王充 (*ca.* 27–100). *Lun heng* 論衡 (Discourses Weighed in the Balance). Shanghai: Commercial Press, 1929. *SPTK* ed.

WANG FU 王黼 (d. 1126) and others. *Hsüan-ho po-ku t'u-lu* 宣和博古圖錄 (Catalogue of Antique Objects in the Imperial Collection of the Sung Dynasty). 30 ts'e. 1752.

WANG HSIEN-T'ANG 王獻唐. *Lin-tzu feng-ni wen-tzu hsü-mu* 臨淄封泥文字叙目 (Inscriptions on Sealing Clay from Lin-tzu, Shantung). Tsinan: Shantung Provincial Library, 1936.

WANG KUO-WEI 王國維 "Chien-tu chien-shu k'ao 簡牘檢署考" (A Study of the Bamboo and Wooden Documents and the System of Sealing), in *WCAIS*, (Shanghai: Commercial Press, 1936), ts'e 26.

———. "Shih shih 釋史" (An Interpretation of the Character *Shih*), in *WCAIS*, ts'e 3.

———. "Wei shih-ching k'ao 魏石經考" (A Study of the Stone Classics Engraved in the Third Century), in *WCAIS*, ts'e 8.

WANG MING 王明. "Sui T'ang shih-tai ti tsao-chih 隋唐時代的造紙" (Paper Manufacture during the Sui and T'ang Dynasties), *KKHP*, No. 11 (1956), pp. 115–26.

———. "Ts'ai Lun yü Chung-kuo tsao-chih ti fa-ming 蔡倫與中國造紙的發明" (Ts'ai Lun and the Invention of Paper in China), *KKHP*, No. 8 (1954), 213–21.

WANG SHIH-TO 汪士鐸 (1802–1889). "Shih po 釋帛" (On the Terms for Silk Textiles), in *Wang Mei-ts'un hsien-sheng chi* 汪梅村先生集 (1881).

WANG SHU-NAN 王樹枬. *Han Wei Liu-ch'ao chuan-wen* 漢魏六朝專文 (Brick Inscriptions of Han, Wei, and Six Dynasties). 2 ts'e. Shanghai: Commercial Press, 1935.

Wang-tu Han-mu pi-hua 望都漢墓壁畫 (Wall Painting of a Han Tomb Discovered at Wang-tu, Hopei). Peking, 1955.

WANG YIN 王隱 (*ca.* 300). *Chin shu* 晉書 (A History of the Chin Dynasty), reconstructed in the *Kuang-ya ts'ung-shu* 廣雅叢書 (1920), ts'e 438–43.

WANG YING-LIN 王應麟 (1223–1296). *K'un-hsüeh chi-wen* 困學紀聞. Shanghai: Commercial Press, 1935. *SPTK* ed.

WANG YÜ-CH'ÜAN王毓銓. "Distribution of Coin Types in Ancient China," *American Numismatic Society Museum Notes*, III (1948), 131–51.

———. *Early Chinese Coinage*. New York: American Numismatic Society, 1951.

———. *Wo-kuo ku-tai huo-pi ti ch'i-yüan ho fa-chan*我國古代貨幣的起源和發展 (The Origin and Development of Ancient Chinese Coinage). Peking: Science Press, 1957.

WEI CHENG魏徵(580–643) and others. *Sui shu* 隋書 (History of the Sui Dynasty). Shanghai: T'ung-wen Shu-chü, 1884.

WEI SHOU魏收(506–572). *Wei shu*魏書(History of the Wei Dynasty). Shanghai: T'ung-wen Shu-chü, 1884.

WEN I-TO聞一多. "Shih shang釋桑" (Decipherment of the Character for Mulberry-tree in the Bone Inscriptions), in *Wen I-to ch'üan-chi* 聞一多全集 (4 vols., Shanghai: K'ai-ming Book Store, 1948), II, 565–72.

*Wen-wu ts'an kao tzu-liao*文物參考資料(Materials for the Study of Cultural Objects). Peking, 1950–58. Continued as *Wen-wu* since 1959.

WHITE, WILLIAM CHARLES. *Bone Culture of Ancient China*. Toronto: University of Toronto Press, 1945.

———. *Bronze Culture of Ancient China*. Toronto: University of Toronto Press, 1956.

———. *Tombs of Old Lo-yang*. Shanghai: Kelly & Walsh, 1934.

WIBORG, FRANK BESTOW. *Printing Ink: A History with a Treatise on Western Methods of Manufacture and Use*. New York and London: Harper & Bros., 1926.

WU CH'ENG-LO吳承洛. *Chung-kuo tu-liang-heng shih*中國度量衡史 (History of Chinese Measuring Standards). Shanghai: Commercial Press, 1936.

WU CH'IU-YEN吾邱衍 (1272?–1312). *Hsüeh ku pien* 學古編 (Studies of Antiquities), in *Shuo fu* (1927 ed.), chüan 97.

WU, K. T.吳光清. "Libraries and Book Collecting in China before the Invention of Printing," *T'ien Hsia Monthly*, V (1937), 237–60.

———. "Scholarship, Book Production, and Libraries, 618–1644." Unpublished Ph.D. dissertation, Graduate Library School, University of Chicago, 1944.

WU SHIH-CH'ANG吳世昌. "On the Marginal Notes Found in Oracle Bone Inscriptions," *TP*, XLIII (1954), 34–74.

WU SHIH-FENG吳式芬(1796–1865) and Ch'en Chieh-ch'i陳介祺(1813–1884). *Feng-ni k'ao-lüeh*封泥考畧(Studies of Inscribed Sealing Clay). 10 ts'e. 1904.

WU TA-CH'ENG吳大澂(1835–1902). *Ku-yü t'u-k'ao*古玉圖考 (Studies and Illustrations of Ancient Jade). 2 ts'e. Shanghai: T'ung-wen Shu-chü, 1889.

*Wu Yüeh ch'un-ch'iu*吳越春秋(Spring and Autumn of the Wu and Yüeh States). Shanghai: Commercial Press, 1929. *SPTK* ed.

YANEDA KENJIRO米田賢次郎. "Kyoen Kankan to sono kenkyu seika居延漢簡とその成果" ("The Etsin-gol Wooden Documents and the Result of the Studies of Them"), *Kodai-gaku*, II, No. 3 (1953), 252–60; III, No. 2 (1954), 174–83.

YANG CHIA-LO楊家駱．*Ssu-k'u ch'üan-shu hsüeh-tien* 四庫全書學典 ("Encyclopedia Quatuor Bibliothecarium"). Shanghai: World Book Co., 1946.

YANG HSIUNG 楊雄 (53 B.C.–A.D. 18). *Fa-yen* 法言 . Shanghai: Commercial Press, 1929. *SPTK* ed.

YANG LIEN-SHENG 楊聯陞. *Money and Credit in China, a Short History*. Cambridge, Mass.: Harvard University Press, 1952.

YANG TIEN-HSÜN 楊殿珣. *Shih-k'o t'i-pa so-yin* 石刻題跋索引 (Index to Writings on Stone Inscriptions). Peiping: National Library of Peiping, 1936.

YAO K'UAN 姚寬. *Hsi-ch'i ts'ung-yü* 西溪叢語, in *Hsüeh-ching t'ao-yüan*, (Han Feng Lou ed.)

YAO MING-TA 姚名達. *Chung-kuo mu-lu-hsüeh shih* 中國目錄學史 (History of Chinese Bibliography). Shanghai: Commercial Press, 1938.

YAO PAO-YU 姚寶猷. *Chung-kuo ssu-chüan hsi-ch'uan shih* 中國絲絹西傳史 (History of the Introduction of Chinese Silk to the West). Chungking: Commercial Press, 1944.

YAO SHIH-AO 姚士鰲. "Chung-kuo tsao-chih-shu shu-ju Ou-chou k'ao 中國造紙術輸入歐洲考" (Introduction of the Method of Paper-making in China to Europe), *Fu-jen hsüeh-chih* 輔仁學誌, I (1928), 1–85.

YEH CH'ANG-CHIH 葉昌熾 (1849–1917). *Yü shih* 語石 (Talks on Stone Inscriptions). Shanghai: Commercial Press, 1936. *KHCPTS* ed.

YEN K'O-CHÜN 嚴可均 (1762–1843). *Ch'üan Chin wen* 全晋文 (Collected Essays of the Chin Dynasty), in *Ch'üan shang-ku Han San-kuo Liu-ch'ao wen* 全上古漢三國六朝文 (1930).

———. *Ch'üan Han wen* 全漢文 (Collected Essays of the Han Dynasty), in *Ch'üan shang-ku Han San-kuo Liu-ch'ao wen* (1930).

Yen-tzu ch'un-ch'iu 晏子春秋 (Spring and Autumn of Master Yen). Attributed to YEN YING 晏嬰 (6th century B.C.). Shanghai: Commercial Press, 1929. *SPTK* ed.

YEN WEN-JU 閻文儒. "Fang-shan Yün-chü-ssu 房山雲居寺" (The Yün-chü Temple of Fang-shan, Hopei), *WWTKTL*, 1955, No. 9, pp. 48–53.

YETTS, W. PERCEVAL. "Bird Script on Ancient Chinese Swords," *JRAS* (1934), pp. 547–52.

———. *The George Eumorfopoulos Collection Catalogue of the Chinese and Corean Bronzes, Sculpture, Jades, Jewellery, and Miscellaneous Objects*. 3 vols. London: Ernest Benn, 1929.

YING SHAO 應劭 (ca. 140–206). *Feng-su t'ung-i* 風俗通義 (Popular Traditions and Customs). 2 vols. Peking: Centre franco-chinois d'études sinologiques, 1943. Text with index.

YÜ HSING-WU 于省吾. *Shuang-chien-i ku ch'i-wu t'u-lu* 雙劍誃古器物圖錄 (Illustrations of Antique Objects in the Yü Collection). 2 ts'e. Peiping, 1940.

YÜ SHIH-NAN 虞世南 (558–638). *Pei-t'ang shu-ch'ao* 北堂書鈔 (An Encyclopedia of the T'ang Dynasty). 20 ts'e. 1888.

INDEX

Academia Sinica, 21, 28, 33, 34, 83, 103, 104, 142; *see also* National Academy of Sciences
Agate, 86
Agrarians, 10
Agricultural implements, 51, 103
Agriculture, 3, 25, 26, 186; works on, 12, 15
Alchemist, 165
Alexandria, 142
Alexandrian merchants, 141
Alloy, 40, 176
Allusions in literature, 118
Amitabba Buddha, 79
Amur cork tree, 152
An-hui, 40, 172
An-i, 51, 188
An Lu-shan, 151, 188
An-yang, 20, 21, 28, 37, 40, 47, 53, 54, 58, 83, 114, 188
Ancestor worship, 3, 4, 20, 42, 128, 186
Ancestors, 3, 4, 8, 29, 91, 117, 122, 124
Ancestral temple, 5
Andersson, J. G., 58
Animal bones, 3, 19, 26, 27 34–37; *see also* Bones and shells; Horns; Skulls
Animals in: ancient writing, 24, 25, 42, 43; decorations, 54, 173, 176; sacrifice, 26; silk paintings, 123, 124, 125, 128; *see also* Deer; Elephant; Horse; Rhinoceros; Tiger; etc.
Anthropology, 22
Antiquarians, 21
Aquilaria agallocha, Roxb., 141
Arabs, 141
Archeological discoveries: bones and shells, 21–22; bronzes, 40; grave tablets, 72; paper, 142–48; quasi-paper, 135; silk, 114, 119–25; tablets of bamboo and wood, 94–102; writing implements, 161–63, 173, 176–78, 179–80
Archeological expeditions: Japanese, 102, 145; Prussian, 145; Russian, 99; Sino-Swedish, 99, 102, 143, 145; of Aurel Stein, 96–97, 119, 143, 147, 163, 168
Archeological materials, 179–80
Archeology, 22, 64
Archery, 7
Archives, 5, 9, 11, 12, 13, 19, 21, 91, 184; *see also* Books; Documents; Libraries

Aristocrats, 6, 7, 9, 10, 184
Arrows, 25, 103
Asia, Central, 96, 97, 102, 119, 147
Asia, Western, 115, 139
Astrology, 97
Astronomical instrument, 83
Astronomy, 22; works on, 15
Athens, 142
Authorship, 10
Avatamsaka sutra, 80, 82

Bacon, Francis, 3
Ballads, 15
Balustrade, 74, 82
Bamboo: books, 90–113, frontispiece; brush-holders, 103; building material, 103; documents, 92–96; implements, 103; ink-slab, 173; musical instruments, 103; papers, 150–51; plant, 102, 150; screen for papermaking, 151; screen for wrapping books, 155–56; stylus, 163, 170, 182; tally, 110; writing on, 1, 79, 85, 90, 103, 117; *see also* Bamboo tablets; Tablets of bamboo and wood; Wood; Wooden tablets
Bamboo Annals, 93
Bamboo-membrane paper, 151
Bamboo tablets, 6, 95, 132; dates of writing, 90–92; differences from wood, 104–5, 109; discoveries, 92–96; drafting, 127; length, 93, 94, 96, 105, 110; memoranda, 85; preparation for writing, 102–4; rare in northwestern region, 103; terminology, 109; treatment, 104; use at court, 6; width, 94, 96, 107; written with lacquer, 170; *see also* Tablets of bamboo and wood; Wood; Wooden tablets
Banners, 117, 129
Barbarian invasion, 16, 121
Bark paper, 151
Barnard, Noel, 122, 194
Basket holding tablets, 175
Bayan Bogdo Mountain, 142
Beacons, 99
Beginners' lexicons, 99, 108, 111
Bergman, Folke, 99, 121, 143, 161, 194, 202
Bibliography: Buddhist, 17–18; earliest known, 14; historical, 128, 180

Index